MEDIA
AND
VOTERS IN
CANADIAN
ELECTION
CAMPAIGNS

~

*This is Volume 18 in a series of studies
commissioned as part of the research program
of the Royal Commission on Electoral Reform
and Party Financing*

MEDIA AND VOTERS IN CANADIAN ELECTION CAMPAIGNS

~

Frederick J. Fletcher
Editor

Volume 18 of the Research Studies

ROYAL COMMISSION ON ELECTORAL REFORM
AND PARTY FINANCING
AND CANADA COMMUNICATION GROUP –
PUBLISHING, SUPPLY AND SERVICES CANADA

DUNDURN PRESS
TORONTO AND OXFORD

ISBN 1-55002-114-1
ISSN 1188-2743
Catalogue No. Z1-1989/2-41-18E

Published by Dundurn Press Limited in cooperation with the Royal
Commission on Electoral Reform and Party Financing and Canada
Communication Group – Publishing, Supply and Services Canada.

Canadian Cataloguing in Publication Data

Main entry under title:
Media and voters in Canadian election campaigns

(Research studies ; 18)
Issued also in French under title: Les Médias et l'électorat dans les
   campagnes électorales canadiennes.
ISBN 1-55002-114-1

   1. Mass media – Political aspects – Canada. 2. Communication in
politics – Canada. 3. Electioneering – Canada. 4. Canada. Parliament –
Elections. 5. Campaign management – Canada. I. Fletcher, Frederick J.
II. Canada. Royal Commission on Electoral Reform and Party Financing.
III. Series: Research studies (Canada. Royal Commission on Electoral Reform
and Party Financing) ; 18.

JL193.M43 1991   324.7'3'0971   C91-090530-4

Dundurn Press Limited
2181 Queen Street East
Suite 301
Toronto, Canada
M4E 1E5

Dundurn Distribution
73 Lime Walk
Headington
Oxford, England
OX3 7AD

CONTENTS

~

FIGURES

TABLES

FOREWORD

~

THE ROYAL COMMISSION on Electoral Reform and Party Financing
was established in November 1989. Our mandate was to inquire into
and report on the appropriate principles and process that should govern the election of members of the House of Commons and the financing of political parties and candidates' campaigns. To conduct such a
comprehensive examination of Canada's electoral system, we held
extensive public consultations and developed a research program
designed to ensure that our recommendations would be guided by an
independent foundation of empirical inquiry and analysis.

The Commission's in-depth review of the electoral system was the
first of its kind in Canada's history of electoral democracy. It was dictated largely by the major constitutional, social and technological
changes of the past several decades, which have transformed Canadian
society, and their concomitant influence on Canadians' expectations
of the political process itself. In particular, the adoption in 1982 of the
Canadian Charter of Rights and Freedoms has heightened Canadians'
awareness of their democratic and political rights and of the way they
are served by the electoral system.

The importance of electoral reform cannot be overemphasized. As
the Commission's work proceeded, Canadians became increasingly
preoccupied with constitutional issues that have the potential to change
the nature of Confederation. No matter what their beliefs or political
allegiances in this continuing debate, Canadians agree that constitutional
change must be achieved in the context of fair and democratic processes. We cannot complacently assume that our current electoral
process will always meet this standard or that it leaves no room for
improvement. Parliament and the national government must be seen
as legitimate; electoral reform can both enhance the stature of national

political institutions and reinforce their ability to define the future of our country in ways that command Canadians' respect and confidence and promote the national interest.

In carrying out our mandate, we remained mindful of the importance of protecting our democratic heritage, while at the same time balancing it against the emerging values that are injecting a new dynamic into the electoral system. If our system is to reflect the realities of Canadian political life, then reform requires more than mere tinkering with electoral laws and practices.

Our broad mandate challenged us to explore a full range of options. We commissioned more than 100 research studies, to be published in a 23-volume collection. In the belief that our electoral laws must measure up to the very best contemporary practice, we examined election-related laws and processes in all of our provinces and territories and studied comparable legislation and processes in established democracies around the world. This unprecedented array of empirical study and expert opinion made a vital contribution to our deliberations. We made every effort to ensure that the research was both intellectually rigorous and of practical value. All studies were subjected to peer review, and many of the authors discussed their preliminary findings with members of the political and academic communities at national symposiums on major aspects of the electoral system.

The Commission placed the research program under the able and inspired direction of Dr. Peter Aucoin, Professor of Political Science and Public Administration at Dalhousie University. We are confident that the efforts of Dr. Aucoin, together with those of the research coordinators and scholars whose work appears in this and other volumes, will continue to be of value to historians, political scientists, parliamentarians and policy makers, as well as to thoughtful Canadians and the international community.

Along with the other Commissioners, I extend my sincere gratitude to the entire Commission staff for their dedication and commitment. I also wish to thank the many people who participated in our symposiums for their valuable contributions, as well as the members of the research and practitioners' advisory groups whose counsel significantly aided our undertaking.

Pierre Lortie
Chairman

INTRODUCTION

~

THE ROYAL COMMISSION'S research program constituted a comprehensive and detailed examination of the Canadian electoral process. The scope of the research, undertaken to assist Commissioners in their deliberations, was dictated by the broad mandate given to the Commission.

The objective of the research program was to provide Commissioners with a full account of the factors that have shaped our electoral democracy. This dictated, first and foremost, a focus on federal electoral law, but our inquiries also extended to the Canadian constitution, including the institutions of parliamentary government, the practices of political parties, the mass media and nonpartisan political organizations, as well as the decision-making role of the courts with respect to the constitutional rights of citizens. Throughout, our research sought to introduce a historical perspective in order to place the contemporary experience within the Canadian political tradition.

We recognized that neither our consideration of the factors shaping Canadian electoral democracy nor our assessment of reform proposals would be as complete as necessary if we failed to examine the experiences of Canadian provinces and territories and of other democracies. Our research program thus emphasized comparative dimensions in relation to the major subjects of inquiry.

Our research program involved, in addition to the work of the Commission's research coordinators, analysts and support staff, over 200 specialists from 28 universities in Canada, from the private sector and, in a number of cases, from abroad. Specialists in political science constituted the majority of our researchers, but specialists in law, economics, management, computer sciences, ethics, sociology and communications, among other disciplines, were also involved.

In addition to the preparation of research studies for the Commission, our research program included a series of research seminars, symposiums and workshops. These meetings brought together the Commissioners, researchers, representatives from the political parties, media personnel and others with practical experience in political parties, electoral politics and public affairs. These meetings provided not only a forum for discussion of the various subjects of the Commission's mandate, but also an opportunity for our research to be assessed by those with an intimate knowledge of the world of political practice.

These public reviews of our research were complemented by internal and external assessments of each research report by persons qualified in the area; such assessments were completed prior to our decision to publish any study in the series of research volumes.

The Research Branch of the Commission was divided into several areas, with the individual research projects in each area assigned to the research coordinators as follows:

F. Leslie Seidle	Political Party and Election Finance
Herman Bakvis	Political Parties
Kathy Megyery	Women, Ethno-cultural Groups and Youth
David Small	Redistribution; Electoral Boundaries; Voter Registration
Janet Hiebert	Party Ethics
Michael Cassidy	Democratic Rights; Election Administration
Robert A. Milen	Aboriginal Electoral Participation and Representation
Frederick J. Fletcher	Mass Media and Broadcasting in Elections
David Mac Donald (Assistant Research Coordinator)	Direct Democracy

These coordinators identified appropriate specialists to undertake research, managed the projects and prepared them for publication. They also organized the seminars, symposiums and workshops in their research areas and were responsible for preparing presentations and briefings to help the Commission in its deliberations and decision making. Finally, they participated in drafting the Final Report of the Commission.

On behalf of the Commission, I welcome the opportunity to thank the following for their generous assistance in producing these research studies – a project that required the talents of many individuals.

In performing their duties, the research coordinators made a notable contribution to the work of the Commission. Despite the pressures of tight deadlines, they worked with unfailing good humour and the utmost congeniality. I thank all of them for their consistent support and cooperation.

In particular, I wish to express my gratitude to Leslie Seidle, senior research coordinator, who supervised our research analysts and support staff in Ottawa. His diligence, commitment and professionalism not only set high standards, but also proved contagious. I am grateful to Kathy Megyery, who performed a similar function in Montreal with equal aplomb and skill. Her enthusiasm and dedication inspired us all.

On behalf of the research coordinators and myself, I wish to thank our research analysts: Daniel Arsenault, Eric Bertram, Cécile Boucher, Peter Constantinou, Yves Denoncourt, David Docherty, Luc Dumont, Jane Dunlop, Scott Evans, Véronique Garneau, Keith Heintzman, Paul Holmes, Hugh Mellon, Cheryl D. Mitchell, Donald Padget, Alain Pelletier, Dominique Tremblay and Lisa Young. The Research Branch was strengthened by their ability to carry out research in a wide variety of areas, their intellectual curiosity and their team spirit.

The work of the research coordinators and analysts was greatly facilitated by the professional skills and invaluable cooperation of Research Branch staff members: Paulette LeBlanc, who, as administrative assistant, managed the flow of research projects; Hélène Leroux, secretary to the research coordinators, who produced briefing material for the Commissioners and who, with Lori Nazar, assumed responsibility for monitoring the progress of research projects in the latter stages of our work; Kathleen McBride and her assistant Natalie Brose, who created and maintained the database of briefs and hearings transcripts; and Richard Herold and his assistant Susan Dancause, who were responsible for our research library. Jacinthe Séguin and Cathy Tucker also deserve thanks – in addition to their duties as receptionists, they assisted in a variety of ways to help us meet deadlines.

We were extremely fortunate to obtain the research services of first-class specialists from the academic and private sectors. Their contributions are found in this and the other 22 published research volumes. We thank them for the quality of their work and for their willingness to contribute and to meet our tight deadlines.

Our research program also benefited from the counsel of Jean-Marc Hamel, Special Adviser to the Chairman of the Commission and former

Chief Electoral Officer of Canada, whose knowledge and experience proved invaluable.

In addition, numerous specialists assessed our research studies. Their assessments not only improved the quality of our published studies, but also provided us with much-needed advice on many issues. In particular, we wish to single out professors Donald Blake, Janine Brodie, Alan Cairns, Kenneth Carty, John Courtney, Peter Desbarats, Jane Jenson, Richard Johnston, Vincent Lemieux, Terry Morley and Joseph Wearing, as well as Ms. Beth Symes.

Producing such a large number of studies in less than a year requires a mastery of the skills and logistics of publishing. We were fortunate to be able to count on the Commission's Director of Communications, Richard Rochefort, and Assistant Director, Hélène Papineau. They were ably supported by the Communications staff: Patricia Burden, Louise Dagenais, Caroline Field, Claudine Labelle, France Langlois, Lorraine Maheux, Ruth McVeigh, Chantal Morissette, Sylvie Patry, Jacques Poitras and Claudette Rouleau-O'Toole.

To bring the project to fruition, the Commission also called on specialized contractors. We are deeply grateful for the services of Ann McCoomb (references and fact checking); Marthe Lemery, Pierre Chagnon and the staff of Communications Com'ça (French quality control); Norman Bloom, Pamela Riseborough and associates of B&B Editorial Consulting (English adaptation and quality control); and Mado Reid (French production). Al Albania and his staff at Acart Graphics designed the studies and produced some 2 400 tables and figures.

The Commission's research reports constitute Canada's largest publishing project of 1991. Successful completion of the project required close cooperation between the public and private sectors. In the public sector, we especially acknowledge the excellent service of the Privy Council unit of the Translation Bureau, Department of the Secretary of State of Canada, under the direction of Michel Parent, and our contacts Ruth Steele and Terry Denovan of the Canada Communication Group, Department of Supply and Services.

The Commission's co-publisher for the research studies was Dundurn Press of Toronto, whose exceptional service is gratefully acknowledged. Wilson & Lafleur of Montreal, working with the Centre de Documentation Juridique du Québec, did equally admirable work in preparing the French version of the studies.

Teams of editors, copy editors and proofreaders worked diligently under stringent deadlines with the Commission and the publishers to prepare some 20 000 pages of manuscript for design, typesetting and printing. The work of these individuals, whose names are listed elsewhere in this volume, was greatly appreciated.

Our acknowledgements extend to the contributions of the Commission's Executive Director, Guy Goulard, and the administration and executive support teams: Maurice Lacasse, Denis Lafrance and Steve Tremblay (finance); Thérèse Lacasse and Mary Guy-Shea (personnel); Cécile Desforges (assistant to the Executive Director); Marie Dionne (administration); Anna Bevilacqua (records); and support staff members Michelle Bélanger, Roch Langlois, Michel Lauzon, Jean Mathieu, David McKay and Pierrette McMurtie, as well as Denise Miquelon and Christiane Séguin of the Montreal office.

A special debt of gratitude is owed to Marlène Girard, assistant to the Chairman. Her ability to supervise the logistics of the Commission's work amid the tight schedules of the Chairman and Commissioners contributed greatly to the completion of our task.

I also wish to express my deep gratitude to my own secretary, Liette Simard. Her superb administrative skills and great patience brought much-appreciated order to my penchant for the chaotic workstyle of academe. She also assumed responsibility for the administrative coordination of revisions to the final drafts of volumes 1 and 2 of the Commission's Final Report. I owe much to her efforts and assistance.

Finally, on behalf of the research coordinators and myself, I wish to thank the Chairman, Pierre Lortie, the members of the Commission, Pierre Fortier, Robert Gabor, William Knight and Lucie Pépin, and former members Elwood Cowley and Senator Donald Oliver. We are honoured to have worked with such an eminent and thoughtful group of Canadians, and we have benefited immensely from their knowledge and experience. In particular, we wish to acknowledge the creativity, intellectual rigour and energy our Chairman brought to our task. His unparalleled capacity to challenge, to bring out the best in us, was indeed inspiring.

Peter Aucoin
Director of Research

PREFACE

~

IN MODERN DEMOCRACIES, election campaigns are contested to a large extent in the mass media. From the days of the openly partisan press to the contemporary multi-media environment, political leaders have relied upon mass media to mobilize electoral support. While the right to vote freely and the credibility of the ballot process are central to democracy, the conduct of campaigns and the flow of information to voters are also important. If campaigns are perceived to be conducted unfairly, the entire electoral process may become suspect. Concern for the legitimacy of the system is one of the primary reasons that most democracies have enacted regulations dealing with aspects of electoral communication. These regulations cover a wide range of media activities, including campaign advertising, election broadcasting and even some aspects of news and public affairs.

The Commission's research program on mass media and elections examined the major developments in electoral communication in Canada and other democratic countries in recent decades, in the context of electoral reform. The research studies were designed to cast light on major aspects of election media, whether amenable to regulation or not. Effective regulation requires an understanding of the entire system of campaign communication.

The results of the research program provided background for the Commission's report. Whatever their substantive focus, the studies examined issues such as fairness in electoral competition and public confidence in the electoral process, issues that are central to electoral reform. Some studies examined central elements in the campaign communication system, while others assessed its effectiveness in meeting the information needs of voters and the communication needs of parties. Several projects considered alternative forms of communication that might contribute to improved information for voters. The studies examined campaign media in the larger sense, including partisan advertising, free broadcast time, candidate communication strategies, new communication technologies and news and public affairs coverage, among other topics.

Research dealing directly with mass media and elections is reported in volumes 18 through 22. Volume 16, on opinion polling, and Volume 17, on the attitudes of Canadians toward the electoral system, were also part of the research program but include material on other subjects as well. Taken together, the seven volumes provide a comprehensive overview of the issues of campaign communication.

Volume 18 presents five studies on various aspects of the relationship between the media and electors. Some are based primarily on data from the Canadian National Election Studies, major surveys of voters during and after federal election campaigns. Others are comparative studies of important features of campaign communication: televised leaders debates and mechanisms for the provision of information to voters with special needs. They all reflect the normative assumption that the right to vote must include the right to sufficient information to make an informed choice.

Jean Crête examines the relationship between campaign publicity on television, including party advertising and news coverage, and electoral behaviour. He addresses the extent to which media exposure is a factor in the level of information held by voters and identifies those voters who are likely to learn the most from television. As a critical assessment of the literature on the effects of campaign television, this study makes a significant contribution. Further, it draws on the 1988 Canadian National Election Study to test propositions. Taking a longer view, Robert MacDermid traces correlates of media use during campaigns since 1965 and examines the relationship between media use, political interest and voter turnout. The major focus of this study is on voter attention to campaign communication and its relationship to demographic factors such as gender, education and income, and to partisanship, among other variables. Both studies discuss methods by which the information flow to electors could be improved.

Cathy Widdis Barr presents a detailed examination of the effects of televised leaders debates on voters, based on data from the 1984 and 1988 campaigns. She explores the effects of the debates on turnout, vote decision and, perhaps most important, knowledge of issues and party leaders. One of her most significant findings is that leaders debates are an important source of campaign information for less-informed voters. Robert Bernier and Denis Monière present the most comprehensive overview of televised leaders debates available, covering Europe, North America and Australia. The study examines patterns of organization, formats, rules of participation, legislative requirements, audience levels and responses to debates, and includes a discussion of research on the effects of such debates on electors. Both of these studies examine difficult policy questions including, for example, the issue of mandatory leaders debates, the appropriate role for minor parties and the desirability of public input regarding the issues discussed.

Lyndsay Green examines various means to improve the information available to electors during campaigns, with emphasis on those with special information needs (as a result of limited vision, hearing or literacy in the official languages). The study establishes criteria for assessing new communication channels and technologies in terms of their capacity to improve the dissemination of information and to promote dialogue among electors. It looks in particular at alternatives to mainstream media, including cost-effective means of providing special services to information-impeded groups.

This volume addresses the issue of electoral democracy in ways that incorporate and reflect new trends in campaign communication and media use. Many of these studies present the most current analysis available, in part because of their use of recent election material but also because many of the issues stem from recent developments in communication technology. For the most part, the studies deal with aspects of election communication not amenable to direct regulation, but they provide important suggestions for self-directed reforms as well as for further research.

The studies published in Volume 18 will be of interest not only to students and scholars examining the mass media and/or election campaigns but also to media practitioners, communications analysts, party strategists and others concerned about voter information. They raise both methodological and normative questions and may stimulate discussion in both areas.

The Commission's research program on mass media and elections drew on the expertise of a wide range of communication scholars and political scientists in addition to those whose work was published in these volumes. Their assistance is greatly appreciated. Among those who participated as peer reviewers and advisers, several deserve special recognition: Peter Desbarats, Dean of the School of Journalism, University of Western Ontario; David Taras, University of Calgary; Holli Semetko, University of Michigan; and Marc Raboy, Laval University. The research program also benefited from the advice of individuals from the parties and the media: John Coleman, President, Canadian Advertising Foundation; Terry Hargreaves, Elly Alboim and Colin MacLeod of the CBC; Geoffrey Stevens, political columnist; Lynn McDonald, sociologist and former MP; and others who prefer to remain anonymous. On behalf of the authors and the Commission, I must also acknowledge our debt to the practitioners from the news media and the parties who attended our seminars or agreed to be interviewed and provided much valuable assistance and advice.

The administration of the research program depended heavily on the work of Cheryl Mitchell, who served as my assistant from the inception of the program, and our research assistants at York University: Catherine Bolan, Claudia Forgas, Marni Goldman, Todd Harris, Sharon Johnston and Sheila Riordon. We were also assisted most ably by the Commission staff. Peter Constantinou and Véronique Garneau had particular responsibilities for research in this area. The staff of the Department of Political Science, the Faculty of Arts, Calumet College, and the Faculty of Environmental Studies at York University were very accommodating.

The authors themselves deserve special acknowledgement for their willingness to try to meet tight deadlines, complicated by their normal academic responsibilities, and in particular to respond with cheerfulness and despatch to our requests for revisions. The conscientious peer reviewers were of major assistance to the authors and ourselves in preparing these studies for publication.

The unfailing good humour and encouragement of Peter Aucoin, the director of research, made an important contribution to the work. It was a privilege to work with the Commissioners, whose willingness to bring their experience to bear on the most esoteric of formulations was an inspiration. Pierre Lortie's overall direction and, in particular, his suggestions for research and incisive comments on various drafts made a vital contribution, which is reflected in these research volumes as well as in the Final Report of the Royal Commission. Working with the other research coordinators was a genuine pleasure. Richard Rochefort and his staff were crucial in bringing these studies to publication.

On a personal note, I wish to thank my wife and frequent collaborator, Martha Fletcher, for encouraging me to undertake this task, which I have found very rewarding, and for her direct advice on many aspects of the work, as well as for bearing more than her share of the burden of domestic management. My son, Frederick, reminded me that work, however important, must be balanced with other aspects of life but also that the future of the democratic process is worth working for.

Cheryl Mitchell brought dedication and skill to the work and must have an ample share of the credit for whatever contribution the research program has made. For errors in design and execution, however, I remain responsible.

Fred Fletcher
Research Coordinator

MEDIA
AND
VOTERS IN
CANADIAN
ELECTION
CAMPAIGNS

~

1

TELEVISION, ADVERTISING AND CANADIAN ELECTIONS

~

Jean Crête

INTRODUCTION

Election propaganda is an integral part of the democratic process. It promotes discussion of ideas that govern society and an appreciation of the people who embody these ideas. The conditions and constraints of propaganda are themselves the subject of discussion, if not controversy. This is nothing new, even though public authorities have intervened in recent years in the way propaganda is distributed. This intervention is explained particularly by the fact that the state governs one of the main election propaganda vehicles: television. Today, it would be unthinkable to study an election campaign without looking at party advertising. This is a relatively new attitude for political analysts, however. For example, the major study on the electoral behaviour of Canadians, *Political Choice in Canada,* mentions election advertising only in passing (Clarke et al. 1979). Although studies published after *Political Choice in Canada* provide a more detailed description of election advertising, they do not evaluate the effect of such advertising on voting behaviour (Fletcher 1981b; Monière 1988). Election advertising, especially televised advertising, eats up a large part of the budget and energy of political parties during election campaigns. Canadian election studies are neither atypical nor leaders in this field.

For political party strategists, advertising is only one of many ways to get a message to all or part of the electorate. Newscasts and public affairs programs are an even more important means of propaganda.

Unlike advertising, newscasts permit partisan organizations no control over many aspects of production and broadcasting. Because the media, and particularly television, face many constraints, partisan organizations can always arrange to participate effectively by offering to cooperate, at least for producing the programs in question. During the televised leaders debates, for example, party strategists are even more important than during newscasts, because their cooperation is absolutely necessary for the program to be produced and broadcast.

In this study, I review literature on the relationship between televised election advertising and media coverage of parties during election campaigns, including leaders debates. I also look at the characteristics of the electorate.

Importance of Election Campaigns

In a country where electoral volatility is high and voters do not have strong party loyalties, election campaigns are important. When party loyalty is weak, more votes can be lost or gained. When *The American Voter* (Campbell et al. 1964) was published almost 30 years ago, most voters identified with one party, which explained voting patterns. Today, the role of the volatile voter is vital. We can no longer assume that people will vote as their parents did, or even as they voted in the last election.

According to American electoral sociology of the 1950s, most voters had made up their minds before the election campaigns actually began. For political parties, therefore, the main purpose of election campaigns was to retain established support by strengthening convictions and motivating their supporters to go out and vote. When voter loyalty declines, however, it is easier to make converts. In the 1974 Canadian general election, for example, an estimated 45 percent of voters made their choice during the campaign itself (Clarke et al. 1979, 276). If voters no longer rely on their affiliation with any particular party when voting, however, they must use other criteria to make a decision. These new criteria may include knowledge of the events and issues at hand, as well as the positions of candidates and parties on these issues. American sociology leads us to believe that voting patterns are now determined by the issues at hand and the characteristics of party leaders.

We also know that television has changed the way people use their time, becoming a substitute for many activities. This substitution is not the same in all segments of society (Comstock 1982). Because television is the most popular medium, the relationship between exposure to television and electoral behaviour is important.

To approach this issue, I refer throughout the study to a number of hypotheses found in election studies. As required, I refer to experimental studies, as they highlight the nature of the relationships between variables better than real-situation studies where the contaminating effects of other elements cannot be controlled. The major drawback of experimental studies, however, is that they provide no information on the prevalence of the phenomenon studied in a real situation.

In this study I refer only to hypotheses that are directly relevant to election campaigns. Although these hypotheses do not cover all communication processes relevant to political persuasion, it is important to begin by unfolding the entire map that, at least implicitly, guides our search for hypotheses. In his writings on public communication, McGuire (1989) presents this map in the form of the classical persuasion model's input–output matrix (figure 1.1).

The model's matrix includes these input variables: the source of communication, the message itself, the channel through which the message moves, the recipient of the message and the goal of the communication. The other axis of the matrix consists of output variables ordered on a unidimensional axis that assumes pure rationality. Although no communication theory actually states this specific model, the model is used as a checklist by most authors. In the following pages, I do not necessarily treat these output variables in the order presented in figure 1.1. For example, given that a generation of voters does not suddenly appear in a given election, but is the product of a slow socialization process beginning in early childhood, it is illusory to think that these voters approach an election campaign without baggage. As we will see, it may be hypothesized that interest (output variable 3) in the election campaign is not necessarily the product of exposure (output variable 1) to election messages; on the contrary, interest could well be the factor that leads to exposure to the media.

In this study, I examine only some of the 60 matrix cells, reflecting the state of knowledge in the field of election communications. In the first part of the study, I deal with the message and channel in the context of media coverage of political parties and candidates during an election period. In the second part, I discuss knowledge of politics (output variable 4) and interest (output variable 3). In the third section, I examine some studies on the relationship between the media and the information that is stored (variable 7) and reactivated (variable 8) to reach a decision. The final section deals more explicitly with the decision and behaviour (variables 9 and 10). In the process, I outline some of the hypotheses on election advertising and draw some practical conclusions from this review of the literature.

Figure 1.1
Input–output model of persuasion

Output: dependent variables \ Input: independent variables	Source	Message	Channel	Recipient	Goal
1. Exposure to communication					
2. Attention given to communication					
3. Attraction to, interest in communication					
4. Understanding–knowledge					
5. Acquisition of skills					
6. Changes in attitude					
7. Accumulation of information					
8. Recovery of information					
9. Decision					
10. Behaviour according to decision					
11. Reinforcement of desired behaviour					
12. Consolidation of skills, attitudes and behaviour					

Source: Adapted from McGuire (1989, 45).

THE MEDIA

Media Coverage of Parties

News broadcasts are the first way for political parties to reach voters. In most liberal democratic countries, election campaign observers have noted that political parties have focused much of their effort on obtaining favourable television coverage, since this is the most popular medium. In an election campaign strategy, television programs, especially newscasts and public affairs programs, are but one way to reach the electorate. It is therefore logical for analysts to check broadcasts on television regularly and, because newscasts are a preferred time to broadcast political information, to note the proportion of the news that was devoted to each political party.

Certain principles govern television networks when producing news broadcasts. Election campaigns put two in particular to the test (Seaton and Pimlott 1987, 133). First, there is the principle of balance, which has no direct bearing in the print media. In practice, balance means giving each of the political parties a specified portion of air time. A television network, for example, will follow the leaders of the three major federal political parties, regardless of their relative newsworthiness. The second principle is objectivity. By objectivity journalists mean a mirror of the real world. However, this mirror can only "reflect" certain events and not others, seeing and presenting them from a specific angle.

Based on objectivity, one assumes that the party of the incumbent government would be in the news more often than the other parties. To support this hypothesis I reason that the party in power must give an account of its mandate and is more likely to have "stars" (ministers) whose actions and statements are newsworthy even outside election periods. Refuting this hypothesis does not necessarily imply a lack of objectivity, given the other related postulates. The hypothesis was accurate in a study of the print media during most Quebec provincial election campaigns (Crête 1984), but not so in the case of television during the 1987 British elections (Axford and Madgwick 1989, 149, table 14.1). What about Canadian federal elections? The relative importance

Table 1.1
Relative importance granted to each party in television news coverage of election campaigns, 1974–88
(percentages)

Party	1974	1979	1980	1984	1988
Liberal	42*	40*	35	43.9*	38.5
Conservative	35	32	36*	35.5	33.7*
NDP	24	28	29	20.7	26.2
Others	n.a.	n.a.	n.a.	n.a.	1.6

Sources: 1974: Fletcher (1981a, 305, table 10-7); 1979 and 1980: Fletcher (1981b, 147, table 6); 1984: Estimated from Wagenberg et al. (1988, 121, table 1); 1988: Based on 1988 Canadian Election Study.

*Designates incumbent government.

n.a. = not available.

accorded by television evening newscasts to each party in elections since 1974 is compared in table 1.1.

Despite the variety of samples and indicators used in these studies, the amount of attention given to the various parties is relatively stable. I therefore reject the assumption that the incumbent government always starts with an advantage. In fact, the figures in the table indicate that when the incumbent is the Liberal party it has an advantage, whereas when the incumbent is the Progressive Conservative party it rarely has an advantage. This "advantage" is based on the time devoted to the various parties in network newscasts, not on the content of the news.

If we start with the premise that the networks are influenced more by the principle of balance, we assume that air time is distributed according to each party's relative popularity with the electorate. For example, using a program sampling taken at the beginning of 1974, Winn (1976, 135) showed that the CBC allotted air time to political parties based on their numbers in the House of Commons. Similarly, Fletcher (1988, 167) showed that during the 1980 and 1984 election campaigns the attention given to political parties during televised newscasts was similar to the division of free air time among the parties. This formula is not based on the popularity of the parties at election time, but rather on their popularity during the previous election.

Although there may be reservations about how the "coverage" variable in table 1.1 is measured, we can try to evaluate the overall bias resulting from the principle of balance. In correlating the importance newscasts gave to each party in election campaigns between 1974 and 1988 (see table 1.1) with the percentages of votes these parties won, we obtain a correlation coefficient of 0.68. If we use the results of the previous rather than the current election, the coefficient is 0.78. In short, when predicting the amount of coverage a political party will receive during televised newscasts, predictions based on the percentage of the vote obtained during the last election are more accurate than those based on current popularity. However, the belief that the news should reflect the present more than the past is itself biased. Because the correlation between the distribution of current news air time and the previous election results is not perfect, we can assume that other factors come into play.

On average, the difference between the percentage of the vote at the previous election and the percentage of televised news air time is not very wide for the Liberal and Conservative parties, as table 1.2 shows. Moreover, if we calculate the absolute average spread between the previous vote and coverage, we notice that the spread, or errors, are

9

TELEVISION, ADVERTISING AND ELECTIONS

Table 1.2
Relative attention paid to the major parties by television networks during election campaigns, 1974–88, compared with election results
(percentages)

Party	Mean current vote	Mean of previous vote	Mean of current media coverage	Mean absolute difference for each election*
Liberal	37.4	38.8	39.9	4.3
Conservative	39.4	37.8	34.4	4.4
NDP	18.2	17.8	25.6	7.8

Sources: Fletcher (1981a, 1981b); Wagenberg et al. (1988); Canada, Elections Canada, various years.

*Mean absolute difference is computed as follows: percentage of coverage for a party at an election minus the percentage of votes for this party at the previous election. This is averaged over elections, ignoring the signs (+, -).

equal between the two parties. Most of the errors come from coverage of the 1988 election campaign. During the 1984 election, the Conservative party won 50 percent of the vote and 74 percent of the seats. If the votes won during the previous election had been the only determining factor in the balance principle, the Conservative party would have had as much air time as all the other parties combined during the 1988 campaign. The distribution of newscast air time during an election, therefore, seems to be based largely, although not solely, on past performance. Past performance is also constrained by the number of parties recognized in the House of Commons. The New Democratic Party (NDP) benefits the most from the balance principle because it gets about 30 percent more air time than its election results warrant. The very small parties, those without enough elected representatives to be recognized as parties in the House of Commons, receive approximately 1.5 percent of newscast air time.

Assessment of Parties and Candidates
According to content analyses of national network news programs during federal election campaigns since 1974, the projected image of both the Liberal and the Progressive Conservative parties is more often negative than positive (table 1.3). The NDP is less often on the news, and the image is more positive than for the other two larger parties. Although data come mostly from the CBC, an examination of the other networks would likely produce the same results. In fact, a comparison of networks during the 1979 elections (Fletcher 1981c, table 10-8) shows that the results are the same, regardless of the channel studied.

Table 1.3
Overall positive and negative orientation of election news on television

Party	1979	1980	1984	1988
Liberal	-	-	-	-
Conservative	-	-	+	-
NDP	+	-	+	-
Others	-	-	n.a.	-

Sources: 1979: Fletcher (1981b, 148, table 7); 1980: Soderlund et al. (1984, 70, table 3-9); 1984: Wagenberg et al. (1988, 123, table 3); 1988: Based on 1988 Canadian Election Study.

Note: The data for 1979, 1980 and 1988 were taken from CBC news bulletins, while the 1984 data are a combination of CBC, SRC, CTV, TVA and Global data.

The often negative impression of parties presented in the news does not necessarily indicate that the networks are biased. In fact, most of the news items are neutral. Also, most negatively interpreted items are merely reports of unfortunate events for a party, such as an opinion poll showing a particular party losing ground or a party member being accused of wrongdoing. I suspect, however, that the media view partisan events with a critical eye, regardless of the party involved.

The image in the broadcast media is no different from the public's image of politicians: "In general, the parties and politicians who run the political system are regarded with distaste by most of the public" (Clarke et al. 1979, 31). Kornberg and Wolfe (1980), who studied coverage of parliamentary proceedings by daily newspapers and the public's regard for Parliament, suggest that the public's low confidence in politicians stems from journalists' reports on parliamentary proceedings. This is all the more important because we generally expect the public to have a more positive attitude toward public figures (Lau et al. 1979).

Issues, Local Candidates and Party Leaders

Before examining the various studies (predominantly American) on the relationship between media coverage, advertising and the electorate, it is appropriate to note a few features of election coverage by the Canadian media. Do the Canadian media give the public information on the issues and the candidates, or do they present the election more as a horse race?

Data on the 1988 federal election show that about half the information broadcast on television dealt with issues (table 1.4), contrary to what we might expect from the American example.

In Canada, as in the United States and other industrialized countries, television and the concentration of ownership of the daily press have "nationalized" politics.[1] Network news items are chosen for their interest to viewers across the entire network. It is not surprising, therefore, that party leaders and central organizations are given more space than local candidates and constituency associations. The space occupied by each of the various players in newscasts is suggested in table 1.5.

Local candidates have more space on Radio-Canada newscasts than on the CBC news, reflecting the more regional character of the Radio-Canada network in Quebec. It also shows the distinct character of federal election campaigns in Quebec. Even when identical themes are covered by both the CBC and Radio-Canada, for linguistic reasons there are often different spokespersons.

Canadian election rules, political culture and media restrictions imposed internally or externally set the Canadian situation apart from

Table 1.4
Election news devoted to issues in 1988
(percentage of time)

	CBC[1]	SRC[1]	CTV, Global, CBC[2]
Issues	53.5	50.2	41.0
Other	46.5	49.8	59.0
N	2 714[a]	2 685[a]	585[b]

Sources:
[1]Based on 1988 Canadian Election Study.
[2]Taken from Frizzell et al. (1989, 84).

[a]The units are statements.
[b]The units are news items.

Table 1.5
Election news time devoted to various players during the 1988 federal election
(percentage of time)

Players	CBC National	SRC Téléjournal
Leaders	59.7	48.7
Parties	15.1	14.5
Candidates	7.5	14.7
Other players	17.1	22.1

Source: Based on 1988 Canadian Election Study.

Note: Percentages may not add up to 100.0 because of rounding.

the American case. The differences cited above should be kept in mind in applying proposals from the American experience to the Canadian situation.

KNOWLEDGE OF AND INTEREST IN POLITICS

Knowledge of Politics

In the United States, political knowledge is usually defined as the ability to remember the names and personal characteristics of candidates, to identify election issues and campaign developments, and to recognize the connection between candidates and issues. In rating the effectiveness of the media, the criterion of voter information gain is primary. As Chaffee notes (1977, 215), this criterion is usually ignored, since researchers find it of little interest.

What do we know about the effectiveness of the media in disseminating political information that the public can use, for example, in exercising its democratic right to elect governments or decide on specific issues during referendums? Several studies on voting patterns have addressed the impact of mass media campaigns on obtaining information.

The reader can have an idea of the level of voter knowledge in Canada by consulting the data in table 1.6.

Table 1.6
Knowledge of local candidates, 1988 federal election campaign
(percentages)

	Number of candidates known			
Week	0	1	2	3
2 October	57.7	28.3	11.4	2.8
9 October	53.1	28.0	13.9	5.0
16 October	51.1	26.2	17.5	5.2
23 October	41.7	28.3	19.9	9.9
30 October	33.1	34.2	21.7	11.0
6 November	30.3	30.1	23.7	16.0
13 November	27.4	22.9	29.0	21.7

Source: Based on 1988 Canadian Election Study.

Note: The knowledge index is the number of local candidates that the interviewees could identify in response to the following questions: Do you know the name of the Conservative candidate in your riding? And the name of the Liberal candidate in your riding? And the name of the NDP candidate in your riding?

Table 1.6 presents an index of the degree of knowledge of candidates' names in local ridings. In the week when the 1988 election campaign began, close to three voters in five (57.7 percent) could not name a single candidate in their riding. However, all the candidates had not yet been chosen by that date. In the week of the leaders debate and the launching of election advertising, a little over four voters in ten could not name a single candidate. By election week, only 27 percent of voters were unable to name at least one candidate. The percentage of those who could name three candidates increased considerably during the campaign.

Overall results confirm that there is a connection between media exposure, especially the print media, and knowledge of the facts related to election campaigns (Berelson et al. 1954; Trenaman and McQuail 1961; Katz and Feldman 1962; Blumler and McQuail 1968). It has been more difficult, however, to show that media exposure increases the level of political knowledge. Nevertheless, some researchers have tackled this problem.

The News

In an experimental study in the United States, Behr (1985) was able to show that television can have decisive effects. In this experiment, people watched television for one week in an area specially prepared by the experimenter. The subjects agreed not to watch television at home. The experimenter divided them randomly into two groups. The experimental group watched local newscasts that included profiles of the candidates in a House of Representatives election; the control group watched the same newscasts, except that any information pertaining to the election or the candidates was deleted. One day after the last viewing session, only 56 percent of those in the control group were able to match candidates with their political party, whereas almost everyone in the experimental group could. This was an experimental study, that is, a study in which the contextual variables were controlled by the random distribution of the subjects. Would results be the same if the controls were relaxed? A British study indicates otherwise.

Three opinion polls were conducted during the 1987 election campaign in Great Britain: one poll done two weeks before the election, another done one or two days before and a third, five or six days after the election. The polls showed that the public's knowledge of certain issues had not increased appreciably. The test was conducted using the election platforms of the three major parties. The researchers identified ten clear and unambiguous political proposals and asked the people interviewed to attribute each proposal to one of the three parties. Two weeks before the election, 42 percent of the interviewees were able to match at least seven out of ten proposals correctly; two days before the election the proportion was 47 percent; one week after the election, the percentage had fallen to 44 percent (McGregor et al. 1989, 183). If we take into account a margin of error in the sampling, we might conclude that there was no significant change from one group to the other. Throughout the experiment, the percentage of respondents who were unable to match more than three proposals to the correct party remained stable. Also, more than half the respondents who had seen something about the election on television were able to match seven proposals correctly, while only one-fifth of those who had not see any televised news reports were that successful (ibid.). Although we can conclude that people who could match proposals with parties are also those who watch programs dealing with the election, we cannot conclude that the number of people who know the positions of the various parties increases during election campaigns.

During this election campaign, an increasingly greater number of television viewers believed that television placed too much importance on the election (McGregor et al. 1989, 176). Compared with the number of viewers before the campaign, the main BBC television newscast lost 25 percent of its viewers, while the private channel ITV lost 11 percent (Blumler et al. 1989, 171). This loss of audience may explain why the number of informed people remains unchanged. In the United States, it has been noted that exposure to television programs dealing with presidential election campaigns depends on whether the election is a close race (Danowski and Ruchinskas 1983). In a tight race, voters follow programs dealing with the election more attentively. Apparently, the 1987 British general election was not very interesting to voters, given that the change in the incumbent party's percentage of votes was the lowest since 1950 (Kavanagh 1989, table 1.1).

Advertising

At the beginning of the 1970s, Atkin and his colleagues (Atkin et al. 1973; Atkin and Heald 1976) and Patterson and McClure (1974, 1976) focused their studies on election advertising and showed that such advertising increases voter knowledge of the issues and the candidates.

Patterson and McClure (1974, 1976) reported that three-quarters of voters who remembered having seen political ads were able to identify the message of the ads. Also, voters who had a great deal of exposure to television were more likely to identify candidates' positions correctly from a list of 10 issues presented in the political ads. On average, among informed viewers, there was a 32 percent shift toward correct identification, while this percentage was 24 percent among less-informed viewers. Atkin et al. (1973) pointed out that voters obtain a great deal of information on issues and candidates through political ads.

Proposition: Election advertising increases voters' knowledge of issues and candidates.

Several studies have identified the conditions that make it easier to acquire political knowledge. Patterson and McClure (1974) showed that election advertising had a greater impact on people who rarely watch television news or read newspapers. Although this conclusion seems at first glance to be the most logical one, it is not completely corroborated by the data, as shown in table 1.7.

Table 1.7 provides data on the degree of knowledge, or rather ignorance, of citizens according to their exposure to the media and advertising during the 1988 federal election campaign. The media exposure index is the number of days per week the interviewee reports having read a newspaper, added to the number of days that person reported having listened to the news on television. A person who listened to the news and read the paper every day obtained the maximum score of 14. On the opposite end of the scale, the person who read no papers and listened to no televised news obtained a score of zero. From the table, it is apparent that the greater the exposure to information sources, the higher the level of knowledge. For example, among people with no exposure to these information sources and who did not see election advertising on television, 70 percent could not name a single candidate in their riding; at the other end of the spectrum – that is, among those who were exposed daily to the media and who saw election advertising – the percentage of those who did not know the candidates fell to 24.

The information in table 1.7 leads to the conclusion that exposure to election advertising substantially increases people's knowledge of the candidates. Thus, the percentage of people who did not know the candidates among those who did not read newspapers and did not listen to televised news dropped from 70 to 63 percent if they saw election advertising. Unlike Patterson and McClure (1974), however, we cannot state that the greatest effect was among people who had little exposure to the media. In fact, if we looked only at people who were more interested in the media (index = 14) and those with no interest (index = 0), we would reach the opposite conclusion. In two different studies, Atkin and his colleagues (Atkin et al. 1973; Atkin and Heald 1976) also showed that voters who pay a great deal of attention to ads

Table 1.7
**Exposure to the media and election advertising, and
degree of knowledge**
(percentages)

Degree of exposure to the media*	Percentage who could not name a single candidate	
	Not exposed to advertising	Exposed to advertising
0	70	63
1	62	50
2	65	61
3	61	41
4	46	48
5	46	46
6	41	35
7	51	41
8	44	37
9	47	29
10	50	29
11	39	28
12	33	30
13	23	17
14	36	24

Source: Based on 1988 Canadian Election Study.

*Number of days per week interviewee reported having read a newspaper, added to number of days that person reported having listened to news on television.

or who seek out information are more likely to increase their level of knowledge through election advertising than people who hear the advertising by accident.

Although we do not have information on the accidental or voluntary nature of exposure to election advertising in the study of the 1988 federal election campaign in Canada, it is reasonable to think that people who are interested or very interested in politics are more likely to retain more of the election advertising than those who have little or no interest in politics. Table 1.8 relates data on the level of knowledge of Canadian citizens during the 1988 election to the degree of interest in politics. It shows that exposure to advertising is associated with an increased level

Table 1.8
Knowledge of candidates and exposure to election advertising, controlling for interest in politics
(percentages)

	Interest in politics					
	Little or none			Some or much		
	Exposure to election advertising			Exposure to election advertising		
Number of candidates known	No	Yes	Diff.	No	Yes	Diff.
0	66.7	52.3	-14.4	37.4	26.8	-10.6
1	19.4	26.1	+6.7	31.1	30.1	-1.0
2	9.2	15.3	+6.1	21.7	26.1	+4.4
3	4.6	6.3	+1.7	9.7	17.1	+7.4
N	(592)	(587)		(852)	(1 554)	

Source: Based on 1988 Canadian Election Study.

Note: Percentages may not add up to 100.0 because of rounding.

of knowledge, regardless of the level of interest in politics. However, the deduction we made on the relationship between interest in politics and gain in information is not supported by the data. Our data are but indirect measures of the concepts used by Atkin and his colleagues (Atkin et al. 1973; Atkin and Heald 1976).

Proposition: Exposure to campaign advertising and interest in politics are correlated.

Channels and Destinations

The study by Hofstetter and his colleagues (1978, 568) gives us a good idea of the relative values of the various means of communication as sources of political information (table 1.9). Reading newspapers has had the greatest impact on the level of information by far. Radio and network television news rank second. The combination of local television news, discussions and commercials ranks third. The impact of newspapers, television news, political ads and discussions is greater with people who are less politically committed.

Proposition: Election advertising is a major source of information for voters.

Proposition: The less politically aware the voter, the more important election advertising becomes.

Table 1.9
Relative importance of various media as sources of political information

Sources of exposure to political information	(Beta)
Television (total)	–0.08
Short advertising (spots)	0.06
Long advertising (program)	0.02*
Newspapers	0.21
Election specials (TV)	0.03*
Network news (TV)	0.10
Local news (TV)	0.07*
Radio	0.10
Campaign discussions	0.05
R multiple coefficient	0.38

Source: Hofstetter et al. (1978, 568, table 3).
*Not significant for $p \leq .05$.

The role of repeated messages was studied by Rothschild and Ray (1974) in an experiment using short ads about candidates. After the message had been presented once, 20 percent of the subjects remembered the candidates; after it had been presented six times, 55 percent of the subjects could name the candidates.

Proposition: Message repetition (frequency) is an important factor in familiarizing voters with candidates and issues.

We know that the attention given to political information, which is the first level of political participation, is linked to the resources individuals have at their disposal. Resources can be divided into two categories, each with the potential to augment or substitute for the other (Uhlaner 1984, 202). First, there are individual resources, such as education and income. Second, there are group resources, such as membership in an association or a union. The latter can offset the gap between individuals from different socio-economic segments of society. Generally, only socio-economic characteristics are taken into account in studies, which tends to lower the perception that people have of the relationship between socio-economic status and political knowledge.

The attention voters give to election campaigns in the newspapers is linked, in part, to education and socio-economic status. Radio is somewhere between newspapers and television (see Clarke et al. 1979, table 9.9). Moreover, there is a correlation (0.3 to 0.4 in 1974) between attention to one medium and to others. In other words, if voters pay attention to an election campaign largely through one medium, they will also tend to follow the campaign in the other media.

Clarke and his colleagues also noted in their 1979 election study that the attention voters give to television coverage of politics is linked to age. Older people are easier to reach through television. Data on the 1988 federal election are presented in table 1.10. Again, the youngest voters, who were between 18 and 30 years old during the 1988 election, were much less likely to listen to news on television every day than were people 65 years of age or more. Exposure to televised news seems to rise with age. The importance granted to televised election news also increases with age, but levels out when voters are over 45 years old. However, the idea that exposure to televised news increases with age may be misleading.

In fact, after the work done by Danowski and Ruchinskas (1983), there is reason to believe that the correlation between age and exposure to programs dealing with election campaigns on television is a generational phenomenon rather than a phenomenon of aging. The question is: Are today's older people attentive to television programs dealing with elections because they have reached a stage in their lives where this is the thing to do (the aging hypothesis), or is it that people from this group (i.e., people born around the same time), as they mature

Table 1.10
Exposure to television by age group during the 1988 federal election
(percentages)

	Age group				
Exposure to television	Born before 1924	1924–33	1934–42	1943–57	1958–70
Watches the news every day on TV	70.9	65.8	53.0	38.1	28.5
Attaches great importance to election news on TV	22.1	22.2	21.5	18.1	11.9
Watched at least one of the two televised leaders debates	65.1	68.8	59.4	49.9	41.2

Source: Based on 1988 Canadian Election Study.

and age together, share similar social experiences (Braungart and Braungart 1989, 20)? American data presented by Danowski and Ruchinskas (1983) show that, indeed, attention paid to television programs dealing with election campaigns has nothing to do with age. Rather, it is a group phenomenon: individuals born between 1900 and 1923 tune in to this type of program the most, more than individuals born either before or after this period.

The generation hypothesis is appealing, but it is not supported by all the data. For example, the 55-to-64 age group was the most attentive to the televised debates during the 1988 election campaign (table 1.10). Nor does the importance given to televised election news appear to be linked to the group born before 1924. The generation hypothesis would certainly bear closer study, given the important consequences that its confirmation could have on the use of mass television (broadcasting) as opposed to specialized television (narrowcasting) or other forms of communication.

Interest in Politics

The role of the mass media in stimulating interest in politics is important, since people who are interested are more likely to vote than those who are not (Milbrath 1965). Interest is generally defined as the amount of attention or psychological commitment in a specific campaign. This variable is loosely linked to exposure to the contents of a campaign (Lazarsfeld et al. 1948; Berelson et al. 1954). Lane (1965) suggests that greater access to political information leads to greater political awareness of society. Since interest in a campaign and exposure to media are correlated (Hofstetter et al. 1978; Clarke et al. 1979, 299, note 21), there is a link between exposure to advertising and interest (Atkin and Heald 1976). As shown in studies on televised debates and on the influence of media, ordinary television programs cannot easily generate an interest in politics; the interest must be there already. Moreover, if this interest exists and is strong enough to motivate an individual to pay attention to the media, it is quite likely that the media will heighten this interest. This explains the wide gap in the level of knowledge between people who show an interest in politics and those who do not (table 1.8).

MEDIA AGENDAS AND POLITICAL PERSONALITIES

Agenda Setting

The effect of political messages on the importance of issues in an election campaign has attracted the attention of a number of researchers. Lazarsfeld and colleagues (1948, 98) noted that the mass media had a significant impact during the 1940 American presidential election campaign by redefining the issues so that "issues about which people had previously thought very little, or had been little concerned, took on a new importance as they were accented by campaign propaganda." Subsequent research on agenda setting focused on the relationship between the relative priority assigned to issues by the media and by the public (McCombs and Shaw 1972; McLeod et al. 1974). Although the correspondence between the media's priorities and those of the general public can be explained otherwise, most observers agree that the media influence what people believe before they reach a decision, particularly an election decision. If candidates can lead voters to believe that their issues and qualities are of top priority, then they may gain the advantage. The goal, therefore, is to focus attention on what fosters the interests of the candidates, rather than to try to convince the voters about a particular issue.

In a series of experimental studies, Iyengar and Kinder (1987, 16) tested the assumption that the issues covered by television news become the most important issues. One experiment consisted of first measuring the opinions of the subjects on the most important issues facing the country. Then the people were divided into two groups. One group viewed newscasts to which a given topic, e.g., national defence, had been added. The second group watched unaltered newscasts. After one week, the opinions of the two groups were measured again. Other experiments consisted of collages of news items presented in a single session, followed by a measurement of opinions. In this second type of experiment, the number of news items on a given topic varied from group to group.

The results of the tests are revealing. The subjects gave more importance to the problems dealt with in the newscasts, except for inflation, which they already considered very important when the experiment began. Follow-up interviews one week after the end of the experiment showed that the effect was still the same.

Another way of tackling the effect of political messages on the importance of issues is to show the relationship between public opinion trends on a given topic over a period of several years and media coverage of the topic during the same period. Studies by Funkhouser (1973), MacKuen (1981, 1984) and Behr and Iyengar (1985) showed similar results. First, they showed that in the United States, there was a correlation between the amount of attention given to a topic by the media within a given period and the importance of this subject to the public. Second, they showed, using different data, periods and techniques, that public opinion changed when the media changed, and not before.

Finally, the studies pointed to the persistent correlation between media coverage and public opinion, even when the economic and political indicators were held constant.

For example, Behr and Iyengar (1985) took into account indicators such as energy costs, U.S. dependency on foreign supplies, OPEC ministers' meetings, speeches on energy by the U.S. president and, of course, media coverage, to explain the bi-monthly fluctuations in American public opinion regarding energy between 1974 and 1980. Also, by using a two-stage regression procedure, they were able to weed out these retroactive effects to obtain the net effect of media coverage on public opinion. They estimated that it took seven news items on energy to increase the importance of energy on the public's agenda by 1 percent. This same 1 percent increase could be obtained, however, with a single news item, if this item led off a newscast. In a televised speech, the president of the United States could generate an average increase of more than 4 percent of the same indicator on the importance of the energy problem to the American public.

Although coverage is not the determining factor influencing public opinion, it does go a long way toward explaining changes in public opinion. Apparently, the people behind the main BBC evening newscast ("Nine O'Clock News") believed this hypothesis when, during the 1987 British election campaign, they decided not to broadcast two reports they had commissioned, because the subjects of the reports ("inner cities" and "divided Britain") had not been raised by the parties themselves. BBC officials were afraid of being accused of focusing on subjects that the parties had not debated (Blumler et al. 1989, 168).

In addition, programs such as televised debates might have decisive effects, not only on the political agenda, but also on the positions voters take on these issues. This was clearly shown in the English-language debate among the leaders of the three major political parties during the 1988 federal election in Canada. In the days immediately following the debate, support for the Free Trade Agreement between the United States and Canada fell by 6 percent (Johnston et al. 1989). Following the first Ford–Carter debate, which took place during the 1976 U.S. presidential campaign, voters were even more supportive of their favourite candidate's position on the question of employment (Abramowitz 1978, 686).

Not only can the media contribute to setting the political agenda and influencing the positions people take on issues, but they can also change the criteria voters use to judge their elected representatives. This is what American authors call "priming." If we look closely at the experimental studies done by Iyengar and Kinder (1987), we see that, in evaluating the performance of the U.S. president, the subjects in the experimental groups tended to place more importance on the theme inserted in the newscasts they watched than did the control groups. The effect is even clearer when the news item relates the theme to government responsibility (ibid., chap. 9).

The power of television in shaping the political agenda is even greater when individuals have fewer resources and political skills. Thus, individuals who take an interest in and are active in politics are influenced very little by ordinary newscasts (Iyengar and Kinder 1987, 90).

To examine the relationship between the political agenda and election advertising, Bowers (1972) compared the contents of newspaper election advertising with data obtained from opinion polls in all U.S. senatorial and gubernatorial election campaigns. He found a strong correlation between the perspective adopted in ads and that of voters. In a study on election advertising and the agenda of voters during the 1972 presidential election campaign, Shaw and Bowers (1973) concluded that the mention of an issue in an advertisement gives added importance to the issue, especially among those who have seen the ad. These associations can be largely explained by the fact that the candidates rely on opinion polls in the preparation of their advertising.

Proposition: There is a correlation between the issues proposed by candidates in their advertising and the issues emphasized by the electorate.

In a survey conducted in Michigan in 1974, Atkin and Heald (1976) showed a clear positive correlation between the importance given to an issue in election advertising and the importance given to that issue by voters. The correlation was even greater when a voter was less informed to begin with and was less exposed to other sources of information. In other words, the less informed voters are, the more likely they are to gain information from election advertising.

The role of political advertising is to sell the image of the candidates, rather than their political positions (Denton and Hahn 1986). In fact, few political ads present in-depth discussions of the issues or candidates' positions on them (Joslyn 1980, 1986). On the contrary, even ads dealing with issues use ambiguous language to express a candidate's interest in a certain issue without presenting the candidate's specific proposals on it. The main purpose of such messages is to cultivate the candidate's image, without alienating voters who disagree with that candidate's specific positions. As Bennett (1977) noted, the ritual limitations of electoral discourse force candidates to deal with the issues: candidates are expected to campaign on the issues, and a candidate who does not deal with the issues is taking an enormous risk. Bennett adds, however, that talking about issues is not the same thing as taking a stand on them. Being too specific on the issues would break a cardinal rule of electoral discourse. Vague messages let voters feel closer to a candidate's position than a precise message with which voters might disagree.

Page (1978, 178) summarizes the problem: "A candidate who takes a specific policy stand is bound to alienate those who disagree; but a candidate who promises peace, progress and prosperity, and projects an image of warmth and honesty, is likely to please almost everyone."

These two rules of the game are readily reflected in political advertising. Candidates develop specific positions on the issues, but election advertising is not the vehicle they use to convey these positions. The presentation of specific positions is normally reserved for forums where these positions are likely to meet with approval and where the message is not likely to be seen or heard by a large number of people. Latimer's work in Alabama (1985), which points out that competition on the issues is stronger at the state level than at the federal level, gives similar results. If the purpose of advertising is to reach a large number of undecided voters and nonpartisans (Shyles 1986), the message must be vague.

Using a vague message is based on the two rules already mentioned. First, the candidate must raise the issues during the election campaign. Second, the message must be sufficiently vague to avoid developing any opposition; voters must believe that the candidate agrees with their position.

There are indications that taking a stand on the issues could be more effective than being noncommittal or indecisive. Patton and Smith (1980), for example, compared candidates who did not take a stand with those who did, concluding that those who abstained were not rated nearly as well. Similarly, Rosen and Einhorn (1972) reported that candidates who were neutral on the issues were considered less honest, less direct and less well informed than their opponents who took a stand. In an experiment, Rudd (1989) showed that when candidates use vague messages and their opponents take a clear stand on the issues, the more precise candidate is rated higher. Mansfield and Hale (1986) concluded that the perceptions of television viewers are formed by a combination of issues and images of candidates. This conclusion is true both for viewers who watch television to obtain information and for those who watch television to relax. As in the case of newscasts, candidates consider that newspaper advertising enables them to deal with more complex subjects than do the broadcast media. One candidate wrote, "A newspaper ad can be read more than once" (Latimer 1989, 341).

Proposition: Candidates who take a position on the issues in their advertising rate higher with the electorate than candidates who do not.

Political Personalities

In the United States, much attention is given to political personalities. To the extent that the role of candidates is seen as important, party labels are not. Election campaigns are designed, therefore, to highlight the qualities of the candidates. For observers of the U.S. political scene, the primary mission of election propaganda is to focus on the image of the candidate and not on the obligations of the legislator (Latimer 1985). The roles of images and issues in advertising have been studied from many angles. In general, these studies show that image dominates (see Mintz 1986; Latimer 1985; Joslyn 1980; Humke et al. 1975; Bowers 1972). When voters are questioned about candidates, it is easier to get answers on the overall evaluation of these candidates' personal images (good or bad, honest or dishonest, hard worker or lazy) than answers on the candidates' positions on issues or their ideology (Clarke and Evans 1983, 89). This observation meshes with Zajonc's thesis (1980), which states that emotional factors come before those of knowledge (figure 1.1). Rhetoric on the duties of the legislator only emphasizes the candidate's qualities.

Televised debates between party leaders or between candidates are the ideal means of comparing the qualities of these personalities. During the debates between candidates for Nebraska state senator in 1988, Wanzenfried and colleagues (1989) measured changes in young voters' perceptions of five candidate characteristics: competence, personality, sociability, composure and extroversion. Their results showed that for the experimental group there was no difference between their evaluation of the competence or sociability of any of the candidates before and after the debate. The evaluation of the other three characteristics varied according to the candidate. Following the first televised debate in the United States, the Kennedy–Nixon debate in 1960, Katz and Feldman (1962) noted a change in viewers' perceptions of the competence and personality of the two candidates.

During the 1988 federal election campaign, it was noted (Johnston et al. 1992) that among people who saw the leaders debates, assessment of the competence and personality of the Liberal party leader, John Turner, improved considerably in the five days following the debates, while assessment of the competence of the NDP leader, Ed Broadbent, deteriorated.

I conclude, therefore, that television viewers can distinguish the various qualities of political personalities and, moreover, that which interests us most here, that television can change people's evaluation of these personalities.

McIntosh (1989) used the second debate between George Bush and Michael Dukakis, the 1988 U.S. presidential candidates, to measure changes in attitudes toward the candidates among a group of junior college students. The subjects' preference was measured using the following question: "Who would you tend to vote for right now?" The answers were coded on a scale of 1 ("Bush, very certainly") to 13 ("Dukakis, very certainly"). The percentage of those who strongly favoured Bush remained the same before and after the debate. The percentage of those who strongly favoured Dukakis increased significantly (from 21 percent to 41 percent). What is relevant here is that this increase simply shows a consolidation of the intention to vote for Dukakis by those who had already expressed the intention of voting for him. In other words, what we witnessed was a reinforcement of the pro-Dukakis vote, with no similar movement on the part of those leaning toward Bush. This reinforcement effect is dominant in these debates, both in the United States (Hagner and Rieselbach 1978) and in Canada (LeDuc and Price 1985; Johnston et al. 1992).

Moreover, it was shown that the U.S. public obtains most of its information on the candidates in the House of Representatives through advertising. In their newscasts and public affairs programs, the media present little information on the constituency candidates, unless one of them provokes a controversy or attracts attention through a dramatic event (Latimer 1989). In Canada, the situation appears similar.

For example, it has been reported that, in 1974, barely 15 percent of election news published in the dailies dealt with people other than the leaders (Clarke et al. 1979, 279), a trend repeated in the 1979 election (Fletcher 1981c, 281). During the 1988 Canadian federal election campaign, the CBC devoted 7.5 percent of its national newscasts to local candidates. There is every reason to believe, however, that the amount of air time devoted to local candidates during local newscasts should be much greater. The Radio-Canada news program "Téléjournal," which in the Canadian context is both a national newscast (Canada) and a regional newscast (Quebec), had, by the same time, devoted twice as much air time to candidates as did the CBC news broadcast.

Tests on the relative effectiveness of election advertising showed that ads dealing with issues were more persuasive than those focusing on the image of the candidates. More specifically, advertisements on issues produced better evaluations of candidates (Kaid and Sanders 1978) and a greater indication of an intention to vote for them (Garramone 1985) than ads pushing the image of a candidate. In an experimental study, Roddy and Garramone (1988) showed that, in the case of attacks and counterattacks through advertising, the most devastating are those that attack the issues.

The authors of U.S. studies (Patterson 1980; DeFleur and Ball-Rokeach 1975; Strouse 1975; Jacobson 1975; Cundy 1986) also agree that when the candidate is not well known, the impact of televised information is even greater. When a candidate has acquired a public image, new information about the candidate is not likely to change people's perception. Election advertising, therefore, is all the more effective when the candidate is not well known, as is the case more at the beginning of a campaign than at the end.

Proposition: The less known the candidate, the more effective election advertising is.

Proposition: For local candidates (as opposed to party leaders or stars), election advertising is one of the few means of gaining exposure.

Proposition: Advertising related to issues seems to produce better results than advertising related to personalities.

MEDIA EFFECTS ON VOTING

The strongest argument against the idea that massive use of radio and television dictates election success comes from studies showing that very few voters change their voting intentions during an election campaign. The literature on the subject has been compiled by Klapper (1960, chaps. 2 and 4) and Weiss (1969), and the conclusions drawn from this literature are well known. Mass media influence the attitudes of audiences only in the absence of mediating factors, such as the previous attitudes of the audience and the social influences on these individuals. When mediating factors are present, the effect of mass communication will most often be to activate existing attitudes and reinforce predispositions (Jacobson 1975). In their study on the attitudes of Canadian voters, the authors of *Political Choice in Canada* conclude, "Evidence of direct effects of media attention and party contact on changing people's voting preference may be lacking, but the data suggest the presence of reinforcement effects" (Clarke et al. 1979, 296).

More recent studies, however, indicate that the effects of the mass media go beyond the simple reinforcement of attitudes. Evidence that election advertising has a significant impact is nevertheless slim. For lack of a better approach, studies have used grouped data indicators, correlations, or in some cases examinations of atypical populations, such as the study conducted on college students (Cundy 1986, 212). The results of these studies tend to be positive. In his study on candidate and party expenses during the 1966 and 1970 Quebec elections, Palda (1973) found a significant link between advertising spending and election results. Using a similar procedure during the elections for the U.S. House of Representatives, Wanat (1974) also found a significant link between the amount spent on television advertising by a particular candidate and the number of votes won.

Using a different approach, Joslyn (1981) pursued the same objective. He compared election advertising expenses with survey data in electoral districts during the 1970, 1972 and 1974 elections. Using multivariate analysis, Joslyn showed that election advertising spending is the third best indicator of voter defection and voter loyalty (the first two being party identification and incumbency). Mulder (1979) used the same basic approach to study the mayoral elections in Chicago in 1975. He reported weak but statistically significant correlations between exposure to political ads and voting preferences. As Jamieson (1989) tried to show, it is the sociopolitical context that gives meaning to a message. We should expect ads that attack a candidate to polarize the debate because of their boomerang effect on voters who favour the candidate attacked. Also, focus group tests tend to show that Canadian voters who are not interested in politics are also less likely to be angered by negative advertising (Wearing 1988, 115). This makes the parties' task even more difficult. Although election advertising and debates between leaders can polarize voters, it is highly unlikely that public affairs programs and newscasts can do the same.

Public affairs programs and newscasts, like advertising and such special events as leaders debates, nonetheless give voters useful information in making their election choices. Among all the types of news categories presented by the media, one demands special attention: the publication of opinion poll results during election campaigns. It is claimed that the information voters derive from polls encourages them to join the ranks of the most popular party – the "bandwagon" effect – or to vote strategically. Voting strategically means voting for a second-choice candidate; for example, take the case of a voter who fiercely opposed the proposed Free Trade Agreement between Canada and the United States and whose normal voting preference would have been the NDP. During the 1988 election campaign, the voter realizes that the party with the best chance of beating the government party and its free trade policy is the Liberal party. If the voter decides to abandon the first choice – the NDP – in order to vote Liberal, the voter is said to be voting strategically. Opinion polls on party popularity give voters information enabling them to make this type of decision.

As seen in the study of the 1988 federal election campaign (Blais et al. 1990), people who kept up to date on poll results had the most accurate perspective on who was going to win or lose the election. These people were therefore potentially better armed to make a strategic decision. And that is what some of them did.

The study by Blais and his colleagues (1990) also draws our attention to a phenomenon that is both comical and revealing. Two weeks before the end of the 1988 election campaign, Gallup published the results of a poll mistakenly showing the Liberals to be ahead of the Conservatives. Publication of these results had a greater effect on people who, during the week preceding the interviews, had no idea of the results of opinion polls on party popularity. Thus, during the final two weeks of the campaign, people who did not know the previous poll results were more likely to believe that the Liberals would win. To the extent that the relationship between publication of the faulty Gallup poll and voters' expectations is not misleading, we may draw conclusions on the virtues of prohibiting the publication of polls for a few days before the election.

Advocacy Advertising

Studies on the mass media remind us that the credibility of the source is an important factor in estimating the impact of the message. Advertising by interest groups lets a party or candidate benefit from support while escaping election spending regulations. It also lets these groups do the "sales pitch" for them. A recent but already classic case of this type linked the Democrats' presidential candidate Michael Dukakis to criminal Willie Horton. Television ads by an organization that was technically independent of the Bush campaign let Americans know about a black prisoner who raped a white woman while on a weekend pass. Weekend passes were part of the prisoner rehabilitation program in the state of Massachusetts, where Dukakis was governor. By the end of the election campaign, one voter in four knew about this issue. At the beginning of the campaign, 36 percent of voters felt that Dukakis was a little soft on criminals. By the end of the campaign, that figure had climbed to 49 percent (Diamond and Marin 1989, 386). The U.S. literature is full of such examples showing that advertising by political action committees and interest groups is effective.

In Canada, an Environics survey conducted in December 1988, the month after the federal election, showed that third-party election advertising is, according to voters themselves, an important factor in voting. Nearly three people in ten (27 percent) consider third-party advertising and leaders debates very important in their voting decisions. Moreover, only 13 percent considered parties themselves as very important, while even fewer considered information distributed to residences (11 percent) and opinion polls (11 percent) as important (Adams 1990).

In a survey conducted four months after the November 1988 election, 31 percent of Canadians admitted that their vote had been influenced by third-party ads, and half of these (14 percent) said the ads had had a significant effect. During the survey conducted by the same company in December 1988, 27 percent said that third-party advertising was important in their electoral choice (Adams 1990). These are, however, raw survey data that called on interviewees' memory of how their voting preferences evolved over the campaign. Moreover, the processing of the data was very elementary. The fact remains that there is a striking parallel between the daily quantity of advertising by the coalition for free trade and the return to power of the party bearing the free trade standard (see Johnston et al. 1992).

From this limited information, we cannot determine whether advertising paid for by third parties is more effective or less effective than that paid for by official agents of the parties or candidates. To the extent that advertising paid for by para-partisan organizations is added to that of the parties and candidates, however, a larger audience is reached or the same audience is reached more often.

CONCLUSION AND DISCUSSION

In this literature review, we have seen that the main focus of television newscasts during election campaigns is the leaders of the main parties and the issues they define. The information retained by the voter certainly depends on the degree of exposure to these information sources. This degree of exposure depends on people's interest in the election campaign, which depends in turn on how exciting the election is perceived to be.

We have also seen that the news coverage of political parties on the public broadcasting network reflects the compromise that political parties themselves reached in the name of the principle of balance. The formula resulting from this compromise serves as an index to measure the distribution of the time allotted to each party in newscasts. Two biases result from applying the compromise: on the one hand, the distribution of time among the parties is based not on the importance of the day's news, but on what happened three, four or five years ago. To the extent that the strength of parties is relatively stable, the consequences are more than negligible. In the case where the relative strength of parties would change radically – as appears to be the case in Canada since the beginning of the 1990s – the bias would be all the more obvious. The second bias is the privilege enjoyed by the New Democratic Party as a result of the compromise formula.

I think it wise that a Crown corporation such as the CBC should seek to distribute air time in such a way that it does not become a greater target for criticism by political parties represented in the House of Commons. Moreover, given that the main parties have agreed on a basic formula and that this formula is not incompatible with the principle of journalistic objectivity, it seems advisable not to intervene in these processes unless it is to confirm the independence of the Corporation relative to the parties and political power.

The general impression of Canadian political parties gained by watching televised news is somewhat negative. Some might blame journalists, producers and broadcasters for presenting politicians and their activities in a bad light. It also may be that the source of this negative impression lies in the discrepancy between the high standards citizens set for their politicians and reality. As long as political parties live on the contributions of private sector corporations, and citizens do not accept this form of party financing as normal, it is likely that politicians and parties will continue to be viewed negatively. If any action should be undertaken to enhance the image of politicians and parties, in my view it must come more from the parties and politicians themselves than from the media, the mirrors that reflect them to society.

Election campaigns are the high points in a democracy. They are periods when candidates, parties and policies are examined closely. It is unacceptable that by the end of an election campaign more than one voter in four still cannot identify a single candidate in his or her riding. What can be done? We have seen that people who watch television news and read newspapers are those most likely to be able to identify candidates. To increase the level of knowledge, it should suffice to increase the quantity (and repetition) of information in the media. The problem lies with those who do not avail themselves of these sources of information. How can they be reached? I have pointed out that it is possible to use advertising to increase the level of knowledge of those who are not interested in politics and who do not follow political news. Holding media events such as leaders debates is also a way of reaching a less attentive group of citizens, particularly youth. These debates provide an opportunity to acquire information on political personalities and their positions on the issues of the day.

In my research review, I drew attention to a specific type of news: polling results. Given people's interest in this subject, it is appropriate to spend some time on the topic. What seduces or dismays in opinion polls during election campaigns is the information on the distribution of voter intentions by party. People who know this information are more likely to predict correctly the respective strength of the parties at the finish line than people who were not informed of the poll results. This is the first effect of the publication of polls. This information is added to other information already held by the voter so that as informed a decision as possible can be reached.

Some people fear, however, that the publication of an erroneous or abnormal poll may deceive voters. This is the origin of the idea of prohibiting the publication of opinion poll results, either entirely or during the last portion of the election campaign. Studies of the 1988 election campaign (Blais et al. 1990; Johnston et al. 1992) lead to two observations. In 1988, the notorious Gallup poll was published two weeks before election day. To avoid problems caused by this poll, it would have been necessary to prohibit publication of polls at least 14 days before the election. Second, this defective Gallup survey had its effect mainly among those who had no direct knowledge of the poll. If a publishing ban had been in effect, people would probably have learned about the poll through rumours, a channel that would become widespread if the media could no longer publish poll results. The study on the 1988 election campaign in Canada confirms that it is the widespread distribution of public information that guarantees better voter judgement.

Within the scope of research on mass media and election campaigns, I focused on election advertising. The advantage offered by television advertising is that it reaches a segment of the electorate that is not very interested in public affairs – and consequently invests little in acquiring political information – but does watch television. This potential election audience can easily avoid exposure to election propaganda by *not* reading newspapers, magazines and brochures, *not* attending political meetings, *not* watching public affairs programs and *not* discussing politics. But because this group watches television a great deal, it cannot escape election advertising. It is therefore the least informed citizens who are likely to learn the most through televised election advertising.

Televised election advertising is to recent election campaigns what neighbourhood meetings were to the campaigns of long ago. Media strategists have replaced election organizers as propagandists of the "good news." They visit homes via television, but for how much longer will this method still be effective? Will the fragmentation of audiences by the advent of many specialized television channels complicate significantly the task of reaching the entire public? Will new generations be as tuned in to television as have been the present generations, for whom television was a great innovation?

In future elections, it will undoubtedly be necessary to advertise through many channels in addition to the traditional television networks to reach all potential voters.

APPENDIX
PROPOSITIONS ABOUT ELECTION ADVERTISING ON TELEVISION

Proposition: Election advertising increases voters' knowledge of issues and candidates.

Proposition: Exposure to campaign advertising and interest in politics are correlated.

Proposition: Election advertising is a major source of information for voters.

Proposition: The less politically aware the voter, the more important election advertising becomes.

Proposition: Message repetition (frequency) is an important factor in familiarizing voters with candidates and issues.

Proposition: There is a correlation between the issues proposed by candidates in their advertising and the issues emphasized by the electorate.

Proposition: Candidates who take a position on the issues in their advertising rate higher with the electorate than candidates who do not.

Proposition: The less known the candidate, the more effective election advertising is.

Proposition: For local candidates (as opposed to party leaders or stars), election advertising is one of the few means of gaining exposure.

Proposition: Advertising related to issues seems to produce better results than advertising related to personalities.

NOTES

This paper was completed in April 1991.

The author wishes to thank two anonymous evaluators and Frederick J. Fletcher, the research coordinator for media and elections, for their comments on an initial version of this text.

1. Other factors, such as the significant development of the public relations and public opinion poll industries, have allowed the leaders of national parties to relegate their ridings and their candidates to a secondary role, both in the parties and, of course, in politics in general (Butler and Kavanagh 1974, 201).

BIBLIOGRAPHY

Abramowitz, A.I. 1978. "The Impact of a Presidential Debate on Voter Rationality." *American Journal of Political Science* 22:680–90.

Adams, Michael (Environics Research Group). 1990. "Public Opinion and Third Party Advertising." Brief to the Royal Commission on Electoral Reform and Party Financing. Ottawa.

Atkin, C., L. Bowen, O. Nayman and K. Sheimkopf. 1973. "Quality versus Quantity in Televised Political Ads." *Public Opinion Quarterly* 37:209–24.

Atkin, Charles, and Gary Heald. 1976. "Effects of Political Advertising." *Public Opinion Quarterly* 40:216–28.

Axford, Barrie, and Peter Madgwick. 1989. "Indecent Exposure? Three-Party Politics in Television News during the 1987 General Election." In *Political Communications: The General Election Campaign of 1987*, ed. I. Crewe and M. Harrop. Cambridge: Cambridge University Press.

Baker K.L., and H. Norpoth. 1981. "Candidates on Television: The 1972 Electoral Debates in West Germany." *Public Opinion Quarterly* 45:329–45.

Behr, R.L. 1985. "The Effects of Media on Voters' Considerations in Presidential and Congressional Elections." Ph.D. diss., Yale University.

Behr, R.L., and S. Iyengar. 1985. "Television News, Real-World Cues, and Changes in the Public Agenda." *Public Opinion Quarterly* 49:38–57.

Bennett, W. Lance. 1977. "The Ritualistic and Pragmatic Bases of Political Campaign Discourse." *Quarterly Journal of Speech* 63:219–38.

Berelson, B.R., P.F. Lazarsfeld and W.H. McPhee. 1954. *Voting*. Chicago: University of Chicago Press.

Bernier, Robert. 1991. *Gérer la victoire? Organisation, communication, stratégie.* Boucherville: Gaëtan Morin.

Bishop, George, Robert Meadow and Marilyn Jackson-Beeck, eds. 1978. *The Presidential Debates: Media, Electoral, and Policy Perspectives.* New York: Praeger.

Blais, A., R. Johnston, H. Brady and J. Crête. 1990. "The Dynamics of Horse Race Expectations in the 1988 Canadian Election." Paper presented to the Canadian Political Science Association annual meeting, Victoria.

Blumler, J.G., and D. McQuail. 1968. *Television in Politics*. Chicago: University of Chicago Press.

Blumler, J.G., M. Gurevitch and T.J. Nossiter. 1989. "The Earnest versus the Determined: Election Newsmaking at the BBC, 1987." In *Political Communications: The General Election Campaign of 1987*, ed. I. Crewe and M. Harrop. Cambridge: Cambridge University Press.

Bowers, Thomas A. 1972. "Issues and Personality Information in Newspaper Political Advertising." *Journalism Quarterly* 49:446–52.

Braungart, R., and M. Braungart. 1989. "Les générations politiques." In *Générations et politique*, ed. J. Crête and P. Favre. Paris: Économica.

Butler, D., and D. Kavanagh. 1974. *The British General Election of February 1974*. London: Macmillan.

Campbell, Angus, Phillip E. Converse, Warren E. Miller and Donald E. Stokes. 1964. *The American Voter*. New York: John Wiley.

Campbell, James E., John R. Alford and Keith Henry. 1984. "Television Markets and Congressional Elections." *Legislative Studies Quarterly* 9:665–78.

Canada. Elections Canada. Various. *Report of the Chief Electoral Officer of Canada*. Ottawa: Minister of Supply and Services Canada.

Canadian National Election Study. 1988. Institute for Social Research, York University. Principal investigators: Richard Johnston, André Blais, Henry E. Brady and Jean Crête. Funded by the Social Sciences and Humanities Research Council.

Caron, André H., Chantal Mayrand and David E. Payne. 1983. "L'imagerie politique à la télévision: les derniers jours de la campagne référendaire." *Canadian Journal of Political Science* 16:473–88.

Chaffee, S.H. 1977. "Mass Media Effects: New Research Perspectives." In *Communication Research – A Half-Century Appraisal*, ed. D. Lerner and L.M. Nelson. Honolulu: University Press of Hawaii.

Chaffee, S.H., and Y. Miyo. 1983. "Selective Exposure and the Reinforcement Hypothesis: An Intergenerational Panel Study of the 1980 Presidential Campaign." *Communication Research* 10:3–36.

Clarke, H.D., J. Jenson, L. LeDuc and J.H. Pammett. 1979. *Political Choice in Canada*. Toronto: McGraw-Hill Ryerson.

Clarke, Peter, and Susan H. Evans. 1983. *Covering Campaigns: Journalism in Congressional Elections*. Stanford: Stanford University Press.

Comstock, George. 1982. "Television and American Social Institutions." In *Television and Behavior*, vol. II. Washington, DC: U.S. Department of Health and Human Services.

Corner, J. 1979. "'Mass' in Communication Research." *Journal of Communication* 29:26–32.

Cotteret, J.M., C. Émeri, J. Gerstlé and R. Moreau. 1976. *Giscard d'Estaing–Mitterrand: 54774 mots pour convaincre.* Paris: Presses universitaires de France.

Crête, J. 1984. "La presse quotidienne et la campagne électorale de 1981." *Recherches sociographiques* 25:103–14.

Crewe, Ivor, and Martin Harrop, eds. 1989. *Political Communications: The General Election Campaign of 1987.* Cambridge: Cambridge University Press.

Cundy, Donald T. 1986. "Political Commercials and Candidate Image." In *New Perspectives on Political Advertising,* ed. L.L. Kaid, Dan Nimmo and Keith R. Sanders. Carbondale: Southern Illinois University Press.

Danowski, J.A., and J.E. Ruchinskas. 1983. "Period, Cohort, and Aging: A Study of Television Exposure in Presidential Election Campaigns, 1952–1980." *Communication Research* 10:77–96.

Dawson, P., and J. Zinser. 1971. "Broadcast Expenditures and Electoral Outcomes in the 1970 Congressional Elections." *Public Opinion Quarterly* 35:398–402.

DeFleur, M.L., and S.J. Ball-Rokeach. 1975. *Theories of Mass Communication.* 4th ed. New York: Longman.

Denton, Robert E., and Dan F. Hahn. 1986. *Presidential Communication: Description and Analysis.* New York: Praeger.

Desmond, R.J., and T.R. Donohue. 1981. "The Role of the 1976 Televised Presidential Debates in the Political Socialization of Adolescents." *Communication Quarterly* 29:302–308.

Devlin, Patrick L. 1986. "An Analysis of Presidential Television Commercials, 1952–1985." In *New Perspectives on Political Advertising,* ed. L.L. Kaid, Dan Nimmo and Keith R. Sanders. Carbondale: Southern Illinois University Press.

———. 1989. "Contrasts in Presidential Campaign Commercials of 1988." *American Behavioral Scientist* 32:389–414.

Diamond, Edwin, and Stephen Bates. 1984. *The Spot: The Rise of Political Advertising on Television.* Cambridge: MIT Press.

Diamond, Edwin, and Adrian Marin. 1989. "Spots." *American Behavioral Scientist* 32:382–88.

Fletcher, Frederick J. 1981a. *The Newspaper and Public Affairs.* Vol. 7 of the research studies of the Royal Commission on Newspapers. Ottawa: Minister of Supply and Services Canada.

————. 1981b. "The Contest for Media Attention: The 1979 and 1980 Federal Election Campaigns." In *Politics and the Media: An Examination of the Issues Raised by the Quebec Referendum and the 1979 and 1980 Federal Elections.* Toronto: Reader's Digest Foundation of Canada.

————. 1981c. "Playing the Game: The Mass Media and the 1979 Campaign." In *Canada at the Polls, 1979 and 1980,* ed. Howard R. Penniman. Washington, DC: American Enterprise Institute for Public Policy Research.

————. 1988. "The Media and the 1984 Landslide." In *Canada at the Polls, 1984,* ed. Howard Penniman. Washington, DC: American Enterprise Institute for Public Policy Research.

Frizzell, A., J.H. Pammett and A. Westell. 1989. *The Canadian General Election of 1988.* Ottawa: Carleton University Press.

Funkhouser, G.R. 1973. "The Issues of the Sixties: An Exploratory Study in the Dynamics of Public Opinion." *Public Opinion Quarterly* 37:62–75.

Garramone, Gina. 1985. "Motivation and Political Information Processing." In *Mass Media and Political Thought,* ed. S. Kraus and R.M. Perloff. Beverly Hills: Sage Publications.

————. 1986. "Candidate Image Formation." In *New Perspectives on Political Advertising,* ed. L.L. Kaid, Dan Nimmo and Keith R. Sanders. Carbondale: Southern Illinois University Press.

Gourevitch, Jean-Paul. 1986. *La politique et ses images.* Paris: Edilig.

Hagner, P., and L. Rieselbach. 1978. "The Impact of the 1976 Presidential Debates: Conversion or Reinforcement?" In *The Presidential Debates,* ed. G. Bishop et al. New York: Praeger.

Hale, Jon F. 1987. "The Scribes of Texas: Newspaper Coverage of the 1984 U.S. Senate Campaign." In *Campaign in the News: Mass Media and Congressional Elections,* ed. Jan Pons Vermeer. New York: Greenwood Press.

Harrison, Martin. 1989. "Television Election News Analysis: Use and Abuse – A Reply." *Political Studies* 37:652–58.

Hofstetter, Richard, and T.F. Buss. 1980. "Politics and Last-Minute Political Television." *Western Political Quarterly* 33:24–37.

Hofstetter, Richard C., Cliff Zukin and Terry F. Buss. 1978. "Political Imagery and Information in an Age of Television." *Journalism Quarterly* 55:562–69.

Humke, Ronald G., Raymond L. Schmitt and Stanley E. Grupp. 1975. "Candidates, Issues and Party in Newspaper Political Advertisements." *Journalism Quarterly* 52:499–504.

Iyengar, Shanto, and Donald R. Kinder. 1987. *News That Matters.*
Chicago: University of Chicago Press.

Jacobson, Gary C. 1975. "The Impact of Broadcast Campaigning on
Electoral Outcomes." *Journal of Politics* 37:769–93.

Jamieson, Kathleen Hall. 1986. "The Evolution of Political Advertising in
America." In *New Perspectives on Political Advertising,* ed. L.L. Kaid,
Dan Nimmo and Keith R. Sanders. Carbondale: Southern Illinois
University Press.

————. 1989. "Context and the Creation of Meaning in the Advertising of
the 1988 Presidential Campaign." *American Behavioral Scientist* 32:415–24.

Jamieson, K.H., and D.S. Birdsell. 1988. *Presidential Debates.* New York:
Oxford University Press.

Johnson, Karen S., and Camille Elebash. 1986. "The Contagion from the
Right." In *New Perspectives on Political Advertising,* ed. L.L. Kaid,
Dan Nimmo and Keith R. Sanders. Carbondale: Southern Illinois
University Press.

Johnston, R.J., A. Blais, H. Brady and J. Crête. 1989. "Free Trade and the
Dynamics of the 1988 Canadian Election." Paper presented to the
Canadian Political Science Association annual meeting, Quebec.

————. 1992. *Letting the People Decide: Dynamics of a Canadian Election.*
Montreal: McGill-Queen's University Press, and Stanford: Stanford
University Press (forthcoming).

Joslyn, Richard A. 1980. "The Content of Political Spots Ads."
Journalism Quarterly 57:92–98.

————. 1981. "The Impact of Campaign Spot Advertising on Voting
Defections." *Human Communication Research* 7:347–60.

————. 1984. *Mass Media and Elections.* Reading: Addison-Wesley.

————. 1986. "Political Advertising and the Meaning of Elections."
In *New Perspectives on Political Advertising,* ed. L.L. Kaid, Dan Nimmo
and Keith R. Sanders. Carbondale: Southern Illinois University Press.

Kaid, L.L., and K.R. Sanders. 1978. "Political Commercials:
An Experimental Study of Type and Length." *Communication Research*
5:57–70.

Kaid, Lynda Lee, and Dorothy K. Davidson. 1986. "Elements of Videostyle."
In *New Perspectives on Political Advertising,* ed. L.L. Kaid, Dan Nimmo
and Keith R. Sanders. Carbondale: Southern Illinois University Press.

Kaid, Lynda Lee, Dan Nimmo and Keith R. Sanders, eds. 1986.
New Perspectives on Political Advertising. Carbondale: Southern Illinois
University Press.

Katz, E., and J. Feldman. 1962. "The Debates in the Light of Research."
In *The Great Debates: Kennedy versus Nixon, 1960*, ed. S. Kraus.
Bloomington: Indiana University Press.

Kavanagh, D. 1989. "The Timing of Elections: The British Case."
In *Political Communications: The General Election Campaign of 1987*,
ed. I. Crewe and M. Harrop. Cambridge: Cambridge University Press.

Kern, Montague. 1989. *30-Second Politics: Political Advertising in the Eighties*.
New York: Praeger.

Klapper, J.T. 1960. *The Effects of Mass Communication*. Glencoe: Free Press.

Kolar, Barry. 1986. "Fighting Back." In *New Perspectives on Political
Advertising*, ed. L.L. Kaid, Dan Nimmo and Keith R. Sanders.
Carbondale: Southern Illinois University Press.

Kornberg, Allan, and J.D. Wolfe. 1980. "Parliament, the Media and the
Polls." In *Parliament, Policy and Representation*, ed. H.D. Clarke,
C. Campbell, F.O. Quo and A. Goddard. Toronto: Methuen.

Kraus, Sidney, ed. 1962. *The Great Debates: Kennedy versus Nixon, 1960*.
Bloomington: Indiana University Press.

———, ed. 1979. *The Great Debates: Carter versus Ford, 1976*.
Bloomington: Indiana University Press.

Labbé, Dominique. 1983. *François Mitterrand: essai sur le discours*.
Paris: La pensée sauvage.

Lane, R.E. 1965. *Political Life*. New York: Free Press.

Lang, Gladys Engel, and Kurt Lang. 1984. *Politics and Television Re-Viewed*.
Beverly Hills: Sage Publications.

Latimer, Margaret K. 1984. "Policy Issues and Personal Images in Political
Advertising for a State Election." *Journalism Quarterly* 61:776–84.

———. 1985. "Political Advertising for Federal and State Elections:
Images or Substance?" *Journalism Quarterly* 62:861–68.

———. 1989. "Legislators' Advertising Messages in Seven State Campaigns
in 1986." *Journalism Quarterly* 66:338–46.

Lau, R.R., D.O. Sears and R. Centers. 1979. "The 'Positivity Bias' in
Evaluation of Public Figures: Evidence against Instrument Artifacts."
Public Opinion Quarterly 43:347–58.

Lazarsfeld, P., B. Berelson and H. Gaudet. 1948. *The People's Choice*.
New York: Columbia University Press.

LeDuc, Lawrence, and Richard Price. 1985. "The Televised Leadership
Debates of 1979." *Canadian Journal of Political Science* 18:135–55.

Lemert, James B., W. Elliott, K.J. Nestvold and G.R. Rarick. 1983.
"Effects of Viewing a Presidential Primary Debate: An Experiment."
Communication Research 10:155–73.

McCombs, M.E., and D.L. Shaw. 1972. "The Agenda-Setting Function
of the Mass Media." *Public Opinion Quarterly* 36:176–87.

McGregor, Robin, Michael Svennenig and Chris Ledger. 1989.
"Television and the 1987 General Election Campaign."
In *Political Communications: The General Election Campaign of 1987*, ed.
I. Crewe and M. Harrop. Cambridge: Cambridge University Press.

McGuire, W.J. 1989. "Theoretical Foundations of Campaigns."
In *Public Communication Campaigns*, ed. R.E. Rice and C.K. Atkin.
Newbury Park: Sage Publications.

McIntosh, E.G. 1989. "Attitude Change and Voting Preference in the
Presidential Debates." *Psychological Reports* 64:422.

MacKuen, M.B. 1981. "Social Communications and Mass Policy Agenda."
In *More than News: Media Power in Public Affairs*, ed. M.B. MacKuen and
S.L. Coombs. Beverly Hills: Sage Publications.

———. 1984. "Exposure to Information, Belief Integration, and Individual
Responsiveness to Agenda Change." *American Political Science Review*
78:372–91.

McLeod, Jack M., L.B. Becker and J.E. Byrnes. 1974. "Another Look at the
Agenda-Setting Function of the Press." *Communication Research* 1:131–66.

McLeod, Jack M., Carl R. Bybee and Jean A. Durall. 1979.
"Equivalence of Informed Political Participation: The 1976 Presidential
Debates as a Source of Influence." *Communication Research* 6:463–87.

Mansfield, Michael W., and Katherine Hale. 1986. "Uses and Perceptions
of Political Television." In *New Perspectives on Political Advertising*,
ed. L.L. Kaid, Dan Nimmo and Keith R. Sanders. Carbondale:
Southern Illinois University Press.

Mickelson, Sig. 1989. *From Whistle Stop to Sound Bite*. New York: Praeger.

Milbrath, Lester. 1965. *Political Participation*. Chicago: Rand McNally.

Miller, W.L., N. Sonntag and D. Broughton. 1989. "Television in the 1987
British Election Campaign: Its Content and Influence." *Political Studies*
37:626–51.

Mintz, Eric. 1986. "Newspaper Advertisements in Canadian Election
Campaigns." *Journalism Quarterly* 63:180–84.

Monière, Denis. 1988. *Le discours électoral*. Montreal: Québec/Amérique.

Mulder, R. 1979. "The Effects of Televisual Political Ads in the 1975
Chicago Mayoral Election." *Journalism Quarterly* 56:335–41.

Nimmo, Dan. 1981. "Mass Communication and Politics."
In *The Handbook of Political Behavior*, vol. 4, ed. Samuel L. Long.
New York: Plenum Press.

Nimmo, Dan, and Arthur J. Felsberg. 1986. "Hidden Myths in Televised
Political Advertising." In *New Perspectives on Political Advertising*,
ed. L.L. Kaid, Dan Nimmo and Keith R. Sanders. Carbondale:
Southern Illinois University Press.

O'Neil, Helen, and Stephen Mills. 1986. "Political Advertising in Australia."
In *New Perspectives on Political Advertising*, ed. L.L. Kaid, Dan Nimmo and
Keith R. Sanders. Carbondale: Southern Illinois University Press.

Page, Benjamin I. 1978. *Choices and Echoes in Presidential Elections: Rational
Man and Electoral Democracy*. Chicago: University of Chicago Press.

Page, Benjamin I., Robert Y. Shapiro and Glenn R. Dempsey. 1987.
"What Moves Public Opinion?" *American Political Science Review* 81:23–43.

Palda, K.S. 1973. "Does Advertising Influence Votes? An Analysis of the
1966 and 1970 Quebec Elections." *Canadian Journal of Political Science*
6:638–55.

Patterson, T.E. 1980. *The Mass Media Election: How Americans Choose Their
President*. New York: Praeger.

Patterson, Thomas E., and Robert D. McClure. 1974. *Political Advertising:
Voter Reaction to Televised Political Commercials*. Princeton:
Citizens' Research Foundation.

———. 1976. *The Unseeing Eye*. New York: G.P. Putnam's Sons.

Patton, Gary W.R., and Bruce Smith. 1980. "The Effects of Taking Issue
Positions on Ratings of Political Candidates." *Political Psychology* 2:20–34.

Quarles, Rebecca Colwell. 1979. "Mass Media Use and Voting Behavior:
The Accuracy of Political Perceptions among First-Time and Experienced
Voters." *Communication Research* 6:407–36.

Ranney, A., ed. 1979. *The Past and Future of Presidential Debates*. Washington,
DC: American Enterprise Institute for Public Policy Research.

Roddy, Brian L., and Gina M. Garramone. 1988. "Appeals and Strategies of
Negative Political Advertising." *Journal of Broadcasting and Electronic
Media* 32:415–27.

Rosen, B., and H.J. Einhorn. 1972. "Attractiveness of the 'Middle of the Road'
Political Candidate." *Journal of Applied Social Psychology* 2:157–65.

Rosenberg, Shawn W., Lisa Bohan, Patrick McCafferty and Kim Harris. 1986.
"The Image and the Vote: The Effects of Candidate Presentation on Voter
Preference." *American Journal of Political Science* 30:108–27.

Rothschild, M.L., and M.L. Ray. 1974. "Involvement and Political Advertising Effect: An Exploratory Experiment." *Communication Research* 1:264–85.

Rudd, Robert. 1989. "Effects of Issue Specificity, Ambiguity on Evaluations of Candidate Image." *Journalism Quarterly* 66:675–82 and 691.

Seaton, J., and B. Pimlott. 1987. *The Media and British Politics.* Aldershot: Avebury.

Shaw, Donald, and Thomas Bowers. 1973. "Learning from Commercials: The Influence of TV Advertising on the Voter Political 'Agenda'." Paper presented to the Association for Education in Journalism.

Shrott, P.R. 1989. "The West German Television Debates: 1972–1987." Paper presented to the American Political Science Association annual meeting, Atlanta, Ga.

Shyles, Leonard. 1986. "The Televised Political Spot Advertisement." In *New Perspectives on Political Advertising,* ed. L.L. Kaid, Dan Nimmo and Keith R. Sanders. Carbondale: Southern Illinois University Press.

Soderlund, W.C., W.I. Romanow, E.D. Briggs and R.H. Wagenberg. 1984. *Media and Elections in Canada.* Toronto: Holt, Rinehart and Winston.

Steinberg, Arnold. 1976. *The Political Campaign Handbook.* Lexington: D.C. Heath.

Strouse, J.C. 1975. *The Mass Media, Public Opinion and Public Policy Analysis.* Columbus: Charles E. Merrill.

Trenaman, J.S.M., and D. McQuail. 1961. *Television and the Political Image.* London: Methuen.

Uhlaner, Carole. 1984. "La participation politique des femmes au Québec: 1965–1977." In *Comportement électoral au Québec,* ed. J. Crête. Chicoutimi: Gaëtan Morin.

Wagenberg, R.H., W.C. Soderlund, W.I. Romanow and E.D. Briggs. 1988. "Campaigns, Images and Polls: Mass Media Coverage of the 1984 Canadian Election." *Canadian Journal of Political Science* 21:117–29.

Wanat, S. 1974. "Political Broadcast Advertising and Primary Election Voting." *Journal of Broadcasting* 18:413–22.

Wanzenfried, J.W., F.C. Powell and L.J. Franks. 1989. "Perceptions of Political Competency and the Impact of a Televised Debate." *Psychological Reports* 64:825–26.

Wearing, J. 1988. *Strained Relations.* Toronto: McClelland and Stewart.

Weiss, W. 1969. "Effects of the Mass Media of Communication." In *Handbook of Social Psychology*, ed. G. Lindzay and E. Aronson. Reading: Addison-Wesley.

Winn, Conrad. 1976. "Mass Communications." In C. Winn and J. McMenemy, *Political Parties in Canada*. Toronto: McGraw-Hill.

Zajonc, R. 1980. "Feeling and Thinking: Preferences Need No Inferences." *American Psychologist* 35:151–75.

2

MEDIA USAGE AND POLITICAL BEHAVIOUR

~

R.H. MacDermid

INTRODUCTION

 M ODERN POLITICAL CAMPAIGNS, unlike their predecessors of as little as thirty years ago, are waged almost entirely through television, radio, newspapers and magazines (Yum and Kendall 1988). Only a small fraction of voters ever meet a party leader or hear a leader or candidate address a crowd. When these infrequent events occur they are tightly scripted and controlled (Cocking 1980; Comber and Mayne 1986; Crouse 1972; Gilsdorf 1981). Only a small percentage of voters ever see local candidates in the flesh, and many will never see them on television, hear about them on radio, or read about them in newspapers, for all of those media tend to feature reports about national campaigns and national political figures rather than local campaigns and local candidates (Fletcher 1987, 359; Soderlund et al. 1984, 54–55).[1] For most people, politics means the short "sound bite" spoken by a party leader and featured in a 45-second story on the national or local television news. Many, of course, read about campaigns in the newspapers, but these stories are often carefully "manufactured" by the parties who are concerned to let as little hard news out as possible (Fletcher 1981c). Print reporters most often produce a stream of commentary on the status of the campaign or the personal characteristics of the leaders, and readers become informed about the details of the race and the personality deficiencies of the candidates rather than what is or is not being talked about by the politicians (Graber 1976; Frizzell and Westell 1989; Wilson 1981). Radio listeners, depending upon where they fit into radio's fragmented market, may hear nothing at all about a political campaign, as radio stations have trimmed news gatherers, cut regular news programs, and moved toward "lifestyle" news (Fang 1985, 235–39; Hedges 1986). Most of us come into contact with television, radio and print on a daily basis, rising and going to work with radio, eating break-fast with a newspaper or television, or using all three media during the evening. Further, the importance of the media to what we say, think or do is hardly ever underestimated. All the more reason to be surprised at how little we know about how media usage affects how people vote, whether they turn out to vote, what they think about the issues of the day, or what they would do if ever it should happen that they wish to take action on a particular problem. Here, almost all we know is untested or partially tested assumption (Fletcher 1988, 1987, 1981a, 1981b, 1981c, 1980, 1975; Iyengar and Kinder 1987; Joslyn 1984; Soderlund et al. 1984).

This study addresses some of the gaps in our knowledge about Canadians' media usage, and especially how that relates to their polit-ical behaviour. As is described later, the measures of media exposure are imprecise, and the research designs ill suited to making causal state-ments about relationships between Canadians' political behaviour and their media usage. Nonetheless, some trends can be analysed using the data gathered by the Canadian National Election Studies: academic opinion research that has followed every federal general election since 1965, with the exception of 1972.

Four questions are addressed and answered in the subsequent sections of the study. First, how closely do Canadians watch political news on television, read about such news in newspapers, or listen to it on radio, and has their attentiveness to the political content of these media changed over time? Second, how do those who do and those who do not pay close attention to politics in the media differ on such characteristics as gender, income, education, language, age, region of residence, and so on? Third, what partisan characteristics are related to attentiveness to political messages in the media? Do strong partisans, for example, follow the media's message more closely than inde-pendently minded voters? And fourth, do those who pay close atten-tion to the political messages in the media know more about politics than those who pay little or no attention to the political content of the media?

The Data
The data reported and analysed in the following pages are drawn from a number of different sources, ranging from Statistics Canada surveys to polls conducted for the British Broadcasting Corporation. The study's main analytic sections employ data gathered by successive Canadian National Election Studies. This database consists of a series of mostly post-election surveys with representative samples of voting age Canadians following every federal general election since 1965, except the 1972 election. With the exception of the 1988 study, all of the surveys

were in-home face-to-face interviews conducted in the weeks and months following election day. The 1988 survey departed from the preceding research designs in that interviews were conducted by telephone. The representative sample of Canadians was contacted first during the campaign, then once more following the campaign, and finally by mail with a self-completion questionnaire. Several research programs, almost completely sponsored by the Social Sciences and Humanities Research Council of Canada and its predecessor, the Canada Council, have gathered a wealth of information about Canadians' voting behaviour, political party identification, political participation, issue positions, attitude toward federal and provincial political parties and party leaders, political efficacy and trust, social class, income, education, occupation, ethnicity, marital status, religion and a large number of other variables. Most of the questionnaires contained items about media usage, but unfortunately, there were no such questions in the 1965 and 1968 studies.[2]

MEDIA ATTENTION

In 1987, the average Canadian watched 3.4 hours of television every day, with women and older people generally watching more than men and younger people (Young 1989, 14). Most of this viewing time was not directly related to politics or the acquisition of political information. On average, viewing time in 1987 consisted of only 17.1 percent Canadian-produced news and public affairs viewing, or about 35 minutes per day. Fifty-four percent of the balance of Canadians' viewing time was composed of drama, comedy and other programming, all of which was produced outside Canada (ibid., 15). The 1987 Statistics Canada General Social Survey (1989) reported similar figures on Canadians' media usage in the course of gathering data on their use of time during one particular day in November and early December of that year. That survey reported that 75 percent of Canadians watched television for an average of 188 minutes on the sampled day. Newspaper readership and radio listening in this survey were much lower; only 4 percent reported listening to the radio and 18 percent reported reading a newspaper. Both of these figures are certain to be underestimates, for as Statistics Canada notes, "respondents could only report a single activity (the primary activity) at any one time. As a result, certain activities which are often done at the same time as something else (e.g., listening to the radio) are not fully reported in this survey" (Canada, Statistics Canada 1989). Other figures suggest that radio listening and newspaper readership are much higher, and are often part of some other activity such as eating or preparing meals and riding to work.

Boden (1990) reports industry figures that show that radio reaches 94.2 percent of all Canadians over the age of seven years, and that individuals listen for an average of 19.1 hours per week.

The 1988 National Election Study (NES) is the only survey in the series that asked Canadians how often in the past week they had watched the news on television or read a daily newspaper.

As table 2.1 shows, 45 percent of the respondents reported watching the news on television every day during the preceding week, 62 percent reported watching a news broadcast at least four times during the preceding week, and only 13 percent said that they had not watched any television news in the past week. By contrast, 40 percent of the sample reported reading a newspaper every day, 52 percent read a newspaper on four or more of the preceding seven days, and 22 percent said that they had not read a newspaper in the past week. Caution is required in interpreting both of these sets of figures. Reading a newspaper does not equate with reading news about a political campaign. No doubt some readers prefer non-political sections of the paper and concentrate solely on them. And there is enough variation in the extent and form of coverage in major newspapers to believe that people could be getting different messages (Frizzell and Westell 1985, 55–73). So frequency of

Table 2.1
Frequency of television news viewing and newspaper reading, NES 1988
(percentage)

Number of days in past week	Watched TV news	Read newspaper
None	13	22
One	05	10
Two	09	09
Three	11	07
Four	07	04
Five	07	04
Six	03	04
Seven	45	40
Total	100	100
N	(3597)	(3603)

Both these questions were asked in the campaign-period survey.

readership may not be a precise measure of attention to political news contained in newspapers. Frequency of television news watching appears to promise a better measure of attention to political news. But there is no way to determine whether the people interviewed watched the entire broadcast (when they watched at all), what they saw on the broadcast, how much attention they paid to it, and so on.

The NES studies contain a number of variables that try to assess attention to the message being received from the media. Since 1974, all of the surveys have contained questions that ask people how much attention they pay to television, print and radio news about the campaign or politics in general. Unfortunately for comparative purposes, the question has changed twice over the years, meaning that comparison is more difficult than is usually the case (i.e., assuming that a question has a stable common meaning over an extended period of use). Tables 2.2–1, 2.2–2 and 2.2–3 display the levels of attention to the three media.

Table 2.2–1, showing newspaper readership, suggests a two-phase interpretation: for the 1974 to 1979 period and probably extending to the 1984 period, campaign news readership appears to remain fairly constant with about 40 percent indicating that they follow campaign newspaper articles quite a bit or often, and about 25 percent choosing the not much, or seldom and never responses. This steady pattern appears to change somewhat in 1988, with the percentage following a "great deal" and "quite a bit" falling slightly, and those following "very little" or "none" of the campaign articles swelling slightly. Not much should be made of this; the movements are small and it is difficult to rule out the possibility that they may in part be caused by the shift to a five-point response scale from the previous four- and three-point scales. On the other hand, the 1970s and 1980s were a period of consolidation in the Canadian newspaper industry. Several papers closed or competing papers were bought out by competitors, generally reducing competition and resulting in the Royal Commission on Newspapers (the Kent Commission) being struck in 1980 (Siegel 1983). Whether this trend, coupled with the growth of tabloid newspapers that do not generally cover politics as extensively as the "highbrow" press, has resulted in voters being less exposed to newsprint coverage is difficult to say without better evidence.

Table 2.2–2 suggests that attention to television campaign programs and advertisements has risen somewhat. Once again, the change in question response sets muddies the interpretation, but by 1988, 57 percent of the respondents are on the same side of the middle point as only about 45 percent were during the 1974 to 1979 period. The 1984 data are rather more difficult to interpret because there is no midpoint

Table 2.2–1
Media use trends across the NES surveys
(percentage)

Read about campaign in newspapers	1974[a]	1979[a]	1980[a]	1984[b]	1988[c]
A great deal	—	—	—	—	12
Quite a bit	39	40	45	—	26
Often	—	—	—	42	—
Something	35	35	30	—	—
Sometimes	—	—	—	31	—
Some	—	—	—	—	31
Not much	27	25	25	—	—
Very little	—	—	—	—	20
Seldom	—	—	—	17	—
Never	—	—	—	10	—
None	—	—	—	—	11
Total	101[d]	100	100	100	100
N	(1254)[e]	(1348)[e]	(843)[e]	(3373)	(2915)[f]

[a]1974, Q38; 1979, Q43A; 1980, Q16.

[b]1984, A10a.

[c]1988, xa3.

[d]Percentages do not add to 100 because of rounding.

[e]Question asked of half-sample only.

[f]Post-election survey. A similar question was asked in the campaign-period wave.

in the 4-point scale, but nearly three-quarters of the respondents said that they often or sometimes watch programs about politics on television. Table 2.2–2 contains the suggestion of growth just as table 2.2–1 suggested a decrease in attention to newspaper coverage. Only speculation can explain the small changes. First, Canadians' television viewing has increased, from 3.2 hours per day in 1976 to 3.4 in 1987, though it is hard to imagine that this increase is made up entirely of news watching (Young 1989, 14). Second, cable television expanded in the 1980s bringing with it the "all news networks," and generally a much greater selection of news programming (though many of these were American signals that do not report Canadian news).

Table 2.2–3 records attention to radio programs and advertisements carried during the campaign. This question was asked following the

Table 2.2–2
Watched campaign news on television
(percentage)

	1974[a]	1979[a]	1980[a]	1984[b]	1988[c]
A great deal	—	—	—	—	22
Quite a bit	—	—	—	—	35
Quite a few	43	42	47	—	—
Often	—	—	—	33	—
Some	38	37	35	—	27
Sometimes	—	—	—	39	—
Almost none	19	21	18	—	—
Very little	—	—	—	—	11
Seldom	—	—	—	19	—
Never	—	—	—	09	—
None	—	—	—	—	04
Total	100	100	100	100	99[d]
N	*(1251)*[e]	*(1346)*[e]	*(843)*[e]	*(3373)*	*(2919)*[f]

[a]1974, Q39; 1979, Q44a; 1980, Q17.

[b]1984, a10b.

[c]1988, xa2.

[d]Percentages do not add to 100 because of rounding.

[e]Question asked of half-sample only.

[f]Post-election survey. A similar question was asked in the campaign-period wave.

Table 2.2–3
Heard campaign news on radio
(percentage)

	1974[a]	1979[a]	1980[a]
Quite a few	21	26	24
Some	33	35	37
Almost none	46	39	39
Total	100	100	100
N	*(1246)*[b]	*(1330)*[b]	*(839)*[b]

[a]1974, Q40; 1979, Q45; 1980, Q18.

[b]Question asked of half-sample only.

1974, 1979 and 1980 campaigns but has not been included in any of the subsequent election studies. The table shows very little trend and confirms radio as the least important media source for news about campaigns. Only about one-quarter of the sample reported hearing "quite a few" programs or advertisements about the parties, candidates or other aspects of the campaign and 40 percent reported hearing almost none. This relative importance accords with daily evidence that suggests that at least for commercial radio, that is, excluding the CBC AM and FM networks, news often has a local focus and is fairly brief. Of course, since the 1970s the radio bands have undergone considerable changes. Prominent amongst these are the migration of listeners to the better reception quality FM band, a marked decrease in the news-gathering capacities of most radio stations, and a move to shorter "lifestyle" news reporting, most of which is not obviously about politics and a good deal of which has American origins (Fang 1985, 236).

Low voter attention to radio news is not necessarily a characteristic of the medium. In the United Kingdom, radio listening is apparently more frequent, and in a 1983 study that coincided with the general election, "over 70 percent claimed to listen to radio news every day" (Wober et al. 1986, 99). However, a downward trend in radio's importance is found in American election studies. Between 1952 and 1978, the percentage of Americans saying that they had heard speeches or discussions about the campaign on radio declined from 70 to 46, though nearly all of the decline occurred with the introduction of television in the early 1950s (Miller et al. 1980, 306).

Variation in Attention over Interviews

It should be pointed out that responses to survey questions are "fragile" data and are often untested for both validity and reliability. It is often difficult to separate real change in attitudes from random variation that may indicate either a meaningless question or that respondents do not have genuine attitudes on particular questions. The NES 1988 study and the NES 1974 to NES 1979 panel of respondents provide two opportunities to examine the robustness of the responses to the questions on newspaper readership and television viewing.

The NES 1988 survey interviewed respondents during the election campaign and again by telephone following the election campaign. The same respondents were asked the same two questions shown in tables 2.2–1 and 2.2–2, both before and after the election. Because the campaign wave of the survey was a rolling sample (interviews were spread out over the length of the campaign), some respondents may have been asked the question separated by only a few weeks at most.

Table 2.3
Response changes to identical TV questions asked of the same respondents before and after election day, NES 1988

Responses[a]	%
Same	45
Different by one[b]	42
Different by two	11
Different by three or more	2
Total	100
N	(2570)

[a]The question wording varied slightly: 1988; a2b, xa2.

[b]Indicates a respondent changing response one position either toward or away from one end of the scale.

Table 2.3 shows that, despite the short interval, there was a good deal of movement in the same individuals' responses to the same questions. Part of this movement may be the result of interviews that took place early in the campaign period, before those respondents had the opportunity to focus on the campaign.

Just under one-half of the respondents gave the same answer on the two occasions that the question was asked. Taking into account the likelihood of interpreting the response set phrases, "a great deal," "quite a bit" and so on, in different ways on different occasions, this seems to indicate an acceptable degree of reliability. The data suggest the possibility that the respondents' first interview may have encouraged them to pay closer attention to the media. In fact, this is suggested in the breakdown of the direction of those changing responses: 66 percent indicated at the second interview that they were paying or had paid closer attention to television campaign news than was the case at the first interview. The figures for the newspaper question were very similar, with the same percentage giving the same response, and 62 percent of movers going "up" the attention scale. Apart from the possible reactive effect of the question, the responses indicate a valid and reliable measure.

The NES 1974 and NES 1979 panel, a reinterview of the *same* individuals, provides another opportunity to observe the stability of individuals' attention to the different media. In both 1974 and 1979, respondents were asked how often they read about politics in the newspapers. The impression given in table 2.4 is again one of stability.

A greater percentage of respondents displayed stable response patterns in table 2.4 than in table 2.3, though this figure needs careful

Table 2.4
Response changes to identical newspaper questions asked of the same respondents following the 1974 and 1979 elections, NES 1974–79 panel

Responses[a]	%
Same	55
Different by one[b]	33
Different by two or more	12
Total	100
N	(607)[c]

[a]1974, Q11a; 1979, Q13a.

[b]Indicates a respondent changing response one position either toward or away from one end of the scale.

[c]Question asked of half-sample only.

interpretation. First, the number of respondents in table 2.4 is quite small because of panel attrition (respondent drop-out) and because the question was asked of a half-sample only. Second, all other things being equal, increased stability might reasonably be expected when the response categories are fewer in number as they are when moving from 1974–79 to 1988. A second contrast to the pattern in table 2.3 is in the direction of movement of individuals. In table 2.4, the direction of movement (not shown) is about equal, with 47 percent of the movers going up the attention scale and 53 percent going down. As these interviews are separated by nearly five years, it suggests that the table 2.3 pattern of movement with the majority increasing in attention to television news might well either be a short-lived artifact of the first interview having caused individuals to pay closer attention to the medium or a result of being interviewed at the outset of the campaign.

Most Important Media

The comments made in discussing table 2.2 are reinforced by examining a question asked in NES 1974, NES 1979 and NES 1984. The respondents were asked which of radio, television and newspapers were the most important source of election information. The data in table 2.5 reflect the limited importance of radio as a source of campaign information and declining voter reliance on newspapers, as well as the increasing importance of television.

Television's growing influence is also apparent in the combinations of important sources. The only response without television (radio and

Table 2.5
Most important media for information
(percentages)

	1974[a]	1979[a]	1984[b]
Radio only	06	07	04
Television only	40	35	42
Newspapers only	31	32	14
Radio and TV equally	04	04	07
Radio and paper equally	01	02	02
TV and paper equally	12	12	19
All equally	06	08	12
Total	100	100	100
N	(1227)[c]	(1300)[c]	(3210)

[a] 1974, Q41; 1979, Q46.

[b] 1984, d4.

[c] Question asked of half-sample only.

paper equally) is the one that did not show a measurable increase between 1974 and 1984.

A 1987 study by Adams and Levitin (1988) reports a similar pattern to that in table 2.5. That survey found that 47 percent of Canadians say that they are informed about the news through television, while 31 and 15 percent chose newspapers and radio (ibid., 5). This study also reported that 42 percent of Canadians thought television to be the most fair and objective medium while only 23 and 18 percent accorded newspapers and radio the same status (ibid., 10; McMonagle 1988).

A small study of the sources of political information in the United States found a similar reliance on television but also underlined the importance of newspapers and magazines as sources of campaign information: "on the average television was the most frequently mentioned source of political information (86 percent), but was mentioned only 4 percent more often than newspapers (82 percent). A significant minority mentioned magazines (30 percent). Although only 18 percent of the respondents mentioned interpersonal sources of political information (friends and/or family), those who did so relied heavily on such sources for information, reporting that they gained more than a third of their political information from such sources. Forty percent of the respondents relied on two sources for political information. The predominant combination of news sources was television and newspapers (35 percent)" (Yum and Kendall 1988, 150).

Yum and Kendall asked about the percentage of information the respondents gained from each media source and found that while television was the most frequently used source, the respondents indicated that on average they gained just 49 percent of their political information from that medium. This reinforces their finding that voters used, on average, 2.6 sources of political information.

THE SOCIODEMOGRAPHIC CORRELATES OF MEDIA ATTENTION

The effects of media usage upon political behaviour are very much under-researched. Despite our daily subjection to a media barrage that tells us the issues of the day and how we should interpret them, we know next to nothing about how these messages interact with other sources of political information and political knowledge to influence political behaviour. The one brief treatment of the subject is found in Clarke et al. (1979). They found that readers, watchers and listeners differed in several ways. Those who got their campaign information from the press were better educated, had a higher socio-economic status, were more likely to have moved, were somewhat more likely to live in an urban area, were somewhat more likely to be anglophones, and thought of themselves as coming from, on average, a higher social class than those who took their information from television or radio. Television watchers were a representative sample of the entire population and, as the high percentage of watchers suggest, did not correlate significantly with any of the background characteristics but age, indicating a slight tendency for watching to increase with age.

Attention to the different media was also correlated with several behavioural and attitudinal variables. For example, interest in politics and interest in the 1974 election itself were most strongly correlated with newspaper readership and less so with television and radio usage. Those respondents who relied upon the print medium were more likely to report participation in politics generally and participation in the 1974 election than were those who relied upon radio or television for their political information. Finally, the authors found no relationship, or a very modest relationship, between the report of the different media users and whether they had switched votes between 1972 and 1974, their strength of partisanship, their consistency of partisanship across federal and provincial levels, and whether they had changed their partisanship in the past.

The authors conclude that media usage had little effect on the 1974 campaign: "Those who saw no programs or party advertisements on television and those who did not read much about the campaign in the newspapers were just about as likely to change their votes from the previous election as were those who avidly followed the campaign. It is, of course, possible that the news reaching people about the campaign had the effect in many cases of reinforcing previously established positions. Nevertheless, the verdict on the impact of the campaign reaching people through the media remains open" (Clarke et al. 1979, 290–91).

This early analysis of the sociodemographic correlates of media usage was restricted to the findings of a single survey and to bivariate analysis, that is, the observation of relationships between just two variables. The question remains open as to whether the same pattern is repeated across the several datapoints now available to us. More importantly, bivariate analysis leaves open many possibilities for spurious, intervening or alternative causal relationships. For example, observing the relationship between only two variables leaves open the possibility that both, and thus their relationship, are caused by a third factor or variable. A hypothetical example might be an observed bivariate relationship between gender and newspaper readership that indicates males are more likely than females to follow political events in the newspaper. Employing a multivariate research strategy and taking income into account may show that both gender and newspaper readership are related to income so that females are likely to be less well off and newspaper readers are likely to be better off, indicating that the bivariate relationship between gender and newspaper readership is caused by the influence of the income variable.

Tables 2.6 through 2.9 extend across time and into multivariate analysis – the early work of Clarke et al. (1979). The tables show the regression coefficients for an equation with first attention to television, then attention to newspapers, attention to radio and attention to all media as the dependent variables in a multiple regression equation. These equations illustrate our success in devising a linear model that tries to predict each respondent's score on the question about how closely they follow the media, from the knowledge of their sociodemographic characteristics. The independent or predictor variables, listed down the left of the page, are chosen because of their presumed relationship to media attention. That is, it is assumed that income, age and education are all related to attention to the different media and all three are to some extent related to each other: low education is related to low income, and age is positively related to income, both usually rising together until retirement. Community size, employment, gender,

Table 2.6
OLS regression coefficients for sociodemographic correlates of attention to television

	1974	1979	1984	1988
Age	.05**	.04**	.15**	.13**
Community size	.01	.01	.03**	—
Education	.03	.04	.21**	.26**
Employed	-.08	-.08	-.05	.02
Gender	.11*	.14**	.18**	.18**
Income	.04	.01	.03	.04
Language	-.05	-.12*	-.05	-.00
Native-born	-.09	.00	-.00	-.05
Union member	-.04	.13*	.05	-.05
Region				
Atlantic	-.03	-.09	.08	.02
Quebec	-.12	-.24**	.02	-.03
Ontario	—	—	—	—
West	-.07	-.03	.14**	.11*
Constant	2.04	2.07	1.78	2.35
R^2	.03	.04	.12	.08
N	(985)	(1213)	(2674)	(2185)

*Less than .05; **less than .005.

language, birthplace, union membership and region may also be expected to be important in predicting media usage, as they have been in predicting many other aspects of political behaviour (western Canadian voters have often cast their ballots very differently from Ontario or Quebec voters). In contrast to bivariate analysis, multivariate techniques assume a complex world where nothing is mono-causal and where the importance of any one factor must be assessed in conjunction with a number of other factors.

Table 2.6 shows near identical multiple regression equations predicting the degree of attention to television news or political advertisements during the campaigns of 1974, 1979, 1984 and 1988.[3] Age was regrouped in seven-year intervals, education into three levels, employment into those working full time and all others, income into quartiles, language into English as a mother tongue and all others, and birthplace into those born in Canada and all others.

Those regression coefficients marked with either one or two asterisks are especially important in predicting attention to television. Age is important across all surveys and its positive coefficient indicates that as age increases attention to campaign news on television increases, even when the influence of all the other variables in the equation is taken into account. Gender is similarly important across all surveys and the coefficients indicate that it is strongly related (in contrast to the other variables) to attention to television news. These are the only two predictor variables that are important across all four elections. The positive relationship with age suggests two factors at work. First, time available for television watching increases with age and especially with retirement. This is especially the case for women whose child and home-care responsibilities may diminish as children age. Second, in most cases increased age brings increased wealth and this may result in the recognition of the importance of politics in wealth creation and preservation. Without more research (surprisingly little has been written on the effects of age on political beliefs), the comments on age must be treated as informed speculation. The strong effect of gender when such considerations as age, income and education are controlled suggests that women do not pay as close attention to television news as do men, possibly because of household responsibilities, or their use of other forms of media or personal networks for obtaining political information. While the difference in attention levels between genders is significant, its effect is not particularly large in either 1974 or subsequent surveys. For example, the equation would predict an average television attention score of 1.99 for a male from Atlantic Canada who scored 1 on all other characteristics, whereas a female resident of the Atlantic region is predicted to have a score of 1.88, where a score of 3 indicates watching quite a few campaign items and 1 indicates watching almost none.

In the 1979 equation, in addition to age and gender, language, union membership and residence in Quebec are significantly related to attention to television news. Those whose mother tongue is not English, and those respondents who lived in Quebec were significantly less likely to watch the television news, while union members were significantly more likely to pay attention to it. Without further detailed analysis, only speculation can be offered on the importance of these variables. Union members, recalling Pierre Trudeau's about-face on wage and price controls following the 1974 election where he campaigned against them, may have paid closer attention to the campaign. Residents of Quebec, preoccupied with the Parti québécois government and the impending referendum on sovereignty-association, may have had their attention focused elsewhere. The English versus other mother tongue variable appears to suggest the same explanation since most of the non-English mother tongue respondents would be francophones. The most sensible interpretation seems a specific event rather than an ongoing process such as Québécois favouring other media for political information, because Quebec residence is important in only the one equation.

In the 1984 equation, in addition to age and gender, community size, education and residence in the West are significant predictors. Many western respondents were probably smarting from the perceived centrist policies of the 1980 to 1984 Trudeau Liberals, chief among which was the National Energy Policy. This much disliked policy probably contributed to concentrating the minds of westerners on the progress of the campaign. Community size, less strongly related to attention than any of the other significant predictors, may be explained by the Mulroney-Progressive Conservative success in the large cities that fashioned his overwhelming majority. Finally, after being an unimportant predictor of attention to television in 1974 and 1979, education becomes strongly significant and remains so in the 1988 equation. Without knowing a great deal more about people's viewing habits it is difficult to explain this increased importance. One purely structural reason may be the advent of cable television and the general increase in television entertainment options. Perhaps television campaign news got closer attention from the entire populace when other viewing options were restricted. When those options multiplied, education became a more powerful determinant of attention.

The 1988 equation is similar to that of 1984 but for the omission of community size. Adding further speculation to the above explanations does not seem reasonable.

There appear to be two patterns in table 2.6: first, the importance of age (increasing in predictive importance) and gender across all surveys, and second, the significance of education and western residence in the 1984 and 1988 surveys. Interestingly, income, being employed and being born in Canada have no significant effect on attention to television campaign news, though most of the coefficient signs are in the intuitively correct direction.

The *R-squared* values in table 2.6 indicate that in nearly every case, the combined sociodemographic variables are not able to explain much of the variance in attention to campaign news on television: in 1974 the predictors explain only 3 percent of the variance, only 4 percent in 1979, then a jump to 12 percent in 1984, and a fall to 8 percent in 1988. The most reasonable explanation is that attention is better determined by other variables, and the study returns to discuss those in subsequent tables.

Table 2.7 uses the same variables as those in table 2.6 to predict attention to campaign news in newspapers. Here, the pattern of significant coefficients is quite different: age, once again, is a significant predictor in all the equations across all the surveys, but now education shares the same importance (and is generally one of the strongest predictors). As well, gender,[4] residence in Quebec and income are important in three of the four surveys. The difference in the pattern of significant predictors suggests that paying attention to television campaign news and paying attention to campaign news in newspapers are somewhat different and are, to a degree, practised by different people.

The fact that the pattern of significant coefficients in table 2.7 is so similar across all four surveys suggests a unified and recurring causal structure. For this reason, all four surveys will be discussed together.

The most important or next-to-most important predictor in all four equations is education, a well-known positive correlate of newspaper readership (Kennamer 1987). The best educated are more likely

Table 2.7
OLS regression coefficients for sociodemographic correlates of attention to newspapers

	1974	1979	1984	1988
Age	.09**	.08**	.13**	.13**
Community size	-.03*	-.03**	-.01	—
Education	.20**	.21**	.29**	.26**
Employed	-.03	-.03	.03	-.01
Gender	.10	.15**	.19**	.18**
Income	.17**	.11**	.11**	.00
Language	.03	-.01	.08	-.02
Native-born	.01	.04	.05	.06
Union member	-.02	-.01	.03	.05
Region				
Atlantic	.02	-.10	-.08	-.01
Quebec	-.27**	-.26**	-.12*	-.06
Ontario	—	—	—	—
West	-.08	-.21**	.02	.00
Constant	1.23	1.43	1.69	2.05
R^2	.14	.12	.14	.06
N	(985)	(1213)	(2674)	(2185)

*Less than .05; **less than .005.

to read about campaign news than are the least educated, an unsurprising fact given the surprisingly high rates of adult illiteracy. The better educated are more likely to have supported opinions and perhaps to have arrived at them through exposure to several different opinions, all as a result of paying attention to the more in-depth and variously opinionated campaign news found in newspapers as compared to television. Age, as with TV attention, is positively correlated with newspaper readership, and probably for the same reasons: increasing time for readership and an increasing stake in political decisions. Income, linked positively to education and age, is a significant determinant of readership for the first three surveys, but its influence is reduced to non-significance during the 1988 election. Gender is again important in determining the readership of campaign news, with males being the more frequent readers. It is easy to speculate why this might be the case. First, women with both jobs and home-care and child-care responsibilities have less time to spend reading about campaign news than do men. In NES 1988, 58 percent of all female respondents were in the workforce, either working full time, unemployed, or laid off. Amongst couples living together or married, female workforce participation was 67 percent. A better understanding of the double-day can be gained by looking at working women with children. In 1988, 49 percent of the women in the workforce had children under the age of 18, meaning that they had both work and very likely all or most of the home-care responsibilities. Second, the majority of female occupations, and especially those pink collar occupations, service sector and unskilled jobs, are, to the holders, not obviously affected by political decisions. By comparison, the management, bureaucratic or financial employment sectors are overwhelmingly male and often immediately affected by political change. To a certain degree these differences are accounted for in the regression equation by the inclusion of income and education controls. Third, female wages are considerably less than male wage rates in similar or comparable jobs. If one accepts the argument that political involvement is affected by concerns for wealth creation and preservation, women, with so much less to preserve, may be less likely to see the relevance of political involvement. To a degree, their observation is accurate because income disparities between genders remain. Fourth, it may be that women rely on other channels of political information such as friendship networks. Finally, the persistent gender difference may be explained by a social desirability bias: males may believe that the socially desirable attitude is for them to report that they follow politics closely.

Living in Quebec has a persistently negative effect on campaign news readership and in three of four surveys it is also significant. This difference cannot be explained by the unique circumstances of any particular election, for it persists across three of four surveys. One plausible explanation of the difference is a purely structural one: Québécois are considerably less likely to subscribe to a newspaper than are the residents of most other provinces. Siegel (1983, 103) reports that in 1981, about the midway point of the period covered by the surveys, newspaper circulation per 100 households was 54 in Quebec. By contrast, only Saskatchewan and Newfoundland had lower circulation figures, and the average for all provinces was 66 per 100 households. The grouping of Newfoundland, Saskatchewan and Quebec together suggests an explanation other than a cultural one, and may be explained by large rural or small town populations in all three provinces. It may be that in some small communities daily newspapers were not available.

Attention to news about the campaign on the radio was only asked in the 1974, 1979 and 1980 surveys. Table 2.8 includes analysis from the first two years because data gathered from the respondents at the third election were somewhat restricted. With only two datapoints, no underlying causal explanation is apparent. While age and living in the Atlantic region are important in 1974, education and gender are important in 1979. Not much can be added to the interpretation of this pattern of coefficients mentioned above. The one important point to keep in mind is the fragmentation of the radio market. While it seems quite likely that Canadians listen to the radio on a daily basis, either travelling to work with it, waking to it, or having it as background to daily activities, it is possible that many do not obtain political information from it because that news is either not available or is very limited. The AM and FM radio bands are populated by stations that favour music over news analysis or talk. Many radio stations (including the CBC) have either reduced news-gathering capacity, news air time, the broadcasting of hard news (as opposed to lifestyle news), or all three. The relatively low percentage of respondents listening to campaign news on the radio may be a reflection of the lack of campaign news being carried by that medium.

In table 2.9, the correlates of attention to all media, the total attention each respondent pays to all three media becomes the dependent variable. Adding together the information contained in the questions about TV, newspaper and radio use allows a clearer picture of the causal structure. Not surprisingly, that pattern is very similar to those discussed above: age, education, gender and income are all important, and living in Quebec continues to have a negative, though somewhat diminished, effect. The explanations given above are once again reinforced. In

Table 2.8
OLS regression coefficients for sociodemographic correlates of attention to radio

	1974	1979
Age	.03*	.01
Community size	-.01	-.01
Education	.05	.09*
Employed	.02	-.10
Gender	.06	.12*
Income	.04	.04
Language	.07	-.01
Native-born	-.04	.13
Union member	-.11	.05
Region		
Atlantic	.19*	.04
Quebec	-.05	-.06
Ontario	—	—
West	.01	.06
Constant	1.45	1.49
R^2	.03	.02
N	(985)	(1213)

*Less than .05; **less than .005.

broader terms, the pattern emphasizes what is known about political participation, that young people are less likely to participate than older people, that females are somewhat less likely to participate than males, and that the poor and the poorly educated show little interest in or knowledge about politics (Clarke et al. 1979; 1991, 37; Mishler 1979; Verba and Nie 1972).

Those who follow campaign news on television, on radio or through newspapers are not a representative cross-section of the Canadian electorate. Such news is more closely watched, read or listened to by males than by females, by the better educated than by the less well educated, by those with higher incomes than by those with lower incomes, and by older people than by younger people. Those people who listen probably have more at stake in the great game of politics – perhaps they know more about politics and campaigns – but how much they are influenced by the news they absorb is difficult to state, and that is something this study returns to in a later section. The above discussion, in emphasizing those sociodemographic characteristics that are impor-

Table 2.9
OLS regression coefficients for sociodemographic correlates of attention to all media

	1974	1979	1984	1988
Age	.17**	.14**	.28**	.25**
Community size	-.02	-.02	.02	—
Education	.27**	.34**	.50**	.53**
Employed	-.09	-.20	-.01	.00
Gender	.27*	.42**	.36**	.36**
Income	.24**	.16**	.14**	.04
Language	.04	-.15	.03	-.02
Native-born	-.12	.17	.05	.01
Union member	-.17	.17	.08	-.01
Region				
Atlantic	.17	-.15	.00	.02
Quebec	-.44*	-.56**	-.10	-.09
Ontario	—	—	—	—
West	-.13	-.18	-.16*	.11
Constant	4.71	4.99	3.47	4.40
R^2	.08	.08	.16	.09
N	(985)	(1213)	(2674)	(2185)

*Less than .05; **less than .005.

tant in explaining media attention, may have unavoidably overstated their importance. As was mentioned earlier and the reader will have noted, the sociodemographic variables are not particularly good predictors of attention to the media, as is shown by the low *R-squared* values in the preceding tables. These low values might be explained in three ways: first, as we know, most of our subjects do pay attention to the media; second, other attitudinal factors are required to explain the differences; or third, media attention is a non-linear function of these factors, suggesting a considerably more complex explanation than a linear model can test.

THE POLITICAL BEHAVIOUR CORRELATES OF MEDIA ATTENTION

In investigating the relationship between sociodemographic characteristics and attention to the media we are discounting political beliefs and actions in favour of explanations derived from economic conditions such as poverty, education and gender. The formative effect that any of these factors has upon political activity can hardly be underestimated. One's gender may establish basic and enduring attitudes toward politics and participation (e.g., Gilligan 1982). Even as role models, female authority figures are far from commonplace. That said, as a rule sociodemographic characteristics do not explain a great deal of the variation in attention to the various media, as shown by the small *R-squared* values in tables 2.6 through 2.9. The following section turns to political behaviour variables as explanations for media attention, and here the first thing to notice is the increase in their predictive power over that of the sociodemographic characteristics.

The following tables, 2.10 through 2.24, analyse the importance of political interest, strength of party identification, voting frequency, vote consistency, the importance of parties, leaders and candidates in the voting decision, and a number of measures of political participation to predict attention to campaign news in the three media. Every table consists of three equations: the left-most includes all variables but one of party, leader or candidate (a series of dummy variables), the centre equation includes all the variables but the participation ones, and the right-most equation includes only the participation variables. Adding and separating the effects of the different groups of variables permits us to observe their effects in different causal explanations. Table 2.24 summarizes the overall pattern of significant coefficients briefly discussed for each table below.

Table 2.10 relates the 1974 regression coefficients for each of three equations where the dependent variable is, as it was in table 2.6, attention to campaign news on television. The pattern of significant coefficients indicates that those who are interested in politics are considerably more likely to watch campaign news than those who are less interested in politics. The standardized regression coefficients or betas (not shown) confirm that political interest is the most important predictor of attention to political information on television. Strength of party identification and consistency of party identification are similarly important predictors. These may be seen as measures of partisanship or emotional involvement in politics: those who strongly identify with a party and have always done so are more likely to watch campaign news than those who switch party allegiance or who are weakly attached to a party. The only significant coefficient among the participation variables (discuss, convince, work, meeting, contact and campaign) is discussing politics with others. Either discussion fuels the watching of campaign news or vice versa, but neither relationship is surprising. What is surprising is the weakness of the remaining participation variables. Trying to convince a friend to vote for your candidate, working to solve a local problem, attending a political meeting or rally, contacting

Table 2.10
OLS regression coefficients for political behaviour correlates of attention to television, 1974

Interest in politics	.27**	.32**	—
Strength of party identity	.12**	.13**	—
Consistent party identity	.13*	.16**	—
Votes always	.06	.07	—
Votes the same	-.06	-.06	—
Voted	.03	.05	—
Party most important	-.02	—	—
Leader most important	—	.03	—
Candidate most important	-.03	-.00	—
Discuss politics	.11**	—	.17**
Convince friends	.01	—	.04
Work in community	.03	—	.05
Attend meeting	.05	—	.05
Contact officials	-.05	—	.01
Campaign for party	-.00	—	.03
Constant	1.01	1.13	1.51
R^2	.19	.15	.11
N	(883)	(893)	(1226)

*Less than .05; **less than .005.

public officials or politicians, or spending time campaigning were not significant predictors of attention to campaign news. The same is true of the right-most equation, featuring only the participation variables. The centre equation, without the participation variables, has the same pattern of significant variables as in the left-most equation. The *R-squared* values indicate the importance of the sets of predictors. While the entire equation predicts 19 percent of the variance, without the participation variables that falls to 15 percent. Using only the participation variables, just 11 percent of the variance is explained. This suggests that the partisanship variables are more important in determining attention to TV campaign news than are the participation variables.

None of the party, leader or candidate variables were significant predictors in table 2.10. These variables measured the "orientation" of the respondents, suggesting whether they concentrated on the local candidate, the political party taken as a whole, or just the party leader. One possibility was that television viewers might disproportionately note leader importance, or those who thought leaders important might pay particular attention to television news. While not borne out in these equations, television remains a medium best suited to projecting leadership characteristics that may not be as effectively communicated through the press. For example, passion, decisiveness and aggression require the immediacy of TV to attain their full force.

Table 2.10 obliquely suggests that TV consumption acts to reinforce partisanship rather than weaken it, a possibility that Clarke et al. suggest in their analysis (1979, 290–91). In other words, those with strong political beliefs apparently have them confirmed rather than upset by exposure to television news. Strictly speaking, the survey research design of the election studies does not allow us to rule out the possibility that the same pattern could not be explained by the observation that strong partisans simply watch more campaign news. While this is obviously true to the extent that those who are strongly partisan do watch more TV, it seems to suggest that TV has a completely passive effect, an argument that most research contests.

Table 2.11 repeats the analysis of table 2.10, but this time for newspaper readership in the 1974 election. Once again, political interest is the dominant explanatory factor while party identification strength is somewhat less important. Consistent party identification is not important at all, discussing politics is similarly again important, and, finally, those who always vote the same are somewhat less likely to bother watching TV campaign news than those who have voted for different parties in the past. The pattern amongst the non-participation variables remains the same when the participation variables are dropped from the equation. When the participation variables are entered by themselves, attending a political meeting or rally becomes a significant factor in determining the degree of attention to campaign news in the newspaper.

The equations in table 2.11 are not a great deal different from those in table 2.10. Once again, political interest is the dominant factor in determining the extent of attention to newspapers. The fact that consistency in voting is now significant and negative suggests that those who habitually vote the same are less likely than others to consult the newspapers for information that will help them make up their minds about the campaign. This also suggests that switchers may be more influenced by newspapers than they are by television. Once again, none of the party, leader or candidate variables is important.

Like table 2.10, the participation variables in table 2.11 explain slightly less of the variation in attention than the remaining variables.

Table 2.11
OLS regression coefficients for political behaviour correlates of attention to newspapers, 1974

Interest in politics	.31**	.43**	—
Strength of party identity	.07*	.11**	—
Consistent party identity	.07	.11	—
Votes always	.03	.06	—
Votes the same	-.16**	-.16*	—
Voted	.04	.06	—
Party most important	-.01	—	—
Leader most important	—	.01	—
Candidate most important	-.03	-.01	—
Discuss politics	.18**	—	.25**
Convince friends	-.02	—	.01
Work in community	.03	—	.03
Attend meeting	.06	—	.10**
Contact officials	-.02	—	.04
Campaign for party	.05	—	.05
Constant	.79	.99	1.14
R^2	.27	.20	.18
N	(883)	(893)	(1226)

*Less than .05; **less than .005.

Table 2.12 employs the same independent variables to explain attention to campaign news on the radio during the 1974 election. The pattern of significant regression coefficients is somewhat different from the ones in the preceding two tables, but, as in those tables, political interest is the dominant factor in explaining attention to radio news about the campaign. By contrast to the preceding tables, the following variables are now significant: trying to convince friends to vote the same as the respondent, working with others to solve a community problem, and citing the political party as the most important factor in determining how a respondent would vote. Unfortunately, the "working with others to solve a community problem" question was dropped from the later surveys, but its significance here hints at the local compass of radio news as compared to the national scope of TV news. In other words, those who have been involved in community problems seem to pay

Table 2.12
OLS regression coefficients for political behaviour correlates of attention to radio, 1974

Interest in politics	.17**	.25**	—
Strength of party identity	.04	.07	—
Consistent party identity	.09	.13*	—
Votes always	.03	.04	—
Votes the same	.02	.02	—
Voted	.01	.02	—
Party most important	-.12*	—	—
Leader most important	—	.11	—
Candidate most important	-.07	.07	—
Discuss politics	.03	—	.08**
Convince friends	.06*	—	.06*
Work in community	.08*	—	.05
Attend meeting	.08	—	.09**
Contact officials	.03	—	.06
Campaign for party	-.05	—	-.02
Constant	.92	.92	1.13
R^2	.11	.07	.08
N	(883)	(893)	(1226)

*Less than .05; **less than .005.

somewhat more attention to the radio, possibly because that is where more local news is to be found. Interestingly, selecting party as the most important factor in voting has a significant negative effect on listening to radio campaign news. This effect is not large and must be read in comparison to the omitted complementary dummy variable for the importance of the party leader in voting. Looked at in this way, it suggests that those who say the party leader is the most important factor in their vote are significantly more likely to listen to radio news than those who place party ahead of leadership.

The pattern of significant coefficients is not altered a great deal by removing first the participation variables and then all variables but the participation ones. When the participation variables enter the equation alone, discussing politics with friends, trying to convince friends and attending meetings are significant predictors of attention to radio news, and together these variables explain a larger proportion of the variance in attention to radio news than do the partisan variables.

Table 2.13 summarizes media attention by combining attention to television, newspapers and radio. As the three media carry different amounts of news, in different forms, and have variously sized geographical areas of coverage, observing each variable separately will allow for the possibility that people specialize in one or two media. Combining them allows for the possibility that some people may pay attention to all three at fairly low levels, but in total that may represent a higher level than a specialist concentrating on only one media source. The significant predictors in table 2.13 are much the same as those in the previous tables. Interest in politics is the most important predictor, while strength of party identification, consistent party identification, discussing politics with others, working in the community, and attending

Table 2.13
OLS regression coefficients for political behaviour correlates of attention to total media, 1974

Interest in politics	.75**	1.01**	—
Strength of party identity	.23**	.31**	—
Consistent party identity	.29*	.40*	—
Votes always	.11	.16	—
Votes the same	-.20	-.20	—
Voted	.07	.13	—
Party most important	-.15	—	—
Leader most important	—	.15	—
Candidate most important	-.13	.06	—
Discuss politics	.32**	—	.49**
Convince friends	.05	—	.11*
Work in community	.13*	—	.12*
Attend meeting	.19*	—	.25**
Contact officials	-.04	—	.11
Campaign for party	-.01	—	.05
Constant	2.72	3.04	3.78
R^2	.31	.24	.21
N	(883)	(893)	(1226)

*Less than .05; **less than .005.

a political meeting or rally are all significant predictors of total media attention. As the importance of all of these factors has been discussed above, it will not be restated here.

The pattern of significant coefficients in the partial equations is very similar to the full equation and therefore requires little comment.

Tables 2.14 through 2.17 apply the same analysis discussed above to the data from the 1979 election. As table 2.24 indicates, the results are not radically different; interest plays the same dominant role as it did in predicting attention to media in the 1974 election data. In table 2.14, as in table 2.10, interest in politics and discussing politics with other people are important factors affecting attention to television. Unlike the similar 1974 table, attending a political meeting or rally and indicating that party leadership was the most important factor in the vote decision were also important predictors of watching campaign news on TV. As discussed above, a leadership focus is now a significant factor

Table 2.14
OLS regression coefficients for political behaviour correlates of attention to television, 1979

Interest in politics	.26**	.35**	—
Strength of party identity	.07	.10*	—
Consistent party identity	.11	.12*	—
Votes always	-.00	.02	—
Votes the same	-.03	-.06	—
Voted	-.02	-.02	—
Party most important	—	—	—
Leader most important	.11*	.10*	—
Candidate most important	.07	.07	—
Discuss politics	.09**	—	.17**
Convince friends	.05	—	.08**
Attend meeting	.08*	—	.10**
Contact officials	-.01	—	.03
Campaign for party	-.00	—	.02
Constant	1.17	1.30	1.41
R^2	.17	.15	.12
N	(861)	(864)	(1315)

*Less than .05; **less than .005.

in determining attention to TV, the medium that most effectively conveys those individual qualities often associated with political leadership. Additional support for the relationship between attention to TV and focus on leadership is found in tables 2.14 and 2.15, where leadership is not significant, and in table 2.16, dealing with attention to campaign news on the radio, where a local candidate focus is a significant though not particularly strong predictor.

When the participation variables are dropped from the full equation in table 2.14, having a constant party identification becomes a significant predictor. While we cannot determine the direction of causality in this instance, it seems that attention to TV reinforces, or at least does not upset, existing partisan allegiances.

The pattern of coefficients in table 2.15 is much like that of table 2.11; interest in politics and discussing politics with others are both significant. A comparison of tables 2.11 and 2.15 (in table 2.24)

Table 2.15
OLS regression coefficients for political behaviour correlates of attention to newspapers, 1979

Interest in politics	.23**	.37**	—
Strength of party identity	.00	.03	—
Consistent party identity	.09	.10	—
Votes always	.04	.08	—
Votes the same	-.09	-.14*	—
Voted	.25*	.25*	—
Party most important	—	—	—
Leader most important	.02	.02	—
Candidate most important	-.05	-.05	—
Discuss politics	.21**	—	.31**
Convince friends	-.01	—	.02
Attend meeting	.06*	—	.09**
Contact officials	-.01	—	.04
Campaign for party	.04	—	.05
Constant	.72	1.00	1.01
R^2	.24	.17	.23
N	(861)	(864)	(1315)

*Less than .05; **less than .005.

indicates that having voted and having attended a meeting are both significant predictors, whereas party-identification strength and a consistent voting record are no longer important determinants of attention to newspapers. Although the latter coefficient remains negative, when the participation variables are dropped from the equation, it becomes a significant predictor. The *R-squared* values in table 2.15 also indicate that the participation variables are explaining more of the variation in attention to campaign news than are the remaining variables.

Table 2.16, like table 2.12, features a weaker political interest coefficient than all of the other tables. This appears to reinforce the earlier suggestion that radio is not a prime medium for political news, or put another way, listening to campaign news on radio is not as closely related to an interest in politics as is watching news on TV or reading about the campaign in the newspaper. As mentioned above, a local candidate focus, as opposed to a leader or party focus, is related to listening to campaign news on radio.

Table 2.16
OLS regression coefficients for political behaviour correlates of attention to radio, 1979

Interest in politics	.15**	.23**	—
Strength of party identity	.05	.07	—
Consistent party identity	.03	.04	—
Votes always	-.02	.02	—
Votes the same	.03	-.00	—
Voted	-.07	-.08	—
Party most important	—	—	—
Leader most important	.05	.05	—
Candidate most important	.15*	.15*	—
Discuss politics	.11**	—	.16**
Convince friends	-.02	—	.01
Attend meeting	.11**	—	.10**
Contact officials	-.02	—	.01
Campaign for party	.01	—	.03
Constant	1.15	1.28	1.23
R^2	.08	.05	.07
N	(861)	(864)	(1315)

*Less than .05; **less than .005.

The political behaviour correlates of total media attention in 1974 and 1979 are again similar, as indicated in table 2.23. Interest is the dominant variable, attending a meeting and discussing politics with friends are both important, while party-identification strength and constancy are not quite significant at the .05 level in table 2.17. Overall, tables 2.13 and 2.17 are very similar, both in the results of the complete equation, and when the set of independent variables is divided.

The 1979 equations repeat many of the patterns discussed in the 1974 data, providing some support for the analysis and its interpretation.

The analysis of the 1984 data is presented in tables 2.18 through 2.20. Once again, table 2.24 indicates the similarities among the 1974, 1979 and the 1988 data. In all instances, political interest and discussion of politics with others are significant. In 1984, attending a meeting and party-identification strength are also significant, as they are, or are very nearly, in the earlier surveys.

Table 2.17
OLS regression coefficients for political behaviour correlates of attention to total media, 1979

Interest in politics	.64**	.95**	—
Strength of party identity	.12	.20*	—
Consistent party identity	.23	.26*	—
Votes always	.02	.12	—
Votes the same	-.09	-.20	—
Voted	.16	.16	—
Party most important	—	—	—
Leader most important	.17	.18	—
Candidate most important	.17	.17	—
Discuss politics	.41**	—	.63**
Convince friends	.02	—	.12*
Attend meeting	.25**	—	.29**
Contact officials	-.04	—	.07
Campaign for party	.05	—	.09
Constant	3.04	3.57	3.65
R^2	.28	.21	.25
N	(861)	(864)	(1315)

*Less than .05; **less than .005.

The equation predicting attention to campaign news in the newspapers in 1984 is once more similar to the earlier two studies and to the subsequent one as well. Table 2.24 shows that many of the significant coefficients in 1984 also appear in previous years, though the major difference appears to be the greater number of significant factors, especially amongst the participation variables. One technical reason for this is that, in general, the standard errors of the regression coefficients in table 2.19 are smaller than those in tables 2.15 or 2.11, and the *R-squared* values in table 2.19 are larger than in the previous tables, suggesting that the model fits the data better, or that the variables chosen are better able to explain attention to newspapers in 1984 than they are in the earlier years.

Table 2.20 is again much like the other tables from 1984 and the comparison tables 2.13, 2.17 and 2.23. Total media campaign attention again depends heavily upon one's interest in politics, several aspects

Table 2.18
OLS regression coefficients for political behaviour correlates of attention to television, 1984

Interest in politics	.40**	.57**	—
Strength of party identity	.07**	.10**	—
Consistent party identity	.06	.12**	—
Votes always	.09	.12*	—
Votes the same	-.00	-.00	—
Voted	.08	.10	—
Party most important	-.07	—	—
Leader most important	—	.05	—
Candidate most important	-.07	-.01	—
Discuss politics	.23**	—	.33**
Convince friends	.01	—	.04
Attend meeting	.10**	—	.15**
Contact officials	.01	—	.05*
Campaign for party	-.01	—	.01
Constant	1.21	1.50	1.71
R^2	.31	.25	.23
N	(2304)	(2304)	(2304)

*Less than .05; **less than .005.

of one's partisan history and the extent of participation in politics and in the campaign.

Finally, tables 2.21 through 2.23 relate similar analyses to those performed in the previous tables. The 1988 analysis is different from that performed on the preceding datasets in that it does not include a number of the participation variables, nor the party, leader or candidate variables, which were omitted from the questionnaire. The fact that the patterns of regression coefficients in the tables are still so similar to the preceding tables reinforces the robustness of the findings.

While the equations in tables 2.10 through 2.23 vary somewhat, as table 2.24 shows, they are sufficiently alike to suggest that the relationship between the independent variables themselves and between those and attention to the various media have not changed much over the 1974 to 1988 period. The dominant factor related to attention to all media is political interest and one can easily see media attention and

Table 2.19
OLS regression coefficients for political behaviour correlates of attention to newspapers, 1984

Interest in politics	.41**	.60**	—
Strength of party identity	-.04	-.01	—
Consistent party identity	.10*	.16**	—
Votes always	.10*	.14*	—
Votes the same	-.02	-.03	—
Voted	.26**	.29**	—
Party most important	.09*	—	—
Leader most important	—	-.12**	—
Candidate most important	.01	-.09*	—
Discuss politics	.27**	—	.38**
Convince friends	-.03	—	-.00
Attend meeting	.07**	—	.12**
Contact officials	.08**	—	.12**
Campaign for party	-.03	—	-.02
Constant	1.17	1.69	1.74
R^2	.34	.26	.25
N	(2304)	(2304)	(2304)

*Less than .05; **less than .005.

Table 2.20
OLS regression coefficients for political behaviour correlates of attention to total media, 1984

Interest in politics	.81**	1.17**	—
Strength of party identity	.03	.09*	—
Consistent party identity	.16**	.28**	—
Votes always	.19*	.26**	—
Votes the same	-.02	-.03	—
Voted	.34**	.39**	—
Party most important	.02	—	—
Leader most important	—	-.08	—
Candidate most important	-.07	-.10	—
Discuss politics	.50**	—	.71**
Convince friends	-.02	—	.03
Attend meeting	.17*	—	.27**
Contact officials	.09*	—	.17**
Campaign for party	-.04	—	-.01
Constant	2.38	3.19	3.45
R^2	.44	.34	.32
N	(2304)	(2304)	(2304)

*Less than .05; **less than .005.

Table 2.21
OLS regression coefficients for political behaviour correlates of attention to television, 1988

Interest in politics	.66**	.70**	—
Strength of party identity	.03	.03	—
Votes always	.04	.03	—
Votes the same	.07	.07	—
Voted	.15	.18*	—
Discuss politics	.18**	—	.52**
Campaign for party	.12	—	.37**
Constant	1.35	1.39	3.10
R^2	.28	.27	.06
N	(1433)	(1433)	(1433)

*Less than .05; **less than .005.

Table 2.22
OLS regression coefficients for political behaviour correlates of attention to newspapers, 1988

Interest in politics	.65**	.69**	—
Strength of party identity	.05	.05	—
Votes always	.09	.07	—
Votes the same	-.02	-.02	—
Voted	.20*	.23*	—
Discuss politics	.22**	—	.55**
Campaign for party	.06	—	.31**
Constant	.95	1.03	2.75
R^2	.26	.26	.06
N	(1433)	(1433)	(1433)

*Less than .05; **less than .005.

Table 2.23
OLS regression coefficients for political behaviour correlates of attention to total media, 1988

Interest in politics	1.31**	1.39**	—
Strength of party identity	.08	.08	—
Votes always	.13	.10	—
Votes the same	.05	.05	—
Voted	.35*	.41*	—
Discuss politics	.40**	—	1.06**
Campaign for party	.18	—	.68**
Constant	2.30	2.42	5.85
R^2	.36	.35	.08
N	(1433)	(1433)	(1433)

*Less than .05; **less than .005.

political interest as different sides of the same coin: interest generates media attention that in turn produces increased interest in politics. Discussing politics is also a significant predictor of media attention in most of the equations. Once again it is easy to see these as being related, for political discussion will generate closer attention to political reports in the media.

Table 2.24
The pattern of significant coefficients in tables 2.10 through 2.23

	1974	1979	1984	1988
Television	Table 2.10	Table 2.14	Table 2.18	Table 2.21
	interest party ID strength party ID same discuss	interest leader discuss meeting	interest party ID strength discuss meeting	interest discuss
Newspapers	Table 2.11	Table 2.15	Table 2.19	Table 2.22
	interest party ID strength vote same discuss	interest voted discuss meeting	interest party ID same votes always voted party discuss meeting contact	interest voted discuss
Radio	Table 2.12	Table 2.16		
	interest party convince work	interest candidate discuss meeting		
Total media	Table 2.13	Table 2.17	Table 2.20	Table 2.23
	interest party ID strength party ID same discuss	interest discuss meeting	interest party ID same votes always voted discuss meeting contact work meeting	interest voted discuss

With the exception of the 1988 data, where the participation variables are restricted, the two sets of variables are of roughly equal importance in predicting attention to the media. This is not surprising given that both sets of variables indicate the same engagement with politics though perhaps in somewhat different ways.

MEDIA IMPACT ON POLITICAL OPINIONS AND POLITICAL BEHAVIOUR

While a great deal has thus far been said about the kinds of people that pay attention to campaign news in the newspaper, on TV or radio, not a great deal has been said about what effects such attention might have. Unfortunately, not much light can be shed on this question. As explained later, the methodology of survey research is not particularly well suited to examining these effects, and the measures we have, both of viewing and its effects, are of the crudest kind. For example, while we have a measure of attention to the different media, we have no indication of what respondents see, read or listen to, or agree or disagree with. The very scanty and disparate empirical information available on the effects of media coverage on voters is presented below. That evidence seems to suggest that there are differences between how the media describe campaigns and how the respondents see them.

Table 2.25 taken from Fletcher (1987, 362) collates tables from several sources, and compares what newspapers, TV and survey respondents thought to be the most important issues in the four elections between 1974 and 1984. There are obvious disparities between the media's interpretation of the most important issues and that given by the respondents. In general, TV and newspapers tend to overplay leadership, national unity and resource issues whereas survey opinion elevates the importance of economic issues such as inflation and unemployment. Some of the biggest differences between the public and media view occurred in 1984, where the public rated economic issues as overwhelmingly important, and the media emphasized other issues such as leadership.

It would not be appropriate to read a great deal into table 2.25, given the fragility of such data. However, it does bolster the argument that viewers are not sponges, indiscriminately soaking up the flow of political information pouring from the media. Just what individuals do absorb from the media or from other sources of political information is difficult to know with current research designs. However, some impression may be drawn from looking at the relationship between media attention and knowledge about politics.

There are few direct measures of political knowledge in the NES datasets. The 1984 NES survey contained a number of direct questions about political knowledge in a battery that asked respondents to identify the premiers of the ten provinces.[5] If respondents receive a great deal of their information from media sources, there may be a strong relationship between attention paid to the media and the respondent's ability to name the provincial premiers in 1984. (This assumes that the media give significant coverage to all the premiers, something that seems unlikely given the relative importance of each of the premiers.) Failure to find a solid relationship between these variables would indicate that respondents either do not get their

Table 2.25
Most important issues, 1974–84

	1974			1979		
Issue	Paper	TV	Survey	Paper	TV	Survey
Economy	92	—	63	62	43	48
inflation	32	—	38	8	14	13
unemployment	3	—	3	15	11	10
Confederation	19	—	6	44	42	28
Resources	25	—	2	21	9	8
Social	23	—	12	13	—	5
Other	37	—	19	80	—	27
foreign relations	2	—	2	3	—	2
leaders	8	—	6	32	32	14
N	(1560)	—	(2445)	(1756)	(1232)	(2668)

	1980			1984		
Issue	Paper	TV	Survey	Paper	TV	Survey
Economy	25	28	48	28	19	86
inflation	6	—	4	2	—	20
unemployment	6	—	4	7	19	43
Confederation	12	9	13	9	8	7
Resources	24	18	32	2	—	4
Social	7	—	2	18	9	13
Other	43	—	32	—	—	33
foreign relations	22	38	3	8	—	3
leaders	12	36	15	11	26	9
N	(984)	(806)	(1786)	(575)	(705)	(2858)

Sources: Clarke et al. (1984), tables 4.1 and 4.3 (1988), table 4.1; Fletcher (1988), table 8.8; Kay et al. (1985); Soderlund et al. (1984), tables 3-1 and 3-2.

political information directly from the media, or that the questions themselves are invalid or unreliable.

Only 1.4 percent of the 1984 respondents were able to name all 10 premiers, the average number of correctly named premiers was 3.5, and the modal category was 1. At the bivariate level, reading about the campaign in the newspaper was more closely related to knowledge ($R = .35$) than was attention to campaign news on the television ($R = .27$). While the difference is not great, the figures seem to reflect the greater depth of political information conveyed by the newspapers. The same fact is reflected in separate regression equations that include a number of sociodemographic variables plus attention to campaign news either on television or in newspapers.

The two regressions indicate the relative importance of the various factors in determining knowledge about the premiers. While both attention to campaign news on television and in newspapers are significant predictors of knowledge, in the case of television, several of the sociodemographic variables are more important. The standardized regression coefficients given in table 2.26 allow a comparison of the relative importance of each of the predictor variables. In the left-hand equation, interest in politics, gender, age and education are all more important predictors of knowledge than is attention to television, suggesting that knowledge of politics is determined more by other factors than by simply paying attention to television news. The right-hand equation in table 2.26 tells a different story: here, attention to newspapers is the most important factor in determining knowledge. Once again, the greater depth of information carried in newspapers is reflected in the higher knowledge scores of those individuals who pay close attention to that medium.

While voters' impressions of the importance of campaign issues parallel if not replicate the relative importance given to issues by the media and, as suggested above, attention to newspapers in particular is related to political knowledge, there is still something to be said about whether attention to the media affects political behaviour.

Tables 2.10 through 2.23 indicate that media attention is related to a range of participation variables including discussing politics, trying to convince a friend, attending a political meeting, contacting officials

Table 2.26
OLS standardized regression coefficients for correlates of political knowledge, NES 1984

Interest in politics	.21**	.16**
Household income	.12**	.09**
Gender	.18**	.17**
Age	.16**	.16**
Education	.23**	.20**
Attention to newspapers	—	.25**
Attention to television	.14**	—
R^2	.29	.32
N	(2675)	(2675)

*Less than .05; **less than .005.

and voting. These variables are often significant predictors of attention to media, and this indicates that they are closely related to it. While the equations suggest a causal direction, participation leading to attention to the media, no such conclusion can be drawn with survey evidence alone. It seems more reasonable to suggest that media attention and the political participation variables measured in the studies are all part of a "participatory complex" with each act "feeding" off the others, so that attention to reports of politics in the media leads to discussion with friends, which leads to closer attention to the media, and that may result in attempting to convince a friend to vote in a certain way. There are many paths through this "complex" and what is known about partic- ipation suggests that individuals will follow different ones, some special- izing in one activity or activities (Verba and Nie 1972).

To this point not much has been said about the relationship between attention to the media and turnout, that is, casting a ballot. While turnout was present (abbreviated to "Voted") in tables 2.10 through 2.23, it was a significant predictor in only five of the full equations. The first expla- nation may be that turnout is not consistently important. A more reason- able explanation is that many of the variables in the equations are correlated (for example, attending a meeting is closely related to voting), and as a result there is some concern about multicollinearity or the possibility of separating out the independent effects of each of the terms in the equation. To address this concern and to determine the relative importance of each of the media variables, the following table presents turnout as the dependent variable (what is being predicted is whether an individual voted or not) and uses as predictor or independent vari- ables all of the sociodemographic variables contained in tables 2.6 through 2.9, plus attention to politics, the strength of identification with a political party and attention to campaign news in newspapers and on television. Table 2.27 analyses only the 1988 National Election Study: there is little reason to suggest that the earlier datasets would produce different results.

The equation in table 2.27 indicates that attention to neither news- papers nor television is a significant predictor of turnout when the effects of the other variables are taken into account. The only significant predictors are age, gender, being born in Canada and being employed. This suggests that demographic characteristics have a more important influence on turnout than do any of the others. Put another way, the effect of aging, the conditioning effect of gender, the influence of being born in Canada as opposed to having immigrated to the country and the effect of being employed as opposed to all other possibilities are more important in determining whether an individual will cast a vote

Table 2.27
OLS regression coefficients for correlates of turnout,
NES 1988

Age	.02**
Education	.01
Employed	.04*
Gender	-.04*
Income	.01
Language	-.00
Native-born	.05*
Union member	.03
Attention to papers	.01
Attention to TV	.01
Strength of party identity	.01
Interest in politics	.01
Region	
Atlantic	-.04
Quebec	.02
Ontario	—
West	-.00
Constant	.60
R^2	.05
N	(1284)

*Less than .05; **less than .005.

than are the media variables and the interest and strength of the partisanship variable. A cautionary note needs to be sounded: as the *R-squared* value suggests, the 15 predictor variables included in the equation account for only 5 percent of the variance in the turnout variable. Clearly, the model in table 2.27 is not the best predictor of voting, but the purpose here was to determine the importance of media attention relative to other well-known influences on turnout.

SUMMARY

The introduction to this study set out four questions to be addressed. The first question asked how closely Canadians follow politics in the media and whether their attentiveness has changed over the past two decades. The evidence indicates that attention is far from concentrated and universal. Only 45 percent of the 1988 respondents watched TV news daily and 5 percent fewer read a newspaper every day of the week. When asked about following campaign news on television and in newspapers, roughly 40 to 50 percent placed themselves in the most attentive category. This same pattern persists across all of the surveys examined, with the caution that changes in close-ended response sets and question wordings may have had some effect on the distributions. Any further interpretation of this evidence requires normative statements or beliefs about what should be. Many democratic theorists would describe this level of engagement with politics as unacceptably low (i.e., Green 1985), but others might describe it as too high (i.e., Berelson 1952). Obviously, the two views contain different assessments of the systemic and individual benefits of citizens' engagement with politics.

The second question asked whether media attentiveness was related to a number of social background variables such as gender, income and education. Tables 2.6 through 2.9 showed that paying attention to campaign news in the media is closely related to education, gender, age and income. This conjunction of characteristics describes not only those who pay most attention to politics, but those who participate most in politics. The most active participants are middle-aged, better-educated males who have higher than average incomes. From a self-interested perspective, this group has more to gain or preserve through political action, and it probably knows more about politics than any other group. This pattern is consistent across all of the surveys from the 1970s and 1980s. Gender, in particular, remains an important determinant of attention to politics in the media despite the politicizing effect of the feminist movement. The noteworthiness of the gender difference does not lie in the fact that it is large – in fact the differences are quite small, though large enough to be significant – but rather that this difference persists. This suggests, along with a great deal of other research (Brodie 1985), that women's engagement with politics may only be increased when the subordinate position of women is addressed through such policies as equal pay, daycare and affirmative action that will permit women access to jobs that are still predominantly male.

The third question asked what partisan characteristics are related to attention to campaign news on television, radio, or in newspapers. Once more, the evidence in tables 2.10 through 2.23 is consistent, and it suggests strongly that those who are most attentive to political messages are likely to be the most partisan. This particular pattern is robust across time and nations. Writing about American voters in the 1950s, Converse (1962) noted that "there is a strong correlation between the mass of stored political information and the motivation to monitor communication systems for additional current information. *The highly involved voter draws a much larger sample of the current information flow than does the uninvolved voter"* (ibid., 586; italics added). Converse also suggested that casual voters, those who live on the fringes of politics, were affected rather differently by exposure to political information through the media or by word of mouth: "the very uninvolved voters, who we have come to expect will tend to 'float' politically, present us with something of a paradox in this regard. On the one hand, such voters show a high susceptibility to short-term change in partisan attitudes *provided that any new information reaches them at all.* On the other hand, when the flow of information through the society is weak, these are the individuals who are *most* likely to experience no new information intake, and hence are individuals *least likely to show changes in patterns of behavior,* if indeed they are constrained to behave at all" (ibid., 586–87).

The evidence presented here seems to reinforce Converse's conclusion: the most politically involved, that is, the most interested, the strongest partisans, the consistent voters, and those who actively take part in the discussion of political matters, are most likely to seek more information. Clearly, entry into political life requires that a number of factors come together and, from this, greater participation and information seeking ensue.

The fourth question addressed the effects of attention to the media on political knowledge and beliefs. While in many ways this is the most important of the four questions, it is also the most difficult to address. Clearly, our knowledge of the effect of the media's message on the political beliefs of citizens is woefully inadequate. Part of this gap is because research designs that can address the content and effect of the messages transmitted through the media are very complex, time-consuming and costly.[6] But the lack of research on this question is also the result of the theoretical orientation of studies in electoral behaviour that have tended to focus on partisanship and social characteristics as a way of explaining electoral behaviour. Unfortunately, this brief study can only address one aspect of the question. The discussion found that while media agendas parallel citizen agendas, they are not identical. Moreover, attention to television news turns out to be a rather weak predictor of political knowledge, while attention to newspapers is a very strong predictor of political knowledge. This should caution us to the differences between the various media while at the same time suggesting the importance of further study of political messages and the media on which they are carried.

THE MEDIA AND POLITICS: SOME CONCLUSIONS

In *The Unreality Industry*, a radical critique of the media, Ian Mitroff and Warren Bennis make the argument that television news, the most common source of political information, the most widely trusted source of information, and the medium most likely to get the facts right (Adams and Levitin 1988), should be seen as an integral part of the television entertainment industry. Television news is first and foremost entertainment that is designed to hold the viewer: "television works by breaking everything down into 15–30 second segments or blips. Since the primary purpose of each blip is to grasp and to hold the attention of the viewer, the content of any blip is nowhere as important as who delivers it and how the presenter looks. The primary purpose of television is not to inform or to educate, and even strangely enough not to entertain, but to keep the viewer from switching dials by holding his or her attention. But to do this requires a never ending series of quick, almost totally unrelated attention grabbers" (Mitroff and Bennis 1989, 178). Whatever "knowledge" viewers derive from television, and here we are particularly interested in political knowledge, is quite different from the knowledge we would expect of an informed citizen of a democracy: "television knowledge is essentially visual, incoherent, frenetic, lacking context, without a larger framework to ground the images that are thrown at the viewer, and contradictory; i.e., essentially it is patternless knowledge, if that can be called knowledge at all in the classic sense of the term" (ibid., 181).

What do voters get from the media? Apart from the suggestion made above, that election information appears to be used to reinforce existing partisan beliefs, apparently voters do not get much in the way of consciously retained information about the candidates or parties. The specific content of television advertisements has a very short life. One study found that the recall of political advertising was low: "34.3 percent of the respondents failed to recall anything from either candidate's television advertising. An additional 22.5 percent were unable to recall anything from one of the two candidate's commercials" (Faber and Storey 1984, 43). As the authors note, "this is consistent with findings indicating that half the people who claimed to have watched one of the network news shows were unable to name even one story within an hour of viewing" (ibid., 43; see also Neuman 1976; Booth 1970).[7]

One of the very few in-depth studies to meet the research design requirements set out in appendix A is Iyengar and Kinder's (1987) *News that Matters*. That study found that television news has an agenda-setting effect in that its choice or placement of news items results in subjects according those issues more or less importance than before the item was viewed (see also McCombs and Shaw 1972; Becker and McCombs 1978; Soderlund et al. 1980; Wagenberg et al. 1983; Weaver 1984). The authors also found that television news draws attention to some aspects of politics at the expense of others, a process they termed priming. "When primed by television news stories that focus on national defense, people judge the president largely by how well he has provided, as they see it, for the nation's defense; when primed by stories about inflation, people evaluate the president by how he has managed, in their view, to keep prices down; and so on" (Iyengar and Kinder 1987, 114–15). They conclude that television news has a decisive effect on the priorities that people attach to various issues and the evaluative criteria citizens use to choose between candidates for office.

Critics of media political reporting have argued that its effects raise issues that go beyond discussions of journalistic techniques. As Joslyn writes, "it appears that the campaign communication that characterizes the contemporary electoral process does more to entertain than enlighten, to reassure than challenge, and to disorient than empower the U.S. public. Although this campaign communication may be functional for all involved, meaningful public choice – and hence self-government – would seem to be less than it might be" (Joslyn 1984, 296). The most important influence television and other media have on the political process is via agenda setting. While table 2.25 indicated that there appears to be some agenda setting, the priorities of the media and public do not agree completely, although there is a high degree of similarity across the issues thought to be important. One conclusion is that the media cause the agenda of individuals to mirror the agenda of the media by choosing certain news stories and highlighting them in certain ways. Perhaps more importantly, the media, as the prime source of political information in a democracy, may also be able to influence the basis upon which decisions are made by focusing on certain character details to the exclusion of others. To the extent that selective emphasis is characteristic of any ideological argument, it suggests that news reports still have far too high a rating of trustworthiness and credibility. Unfortunately, network news compounds the average citizen's lack of critical reading of the news through emphasis on the credibility and veracity of its anchors, reporters and news package.

To the extent that television is able to prime the evaluative powers of citizens, it must also be able to influence elections by shifting the ground over which they are fought. "Consequently, insofar as television news contributes, if unwittingly, to the success of one candidate over another, the results on priming ... are politically important" (Iyengar and Kinder 1987, 122). While this suggestion remains only partially tested, there can be little doubt that the selection and presentation of news stories can influence how people evaluate political candidates. One of the best Canadian examples is the CBC coverage of the Liberal "coup" of the 1988 election. In choosing to report in unusual length a rumoured movement to replace John Turner in mid-campaign, the network not only set the agenda as Turner's leadership abilities, but it also made the issue a prominent evaluative dimension for assessing other aspects of the Liberal campaign (Frizzell and Westell 1989).

The suggestion that the media have the ability to establish evaluative criteria for assessing political leaders and goals has further implications, for it is often argued that television news in particular promotes superficial ways of understanding politics (Mitroff and Bennis 1989; Patterson and McClure 1976). These critics argue that television news in particular and print to a lesser extent concentrate on personalities and aspects of the race such as campaign events, polls and management of the campaign itself, and exclude all but the most superficial treatments of policy issues. "What the viewer watches – the campaign trivia the networks so prominently display – is precisely how the viewer describes and defines the election world he cannot see with his own eyes" (Patterson and McClure 1976, 76).

Unfortunately, the limited evidence presented in this study cannot confirm the implications just discussed. But insofar as the content of media reporting of elections constitutes nearly the entire information flow for most citizens, it surely gives cause for concern about how that information is being shaped. On the other hand, all communication is subject to manipulation, either because of technical constraints or conscious or unconscious bias (Merrill 1965). This suggests in the strongest terms the need to ensure a broad diversity of methods of communication and viewpoints being communicated. Such diversity is a minimal condition for a meaningful democracy.

RECOMMENDATIONS

Assuming the Commission's goal to be the increased attention to media reports on political matters, the following recommendations are offered.

1. Attention to political news is not as widespread as it could be. Recognizing the inability of the Commission to address social obstacles to participation such as gender, age, education and income, the next best course of action is a proliferation of campaign information. This cannot be achieved through existing media alone, for many citizens are not attentive to those messages. The Commission must encourage a proliferation of

political communication on the assumption that the greater the number of opportunities to learn about and discuss politics, the more knowledge citizens will have about politics.

2. As the most closely followed and trusted medium, television has a particularly important role to play in informing citizens about campaigns. The Commission should encourage more in-depth television coverage of the electoral process.

3. The Commission should encourage the political parties to take advantage of free-time election broadcasting to inform voters about the issues. Legislation to require such a change would be problematic, but it might be accomplished by extending the time of each individual advertisement, or running the different parties' ads in succession so that comparisons are invited.

APPENDIX A
METHODOLOGICAL PROBLEMS

Despite concern over the ability of the media to tailor and bias information and so potentially to mislead voters, as one researcher recently noted, the "jury is still out on the precise usefulness of media communication in voting decisions" (Latimer 1987, 812). Frustratingly, this comment finds substantial support: "despite the assumed influence of media ..., attempts to establish a direct cause and effect relationship between media messages and voter attitudes or behaviour have been inconclusive" (Soderlund et al. 1984, 35).

One of the reasons that we know so little about the effect of the media's message upon those who receive it is because of inadequate research designs. Determining the effects of mass media communications upon the political opinions and behaviour of voters would require a research design of considerable complexity. Think for a moment of some of the problems such a research project would face if it were to provide an answer to the questions. First, a detailed account of what each respondent has read or seen would need to be available. At present, we have nothing but very general questions about media usage that are couched in terms of attention to the different media. A much more detailed record of what specifically was seen on television or read in the paper would need to be gathered. Differences in opinion or behaviour might well be predicted on the basis of what has been seen or read. Second, what information available in the media has been received second-hand, from close associates? The filtering effect of two-stage information processes is well illustrated in the literature on political debates, where non-watchers have their opinions formed by those who have watched the debate, or by the media's interpretation of the event. Second-hand information is likely to be partial and distorted and so will differ in content from that transmitted or read firsthand. Third, not all people receive the same information in the same way: thinking of the media as somehow inoculating the public with political information is a simplification of the individual differences likely to be present in the electorate. Some people, for example, will be more willing to critically assess the message than others. Some will already possess a large store of information on the topic and so be able to assess it in the light of the information already known. Fourth, not all information is of equal importance to all individuals; some will find media treatment of daycare issues to be far more important than its treatment of political personalities. Inevitably, this will affect what is remembered from any particular media exposure. Fifth, media exposure, like many activities, is selective. As is shown, those who watch, listen to and read the media are on average better educated, have higher incomes, are more politically active and are more partisan than those people who report lower attention to media sources. This will affect how different groups receive the message. Partisanship, for example, will influence what information is received, how it is processed and how it is eventually used. It is said that partisanship filters incoming messages, rejecting favourable news about the opposition and placing unfavourable news about one's own group in a much more favourable light. In other words, good things about one's own views and bad things about the opposing team's views get through the filter, and all else is translated by it to accommodate the reigning beliefs. Sixth, to properly assess the influence of the media would necessitate an experimental design with before and after measures that would confirm whether the media exposure had any effect at all upon opinions or behaviour. Seventh, a control group having had no exposure to the media would have to be present to ensure that any change said to be caused by the exposure was not caused by some other factor. Finally, some indication of the context in which the individual receives the information may be necessary. Television, and to a lesser degree newspapers, have become or are, overwhelmingly, entertainment media. There is reason to believe that television news may be treated as entertainment, for it occurs in just that context. Imagine for a moment the difference in how we treat a television newscast encountered while channel hopping between a hockey game, three sitcoms and a nature show, and sitting down to read the *Manchester Guardian*. Surely the context in which the information is placed will have some effect on how it is treated.

Constructing a research design to meet these requirements is crucial to addressing many of the more difficult questions about the relationship between media attention and political beliefs and behaviour. Admittedly, such research might be expensive and difficult, but more sophisticated research on media effects holds the promise of considerable returns on our understanding of the way people fashion their own political worlds.

APPENDIX B
QUESTION WORDINGS

1974

Name	Variable	Question	Wording
Interest	v11	q2	We would also like to know whether you pay much attention to politics generally.

			I mean from day to day, when there isn't a big election campaign going on. Would you say that you follow politics very closely, fairly closely, or not much at all?
News att	v33	q11a	Now would you please tell me how often you have done any of these things generally in federal politics, not just in this recent election. How often do you read about politics in the newspapers? Often, sometimes, seldom, or never?
Media imp	v155	q41	Which would you say is most important to you in getting information about politics, radio, television, or the newspapers?
Paper att	v152	q38	During the election campaign, would you say that you read quite a bit, something, or not much at all about the parties, candidates, or other aspects of the election campaign in the newspapers?
TV att	v153	q39	How about television? During the election campaign did you watch programs or advertisements about the parties or candidates or other aspects of the campaign? Would you say that you saw quite a few, some, or almost none?
Radio att	v154	q40	How about radio? During the election campaign did you hear programs or advertisements about the parties or candidates or other aspects of the campaign? Would you say that you heard quite a few, some, or almost none?
Pid str	v131	q30b	How strongly (Liberal, Conservative, NDP, Social Credit or other) do you feel, very strongly, fairly strongly, or not very strongly?
Pid same	v134	q32a	Still thinking of federal politics, was there ever a time when you felt closer to any other party?
Vote always	v156	q 42a	In federal elections since you have been old enough to vote in Canada, including the one held this July, would you say that you have voted in all of them, most of them, some of them, or none of them?

Vote always	v157	q42b	Have you always voted for the same party in federal elections, or have you voted for different parties?
Voted	v160	q43a	Now, thinking about this year's July federal election, we find that a lot of people weren't able to vote because they were away, or had some other reason for not voting. How about you? Did you vote this time, or did something happen to keep you from voting?
Leader Party Candidate	v164	q44a	In deciding how you would vote in the recent July election, which was the most important to you: the party leaders, the candidates here in the constituency, or the parties taken as a whole?
Discuss	v34	q11b	Now, could you please tell me how often you have done any of these things generally in federal politics, not just in this recent election. Discuss politics with other people?
Convince	v35	q11c	Try to convince friends to vote the same as you?
Work	v36	q11d	Work with other people in this community to try to solve some local problem?
Meeting	v37	q11e	Attend a political meeting or rally?
Contact	v38	q11f	Contact public officials or politicians?
Campaign	v39	q11g	Spend time working for a political party or a candidate?

1979

| Interest | v1022 | q2 | We would also like to know whether you pay much attention to politics generally. I mean from day to day, when there isn't a big election campaign going on. Would you say that you follow politics very closely, fairly closely, or not much at all? |
| News att | v1052 | q13a | Now would you please tell me how often you have done any of these things generally in federal politics, not just in this recent election. How often do you read about politics in the newspapers? Often, sometimes, seldom, or never? |

Pid str	v1193	q35b	How strongly (Liberal, Conservative, NDP, Social Credit or other) do you feel, very strongly, fairly strongly, or not very strongly?
Pid same	v1196	q37a	Still thinking of federal politics, was there ever a time when you felt closer to any other party?
Paper att	v1216	q43a	During the election campaign, would you say that you read quite a bit, something, or not much at all about the parties, candidates, or other aspects of the election campaign in the newspapers?
TV att	v1220	q44a	How about television? During the election campaign did you watch programs or advertisements about the parties or candidates or other aspects of the campaign? Would you say that you saw quite a few, some, or almost none?
Radio att	v1225	q45	How about radio? During the election campaign did you hear programs or advertisements about the parties or candidates or other aspects of the campaign? Would you say that you heard quite a few, some, or almost none?
Media imp	v1226	q46	Which would you say is most important to you in getting information about politics, radio, television, or the newspapers?
Vote always	v1229	q48a	In federal elections since you have been old enough to vote in Canada, including the one held this May, would you say that you have voted in all of them, most of them, some of them, or none of them?
Vote always	v1230	q48b	Have you always voted for the same party in federal elections, or have you voted for different parties?
Voted	V1233	q49a	Now, thinking about this year's May federal election, we find that a lot of people weren't able to vote because they were sick, or didn't have time, or had some other reasons for not voting. How about you? Did you vote this time, or did something happen to keep you from voting?

Party Leader Candidate	v1236	q50a	In deciding how you would vote in the recent federal election, which was the most important to you: the party leaders, the candidates here in this constituency, or the parties taken as a whole?
Discuss	v1053	q13b	Now, could you please tell me how often you have done any of these things generally in federal politics, not just in this recent election. Discuss politics with other people?
Convince	v1054	q13c	Try to convince friends to vote the same as you?
Meeting	v1055	q13d	Attend a political meeting or rally?
Contact	v1056	q13e	Contact public officials or politicians?
Campaign	v1057	q13f	Spend time working for a political party or a candidate?

1980

Interest	v2015	q2	We would also like to know whether you pay much attention to politics generally. I mean from day to day, when there isn't a big election campaign going on. Would you say that you follow politics very closely, fairly closely, or not much at all?
Pid str	v2044	q11b	How strongly (Liberal, Conservative, NDP, Social Credit or other) do you feel, very strongly, fairly strongly, or not very strongly?
Pid same	v2047	q13a	Still thinking of federal politics, was there ever a time when you felt closer to any other party?
Paper att	v2058	q16	During the election campaign, would you say that you read quite a bit, something, or not much at all about the parties, candidates, or other aspects of the election campaign in the newspapers?
TV att	v2059	q17	How about television? During the election campaign did you watch programs or advertisements about the parties or candidates or other aspects of the campaign? Would you say that you saw quite a few, some, or almost none?

Radio att   v2060   q18   How about radio? During the election campaign did you hear programs or advertisements about the parties or candidates or other aspects of the campaign? Would you say that you heard quite a few, some, or almost none?

Voted   v2061   q19a   Now, thinking about this year's February federal election, we find that a lot of people weren't able to vote because they were sick, or didn't have time, or had some other reasons for not voting. How about you? Did you vote this time, or did something happen to keep you from voting?

Party Leader Candidate   v2065   q20a   In deciding how you would vote in the recent federal election, which was the most important to you: the party leaders, the candidates here in this constituency, or the parties taken as a whole?

1984

Interest   var017   a2   Do you pay much attention to politics generally – that is, from day to day, when there isn't a big election campaign going on? Would you say that you follow politics very closely, fairly closely, or not much at all?

Paper att   var038   a10a   Some people do quite a lot in politics while others find they haven't the time or the interest. Thinking about federal politics, how often, if at all, have you done any of the following things – often, sometimes, seldom, or never? How often do you read about politics in the newspapers and magazines?

TV att   var039   a10b   Some people do quite a lot in politics while others find they haven't the time or the interest. Thinking about federal politics, how often, if at all, have you done any of the following things – often, sometimes, seldom, or never? Watch programs about politics on television?

Pid str   var082   c1b   How strongly (Liberal, Conservative, NDP, Social Credit or other) do you feel, very strongly, fairly strongly, or not very strongly?

Pid same	var087	c3a	Was there ever a time when you felt closer to any other federal party?
Media imp	var114	d4	Which source would you say was most important to you in getting information about the federal election campaign – radio, television, or the newspapers?
Vote always	var125	e1b	For which party did you vote? (1984)
Vote always	var156	e6a	The last federal election before this one was in February 1980. Do you remember for sure whether or not you voted in that election?
Vote always	var157	e6b	Which party did you vote for then? (vote in 1980 recalled in 1984)
Vote always	var160	e7a	The federal election before that was in 1979. Do you remember for sure whether you voted in that election?
Vote always	var161	e7b	Which party did you vote for then? (vote in 1979 recalled in 1984)
Voted	var124	e1a	Now, thinking about this year's federal election, we find that a lot of people weren't able to vote because they were sick, or didn't have time, or had some other reasons for not voting. How about you? Did you vote this time, or did something happen to keep you away from voting? (1984)
Party Leader Candidate	var128	e2a	In deciding how you would vote/would have voted in the 1984 federal election, which was the most important to you: the party leaders, the candidates here in this constituency, or the parties taken as a whole?
Discuss	var040	a10c	Some people do quite a lot in politics while others find they haven't the time or the interest. Thinking about federal politics, how often, if at all, have you done any of the following things – often, sometimes, seldom or never? Discuss politics with other people?
Convince	var041	a10d	Try to convince friends to vote the same as you?
Meeting	var042	a10e	Attend a political meeting or rally?

| Contact | var043 | a10f | Contact public officials or politicians? |
| Campaign | var044 | a10g | Spend time working for a political party? |

1988

TV watch	a2	a2 cps[8]	How many days in the past week did you watch the news on TV?
Paper read	a4	a4 cps	How many days in the past week did you read a daily newspaper?
Paper att	xa3	xa3 pes[9]	How much attention did you pay to articles in the newspaper about the election campaign? Would you say a great deal, quite a bit, some, very little, or none?
TV att	a2b	a2b cps	How much attention did you pay to news on TV about the election campaign? Would you say a great deal, a bit, some, very little, or none?
TV att	xa2	xa2 pes	How much attention did you pay to news on TV about the federal election campaign? Would you say a great deal, a bit, some, very little, or none?
Interest	a7	a7 cps	We would like to know whether you pay much attention to politics generally, whether there is an election campaign going on or not. Would you say that you follow politics very closely, fairly closely, not very closely, or not at all?
Pid str	xl5	l5 pes	How strongly (Liberal, Conservative, NDP, Social Credit or other) do you feel, very strongly, fairly strongly, or not very strongly?
Voted	xb1	b1 pes	We find that in every election, a lot of people don't vote because they are sick, don't have time, or for some other reason. How about you? Did you vote in this election?
Vote always	b7	b7 cps	Which party did you vote for? (in 1984)
	xb2	xb2 pes	Which party did you vote for? (in 1988)
Vote always	b6	b6 cps	Now, thinking back to the last federal election, in 1984, did you vote in that election?

Discuss	xc1	c1 pes	During the federal election campaign did you discuss politics with other people? (yes or no)
Campaign	xc2	c2 pes	During the campaign did you help a party, for example, by going to a meeting or rally, by working for a candidate, by putting a sticker on your car, or by putting up a lawn sign? (yes or no)

NOTES

I would like to thank Fred Fletcher for his comments on an earlier version of this paper.

1. In 1988 for example, 60.8 percent of the sample could not say whether one of the candidates was their incumbent member of Parliament.

2. The data from the 1965 and 1968 Canadian National Election Studies were made available by the Institute for Social Research (ISR), York University. The 1965 data were originally collected by Philip Converse, John Meisel, Maurice Pinard, Peter Regenstreif and Mildred Schwartz. The 1968 data were originally collected by John Meisel. Neither the original collectors of the data nor ISR are responsible for analyses or interpretations presented here. Data from the 1974, 1979 and 1980 Canadian National Election Studies, which were funded by the Social Sciences and Humanities Research Council of Canada (SSHRC), were made available by the study's principal investigators. The data were collected by Harold D. Clarke, Jane Jenson, Lawrence LeDuc and Jon H. Pammett. The original collectors of the data and the SSHRC bear no responsibility for the analyses and the interpretations presented here. Data from the 1984 Canadian National Election Study, which was funded by the Social Sciences and Humanities Research Council of Canada, were made available by the study's principal investigators. The data were collected by R.D. Lambert, S.D. Brown, J.E. Curtis, B.J. Kay and J.M. Wilson. The original collectors of the data and SSHRC bear no responsibility for the analyses and interpretations presented here. The 1988 Canadian National Election Study was funded by the Social Sciences and Humanities Research Council. The principal investigators were André Blais, Henry Brady, Jean Crête, and Richard Johnston. The original collectors of the data and the SSHRC bear no responsibility for the analyses and interpretations presented here.

3. The 1980 datapoint is not included because a number of the independent variables are missing from that cross-section survey. The 1988 questions vary somewhat from the earlier studies and did not include a variable measuring community size.

4. In the 1974 survey the regression coefficient for gender is significant at the .0574 level.

5. We are interested in how well known the provincial premiers are across Canada. Can you think of their names? (The names of provinces were then read to the respondent.) Question L21.

6. See the discussion in appendix A.

7. Ibid. The authors are referring to Robinson (1972).

8. Refers to campaign period survey.

9. Refers to post-election survey.

BIBLIOGRAPHY

Adams, M., and J. Levitin. 1988. "Media Bias as Viewed by the Canadian Public." In *Canadian Legislatures, 1987–88*, ed. R. Fleming. Ottawa: Ampersand.

Atwood, L. 1980. "From Press Release to Voting Reasons: Tracing the Agenda in a Congressional Campaign." In *Communication Yearbook 4*, ed. D. Nimmo. New Brunswick: Transaction Books.

Becker, L., and M. McCombs. 1978. "The Role of the Press in Determining Voter Reactions to Presidential Primaries." *Human Communication Research* 4:301–307.

Berelson, B. 1952. "Democratic Theory and Public Opinion." *Public Opinion Quarterly* 16:313–30.

Boden, A. 1990. "Radio Still Has Canada's Ear, BBM Confirms." *Marketing* 95:14.

Booth, A. 1970. "Recall of News Items." *Public Opinion Quarterly* 34:604–10.

Brodie, J. 1985. *Women and Politics in Canada*. Toronto: McGraw-Hill Ryerson.

Canada. Statistics Canada. 1989. *General Social Survey. Preliminary Data. Cycle 2: Time Use and Social Mobility Modules*. Ottawa: Minister of Supply and Services Canada.

Clarke, H., J. Jensen, L. LeDuc and J. Pammett. 1979. *Political Choice in Canada*. Toronto: McGraw-Hill Ryerson.

———. 1984. *Absent Mandate: The Politics of Discontent in Canada*. Toronto: Gage.

———. 1991. *Absent Mandate: Interpreting Change in Canadian Elections*. 2d ed. Toronto: Gage.

Cocking, C. 1980. *Following the Leaders: A Media Watcher's Diary of Campaign '79*. Toronto: Doubleday.

Comber, M., and R. Mayne. 1986. *The Newsmongers: How the Media Distort the Political News*. Toronto: McClelland and Stewart.

Converse, P. 1962. "Information Flow and the Stability of Partisan Attitudes." *Public Opinion Quarterly* 26:578–99.

Crouse, T. 1972. *The Boys on the Bus.* New York: Ballantyne Books.

Elkin, F. 1972. "Communications Media and Identity Formation in Canada." In *Communications in Canadian Society,* ed. B. Singer. Toronto: Copp Clark.

Faber, R.J., and M.C. Storey. 1984. "The Recall of Information from Political Advertising." *Journal of Advertising* 13:39–44.

Fang, I. 1985. *Television News, Radio News.* 4th ed., rev. St. Paul: Rada Press.

Fletcher, F. 1975. "The Mass Media in the 1974 Canadian Election." In *Canada at the Polls: The General Election of 1974,* ed. H. Penniman. Washington, DC: American Enterprise Institute for Public Policy Research.

———. 1980. "The Crucial and the Trivial: News Coverage of Provincial Politics." In *The Government and Politics of Ontario,* ed. D.C. MacDonald. Toronto: Van Nostrand Reinhold.

———. 1981a. "The Contest for Media Attention: The 1979 and 1980 Federal Election Campaigns." In *Politics and the Media: An Examination of the Issues Raised by the Quebec Referendum and the 1979 and 1980 Federal Elections.* Toronto: Reader's Digest Foundation of Canada.

———. 1981b. *The Newspaper and Public Affairs.* Vol. 7 of the research studies of the Royal Commission on Newspapers. Ottawa: Minister of Supply and Services Canada.

———. 1981c. "Playing the Game: The Mass Media and the 1979 Campaign." In *Canada at the Polls, 1979 and 1980,* ed. H. Penniman. Washington, DC: American Enterprise Institute for Public Policy Research.

———. 1987. "Mass Media and Parliamentary Elections in Canada." *Legislative Studies Quarterly* 12:341–72.

———. 1988. "The Media and the 1984 Landslide." In *Canada at the Polls, 1984,* ed. H. Penniman. Durham: Duke University Press.

Frizzell, A., and A. Westell. 1985. "Who Shot J.T.? – The Media Coverage." In A. Frizzell and A. Westell, *The Canadian General Election of 1984: Politicians, Parties, Press and Polls.* Ottawa: Carleton University Press.

———. 1989. "The Media and the Campaign." In A. Frizzell, J.H. Pammett and A. Westell, *The Canadian General Election of 1988.* Ottawa: Carleton University Press.

Gilligan, C. 1982. *In a Different Voice.* Boston: Harvard University Press.

Gilsdorf, W. 1981. "Getting the Message Across: Media Strategies and Political Campaigns." In *Communications Studies in Canada,* ed. L. Salter. Toronto: Butterworths.

Glynn, C., and J. McLeod. 1986. "Public Opinion, Communication Processes, and Voting Decisions." In *Communication Yearbook 6*, ed. M. Burgoon. Beverly Hills: Sage Publications.

Graber, D. 1976. "Press and TV as Opinion Resources in Presidential Campaigns." *Public Opinion Quarterly* 40:285–303.

—————, ed. 1984. *Mass Media and American Politics*. 2d ed. Washington, DC: Congressional Quarterly Press.

Green, P. 1985. *Retrieving Democracy: In Search of Civic Equality*. Totowa: Rowman and Allanheld.

Hedges, M. 1986. "Radio's Lifestyles." *American Demographics* 8:32–35.

Iyengar, S., and D.R. Kinder. 1987. *News that Matters: Television and American Opinion*. Chicago: University of Chicago Press.

Joslyn, R. 1984. *Mass Media and Elections*. Reading: Addison-Wesley.

Kay, B., S. Brown, J. Curtis, R. Lambert and J. Wilson. 1985. "The Character of Electoral Change: A Preliminary Report from the 1984 Election." Paper presented at the Canadian Political Science Association annual meeting.

Kennamer, J. 1987. "How Media Use during Campaigns Affects the Intent to Vote." *Journalism Quarterly* 64:291–300.

Latimer, M. 1987. "The Floating Voter and the Media." *Journalism Quarterly* 64:805–12.

Lemert, J. 1981. *Does Mass Communication Affect Public Opinion After All?* Chicago: Nelson-Hall.

McCombs, M., and P. Poindexter. 1983. "The Duty to Keep Informed: News Exposure and Civic Obligation." *Journal of Communication* 33:95.

McCombs, M., and D. Shaw. 1972. "The Agenda-setting Function of Mass Media." *Public Opinion Quarterly* 36:176–87.

McMonagle, D. 1988. "TV Favoured as Source of News, Poll Finds." *Globe and Mail*, 27 January, A8.

Meisel, J. 1985. "The Boob-tube Election: Three Aspects of the 1984 Landslide." In *The Canadian House of Commons: Essays in Honour of Norman Ward*, ed. J. Courtney. Calgary: University of Calgary Press.

Merrill, J. 1965. "How Time Stereotyped Three U.S. Presidents." *Journalism Quarterly* 42:563–670.

Miller, W., A. Miller and E. Schneider. 1980. *American Election Studies Data Sourcebook, 1952–1978*. Cambridge: Harvard University Press.

Mishler, W. 1979. *Political Participation in Canada*. Toronto: Macmillan.

Mitroff, I., and W. Bennis. 1989. *The Unreality Industry. The Deliberate Manufacturing of Falsehood and What It Is Doing to Our Lives*. New York: Carol.

Neuman, R. 1976. "Patterns of Recall Amongst Television News Viewers." *Public Opinion Quarterly* 40:115–23.

Patterson, T., and R. McClure. 1976. *The Unseeing Eye: The Myth of Television Power in National Elections.* New York: G.P. Putnam.

Reader's Digest. 1981. *Politics and the Media: An Examination of the Issues Raised by the Quebec Referendum and the 1979 and 1980 Federal Elections.* Toronto: Reader's Digest Foundation of Canada.

Robinson, J.P. 1972. "Mass Communication and Information Diffusion." In *Current Perspectives in Mass Communications Research,* ed. F.G. Kline and P.J. Tichenor. Beverly Hills: Sage Publications.

Robinson, M., and M. Clancey. 1985. "Teflon Politics." In *The Mass Media in Campaign '84: Articles from Public Opinion Magazine,* ed. M. Robinson and A. Ranney. Washington, DC: American Enterprise Institute for Public Policy Research.

Siebert, F., T. Peterson and W. Schramm. 1973. *Four Theories of the Press.* Urbana: University of Illinois Press.

Siegel, A. 1983. *Politics and the Media in Canada.* Toronto: McGraw-Hill Ryerson.

Soderlund, W., W. Romanow, D. Briggs and R. Wagenberg. 1984. *Mass Media and Elections in Canada.* Toronto: Holt, Rinehart and Winston.

Soderlund, W., R. Wagenberg, D. Briggs and R. Nelson. 1980. "Regional and Linguistic Agenda-setting in Canada: A Study of Newspaper Coverage of Issues Affecting Political Integration in 1976." *Canadian Journal of Political Science* 13:347–56.

Swindel, S., and M. Miller. 1986. "Mass Media and Political Decision Making: Application of the Accumulated Information Model to the 1980 Presidential Election." In *Communication Yearbook 9,* ed. M. McLaughlin. Beverly Hills: Sage Publications.

Verba, S., and N. Nie. 1972. *Participation in America: Political Democracy and Social Equality.* New York: Harper and Row.

Wagenberg, R., W. Soderlund, E. Briggs and W. Romanow. 1983. "Media Agenda Setting in the 1979 Canadian Federal Election: Some Implications for Political Support." In *Political Support in Canada: The Crisis Years,* ed. A. Kornberg and H. Clarke. Durham: Duke University Press.

Wagenberg, R., W. Soderlund, W. Romanow and E. Briggs. 1988. "Campaigns, Images and Polls: Mass Media Coverage of the 1984 Election." *Canadian Journal of Political Science* 21:117–29.

Wagner, J. 1983. "Media Do Make a Difference: The Differential Impact of Mass Media in the 1976 Presidential Race." *American Journal of Political Science* 27:407–15.

Weaver, D. 1984. "Media Agenda-setting and Public Opinion: Is There a Link?" In *Communication Yearbook 8*, ed. R. Bostrom. Beverly Hills: Sage Publications.

Wilson, J. 1981. "Media Coverage of Canadian Election Campaigns: Horserace Journalism and the Meta-campaign." *Journal of Canadian Studies* 15:56–68.

Witt, E. 1983. "Here, There and Everywhere: Where Americans Get Their News." *Public Opinion* (August/September): 45–48.

Wober, M., M. Svennevig and B. Gunter. 1986. "The Television Audience and the 1983 General Election." In *Political Communications: The General Election of 1983*, ed. I. Crewe and M. Harrop. Cambridge: Cambridge University Press.

Young, A. 1989. "Television Viewing." *Canadian Social Trends* 4 (Autumn): 13–15.

Yum, J., and K. Kendall. 1988. "Sources of Political Information in a Presidential Primary Campaign." *Journalism Quarterly* 65:148–51.

3

THE IMPORTANCE AND POTENTIAL OF LEADERS DEBATES

~

Cathy Widdis Barr

I T HAS BEEN almost 25 years since the first televised leaders debate in Canadian history, and it finally seems possible to conclude that debates between the leaders of the major political parties are becoming a regular part of Canadian federal election campaigns. The history of leaders debates in this country has, however, been rather erratic, and the role of debates in future elections is not assured. The first televised debate in Canada was held during the federal election of 1968. This debate did not mark the beginning of a trend, however, because no leaders debates were held during the 1972 or 1974 elections. Canadians had to wait 11 years for another debate between the leaders of the major federal parties. The 1979 debate did not start any trends either; debates were not part of the 1980 election, which was held only nine months after the 1979 campaign. Debates were, however, a major focus of both the 1984 and 1988 federal elections.

In Canada, the decision to debate is left to the individual party leaders and their advisers. Challengers for the position of prime minister are almost always eager to debate, because debates are generally considered to favour challengers over incumbents. Debates place all candidates on an equal footing – challengers share the stage with incumbents and get equal time to put forth their views. In addition, debates draw large audiences and thus provide the wide media exposure that is crucial for challengers, who are usually less well known than incumbents. Although challengers have much to gain and little to lose from participating in debates, the decision whether a debate will occur in a given election usually rests with the incumbent prime minister. The conventional wisdom used to be that incumbents should not debate unless they were in danger of losing the election. This reasoning appears to have been followed by Prime Minister Pierre Trudeau, who declined to debate in 1972, 1974 and 1980, when his party was leading the polls, but agreed to debate in 1979, when his party was behind in the polls. Trudeau chose to debate in 1968 even though his victory seemed assured, but it could be argued that Trudeau was not then a "true" incumbent – he had not led his party to victory in a general election but rather had become prime minister by becoming leader of the ruling Liberal party.

Despite the conventional wisdom, recent trends in both Canada and the United States indicate that it is becoming more and more difficult for incumbents to refuse to debate. Televised debates are increasingly considered by the public and the media to be a normal part of an election campaign. Moreover, a candidate's refusal to participate can itself become an election issue, as happened in Ontario in 1985 when Premier Frank Miller refused. Although debates are not institutionalized in the United States, they have occurred in the past four presidential elections, and all but the 1988 debate involved an incumbent president. The Canadian record is less consistent, but debates have been held during three of the past four federal elections, including the two most recent campaigns. In 1984, John Turner was in a position similar to that of Pierre Trudeau in 1968: he was prime minister by virtue of having been chosen Liberal leader, and his party was ahead in the polls. Turner, however, had to face an additional consideration. According to Jeffrey Simpson, Turner did not want to debate, but his advisers "believed the political risk in refusing to debate outweighed that of losing a narrow decision to Mulroney" (1985, 25). The circumstances surrounding the 1988 debate are even more revealing. Brian Mulroney had been prime minister for four years, his Progressive Conservative party led the pre-election polls, and the Conservatives continued to lead the polls during the three weeks of the campaign that preceded the debates. In the past, this would have been considered a classic scenario for an incumbent to refuse to debate. Nevertheless, Robert Krause (1989) reports that the Conservatives did not consider refusal a viable option.[1]

As televised debates become a regular feature of Canadian elections, it becomes more important to understand their value and role and to consider whether Canadian party leaders should be required by law to participate, as leaders in Sweden and Germany are. To do this, however, we must first understand the nature and extent of the impact of debates. In the United States, there is a lively and sustained scholarly discussion about the value of presidential debates, their role in the campaign and whether they should be mandatory.[2] These discussions draw on an extensive body of research on the impact of debates. Perhaps because they have – at least until recently – been sporadic occurrences, Canadian campaign debates have not been the focus of much scholarly attention. There has been little discussion among Canadian scholars about the value of televised debates and even less empirical investigation of the effects of such events.[3] There are several ways in which debates could influence voters. The impact that most interests politicians and their handlers, as well as media commentators, is the potential for debates to influence how voters cast their ballots. Obviously, the opportunity to win votes is the major reason political parties agree to participate in televised debates. And the media, although arguing that debates are important because they inform voters, usually focus their attention on who "won" and who "lost" and on how this will affect the outcome of the election.[4]

Despite the attention given to the impact of debates on how people vote, this is only one of many possible debate effects. Indeed, given what we know about the large number of factors that contribute to the vote decision, isolating the impact of debates from other factors is one of the most difficult tasks faced by anyone who studies televised debates.[5] In addition, from the perspective of determining the value of debates, their influence on how people vote is one of the least important of their potential effects. Televised debates are major campaign events. They attract large audiences and are covered extensively by the media. They may, therefore, stimulate interest in the campaign and thereby increase voter turnout. In other words, regardless of whether debates influence *how* people vote, they may influence their decision *to* vote. Debates could also affect political attitudes. For example, they could influence voters' perceptions of the personal characteristics of the party leaders and affect voters' overall evaluations of those leaders. Finally, and most important, debates could provide information to the electorate and thus increase voters' knowledge about the leaders, parties and issues. As was noted above, members of the media often claim that debates are important, even essential, for informing voters. *Globe and Mail* columnist Jeffrey Simpson (1989), for one, has argued that debates should be mandatory because they are "important vehicles to let voters hear nation-wide discussions of public issues during campaigns." Although such claims are frequently made, we know very little about what, if anything, voters actually learn from televised debates.

This study examines the impact of the 1984 and 1988 leaders debates in the four areas mentioned above. First, it investigates the effect of the debates on individual vote decisions. Second, it examines the influence of the debates on voter turnout. Third, the study explores the impact of the debates on opinions about the personal qualities of the major party leaders, and on overall evaluations of those leaders. Finally, it examines the influence of the debates on the levels of knowledge Canadians possess about the central factors of any federal election campaign: the party leaders, parties and issues. Findings are used to assess the value of debates and their role in the Canadian electoral process, as well as to draw conclusions about the question of mandatory debates. Analysis of the 1984 election is based on data collected for the 1984 National Election Study (NES), a single-wave, post-election survey of a representative sample of the Canadian electorate. Analysis of the 1988 election is based on two data sets: a re-interview of respondents from the 1984 NES conducted following the 1988 election and the 1988 NES. Unlike previous NESs, the 1988 study was a three-wave survey. The first wave was a campaign-period survey employing a research design known as a rolling cross-section – interviews were conducted with a small sample on each day of the campaign, beginning 4 October and ending 20 November. The second wave was a post-election survey, and the third was a mailback survey.[6]

AN OVERVIEW OF THE 1984 AND 1988 ELECTIONS

Before beginning our examination of the impact of leaders debates, we will take a brief look at the two elections serving as case studies for this purpose. The 1984 election was a landslide victory for the Progressive Conservative party. The Conservatives, led by Brian Mulroney, won 50 percent of the popular vote and 211 seats in the House of Commons. The Liberals, under John Turner, were reduced to 40 seats and 28 percent of the vote, and the New Democratic Party (NDP), led by Ed Broadbent, won 30 seats with 19 percent of the vote. Before election day, 4 September, three televised debates were held between the leaders of these three parties: a debate in French on 24 July, one in English on 25 July and a bilingual debate on women's issues on 15 August. The 1988 election was also won by the Conservatives, although the size of their victory was more modest than it had been four years earlier. In 1988, the Conservatives won 43 percent of the popular vote and 169 House of Commons seats – a major reduction from 1984, but still enough to form a majority government. The Liberals more than doubled their seats to 83 and won 32 percent of the popular vote; the NDP won 43 seats with 20 percent of the popular vote. All three parties had the same leaders in 1988 as in 1984, and during the campaign these men faced each other in two televised debates. The first debate, in French, was held on

24 October; the second, in English, was held on 25 October. Election day in 1988 was 21 November.

In both 1984 and 1988, the leaders debates were treated by the parties and the media as major campaign events, and the public apparently agreed. As can be seen from table 3.1, 49 percent of all 1984 NES respondents and 60 percent of English-speaking respondents reported watching the English debate, 23 percent of all respondents and 55 percent of French-speaking respondents watched the French debate and 38 percent of all respondents watched the women's issues debate. In all, 67 percent of respondents reported watching at least one of the three debates held during the 1984 campaign. The percentage of 1988 re-interview respondents who reported watching the debates is slightly higher: 52 percent of all respondents and 60 percent of English-speaking respondents watched the English debate, 26 percent of all respondents and 69 percent of French-speaking respondents watched the French debate and 65 percent saw one of the two debates. The larger audience in 1988 is due primarily to a larger proportion of French-speaking respondents watching the French debate and secondarily to slightly more people watching the debate in the "other" official language.

Table 3.1
Debate exposure, 1984 and 1988
(percentages)

	All respondents	English	French
1984 NES (*N = 3 359*)			
English debate	49	60	17
French debate	23	13	55
Women's issues debate	38	38	37
At least one debate	67	67	67
Any two debates	34	35	31
All three debates	9	9	10
1988 re-interview (*N = 1 197*)[a]			
English debate	52	60	23
French debate	26	15	69
Either debate	65	63	70
Both debates	14	12	22

[a]Refers to 1988 re-interview of 1984 NES respondents.

Because they attract such large audiences, leaders debates clearly have the *potential* to affect the course of the campaign and the outcome of the election. Several commentators have argued that the 1984 debates were the turning point of that election (e.g., Fletcher 1988; Perlin 1988). The most memorable exchange of the 1984 debates occurred in the English debate when Mulroney attacked Turner over a series of patronage appointments the latter had made shortly after becoming prime minister. The appointments were made at the request of outgoing Prime Minister Pierre Trudeau, and in response to Mulroney's request to apologize for making the appointments, Turner answered that he "had no option." Mulroney replied with all the indignation he could muster: "You had an option, sir. You could have said: 'I'm not going to do it. This is wrong for Canada. And I am not going to ask Canadians to pay the price.' You had an option, sir, to say no, and you chose to say yes, yes to the old attitudes, and the old stories of the Liberal party" (quoted in Sears 1985, 33). Ian MacDonald called this exchange "two of the most electrifying minutes in the history of televised political debates" (1984, 289). Clips of the exchange were repeated for days on television news programs, and the Conservatives referred to Turner's "had no option" response throughout the remainder of the campaign.

Largely because of the patronage exchange, the media declared Mulroney the winner of the English debate. He was also felt to have performed better than his opponents in the French debate. As can be seen from table 3.2, the majority of respondents to the 1984 NES agreed with this assessment: 52 percent rated Mulroney's debate performance as superior to Turner's and Broadbent's.[7] A mere 5 percent evaluated Turner's performance as superior to the performances of his opponents. Following the English and French debates, the Conservatives pulled ahead of the Liberals in all the major public opinion polls and continued to hold the lead for the rest of the campaign.[8] Of course, none of this means that the debates actually influenced the outcome of the 1984

Table 3.2
Leader chosen as debate winner, 1984 and 1988
(percentages)

Year and sample	Turner	Mulroney	Broadbent
1984 NES (*N = 1 671*)	5	52	43
1988 re-interview (*N = 573*)[a]	67	25	8
1988 NES (*N = 2 296*)	68	24	8

[a]Refers to 1988 re-interview of 1984 NES respondents.

election. Other events may have resulted in a Conservative victory, even if the debates had not been held or if Mulroney's performance had been judged less favourably. Indeed, the mid-August women's issues debate apparently had little effect on Conservative fortunes, despite the fact that Mulroney's performance in that debate was heavily criticized. Nevertheless, the debates were clearly viewed by observers at the time as significant events, and this conclusion is supported by the poll results – at least with respect to the French and English debates – and by the outcome of the election.

The 1988 debates are also generally considered to have been important events in that they significantly altered the course, although ultimately not the outcome, of the 1988 election (e.g., Frizzell et al. 1989; Johnston 1990). As in 1984, the most notable exchange of the debates took place between Brian Mulroney and John Turner in the English debate. The topic was the Free Trade Agreement (FTA), which had been negotiated by the Mulroney government with the United States. The exchange began when Turner, who opposed the agreement, declared: "I happen to believe you sold us out as a country." He then proceeded to enumerate the powers that he believed Canada had given up under the FTA, while Mulroney interrupted several times to deny that these powers had been lost. Both men became more and more impassioned. Mulroney claimed that he loved Canada and that the FTA would benefit Canada, to which Turner responded in part: "We built a country east and west and north. We built it on an infrastructure that deliberately resisted the continental pressure of the United States. For 120 years we've done it. With one signature of a pen, you've reversed that, thrown us into the north–south influence of the United States and will reduce us, I am sure, to a colony of the United States because when the economic levers go, the political independence is sure to follow" (quoted in Maser 1989, 63).

Many journalists commenting on the English debate immediately after its conclusion noted the exchange on free trade, but most concluded that the debate had no clear winner. The public, however, did not agree. Forty percent of those who were interviewed for the 1988 NES on the day following the English debate felt that Turner had won, and the next day a clear majority (54 percent) of respondents declared Turner the winner (figure 3.1). As figure 3.1 illustrates, the public declared Turner the winner of the debates immediately, and this belief was sustained throughout the campaign.[9] Indeed, as table 3.2 indicates, more than two-thirds of respondents to the 1988 post-election surveys believed that Turner won the debates, approximately one-quarter believed that Mulroney won and fewer than one-tenth felt that Broadbent won.

Figure 3.1
Leader chosen as debate winner, 25 October–20 November 1988

Percentage of respondents

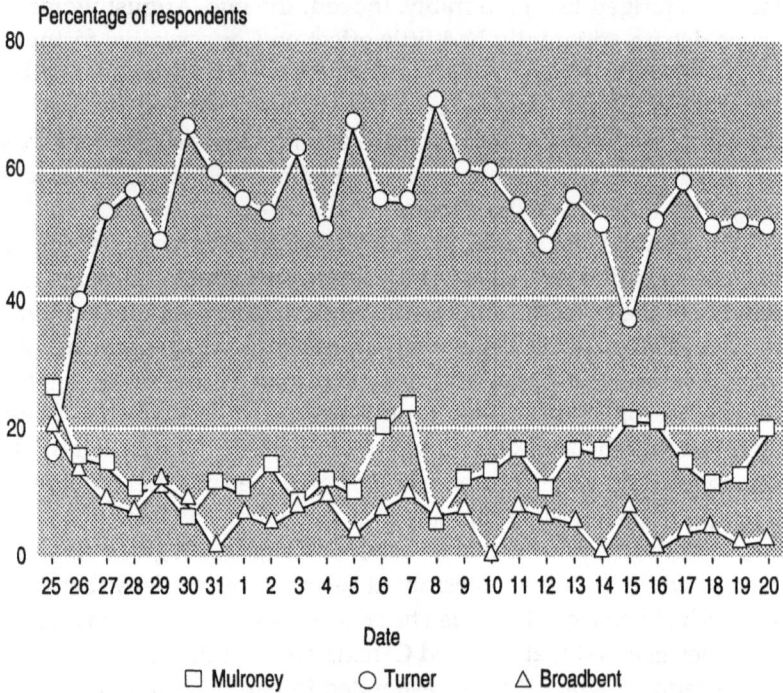

Date

☐ Mulroney   ○ Turner   △ Broadbent

Notes: Data are derived from the 1988 NES. Results for 25 October are based on 19 respondents whose assessments are based on the French debate only. Results for all other dates are based on an average daily sample of 80 respondents whose assessments are based on the French and/or English debates.

Both public opinion polls released during the campaign and the 1988 NES data support the conclusion that Turner's performance in the 1988 debates revived the flagging fortunes of the Liberal party. In the nine polls released between the start of the campaign and the debates, the Conservatives led the Liberals by an average of 15 percent. Of the four polls released in the week following the debates, two gave the Conservatives a slight lead over the Liberals, and two gave the Liberals a slight lead over the Conservatives. This see-saw battle continued throughout most of the rest of the campaign, until the Conservatives regained a solid lead in the final week.[10] Figure 3.2 tracks the vote intentions of the 1988 NES campaign period survey respondents; the debates took place during the seventh interval.[11] As this graph indicates, the gap between the Conservatives and the other two parties before the debates is quite substantial. In the two intervals immediately following the debates, the gap between all three parties narrows, and from

Figure 3.2
Vote intention, 1988

Percentage of respondents

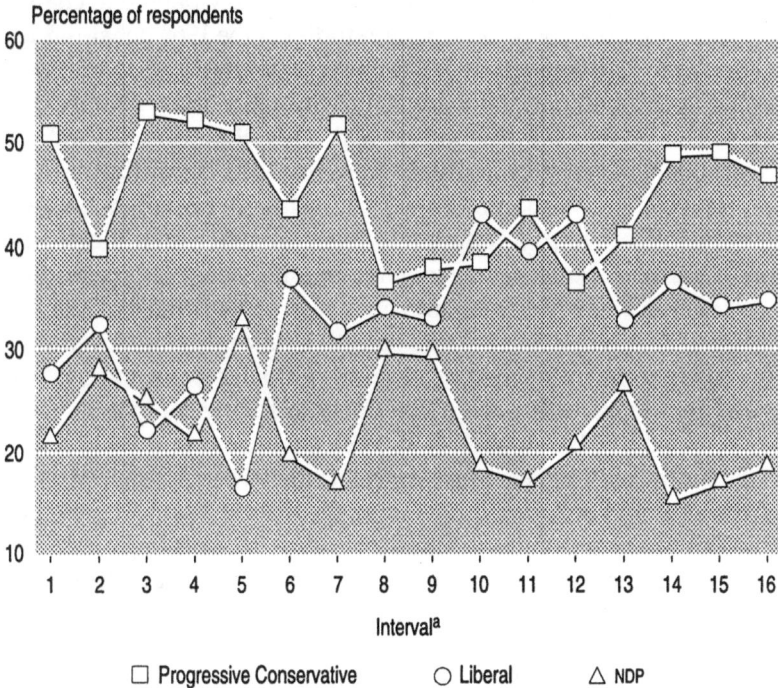

Interval[a]

☐ Progressive Conservative   ◯ Liberal   △ NDP

Notes: Data are derived from the 1988 NES.

[a]Intervals start on 4 October and end on 20 November. All but the sixteenth are three-day intervals; the sixteenth is a two-day interval. No data were gathered on 10 October. The average sample size of the intervals is 226 respondents. The debates occurred during the seventh interval.

the tenth interval on it is clear that the Liberals and Conservatives are battling it out for first place, with the New Democrats a distant third. From this evidence, it seems clear that the debates made the 1988 election a much closer contest than it would otherwise have been. In addition, Turner's vehement attack on the FTA made free trade the dominant issue of the campaign and Turner himself its most credible opponent.

THE EFFECT OF LEADERS DEBATES ON VOTE DECISIONS

The first televised debates in American history were four debates between John Kennedy and Richard Nixon during the 1960 presidential campaign. Dubbed "the Great Debates" by the commentators of the day, the encounters were the focus of a great deal of attention from both the public and the media, as well as from political scientists and communications researchers. Most research on the Kennedy–Nixon debates focused on their impact on individual vote decisions and the outcome of the election. Little evidence, however, was found to indicate that viewing the debates actually caused many people to change their vote. After reviewing 31 separate studies of the 1960 debates, Katz and Feldman (1962) concluded that their major effect was to reinforce existing vote intentions and to crystallize the intentions of undecided voters. This conclusion was in line with prevailing theories in both electoral-behaviour and communications research. According to these theories, election campaigns have little influence on voters because those most likely to pay attention to them are party identifiers, who tend to perceive campaign events in a manner consistent with their party identification. Independent voters were considered less likely to engage in selective exposure and selective perception and therefore more likely to be influenced by election campaigns; however, it was argued that these voters were less likely to follow campaigns (e.g., Berelson et al. 1954; Campbell et al. 1960; Lazarsfeld et al. 1944).

By the time researchers began analysing the 1976 presidential debates between Gerald Ford and Jimmy Carter, the theories that had prevailed in the 1960s were under attack. Researchers were documenting the decline of party identification and the rise of a new type of independent voter: interested, attentive, concerned with policy issues and willing to wait until the campaign period before deciding how to vote (e.g., Chaffee and Choe 1980; Miller et al. 1976; Nie et al. 1979). Despite this new perspective on the potential of debates to influence vote decisions, most researchers who studied the 1976 debates concluded that their major effect was to reinforce existing vote intentions (e.g., Dennis et al. 1979; Hagner and Rieselbach 1978; Lang and Lang 1978; Sears and Chaffee 1979). A few researchers, however, have found more significant effects. Davis (1979), for example, found that the 1976 debates helped undecided voters make up their minds. Davis (1982) concluded that the 1980 debates had a significant positive effect on intentions of voting for Reagan. After studying the 1976 and 1984 debates, Geer concluded that debates not only reinforce preferences but also "cause many cross-pressured and weakly committed individuals to change their preference for president" (1988, 495–96). Finally, a recently published study of debates in West Germany found that German debate watchers were more likely to vote for the party of the leader they felt had "won" the debate, even after party identification was taken into account (Schrott 1990).

LeDuc argues that the volatility of the Canadian electorate means that debates have the potential to influence Canadian voting behaviour: "Partisanship is relatively weak and unstable for large numbers of Canadian voters, and short-term factors are consistently found to be more important elements in voting behaviour in Canada than are socio-demographic or other longer term forces" (1990, 136). Despite the potential of Canadian leaders debates to influence voting behaviour, most studies have concluded that these debates have little impact on how Canadians vote. LeDuc and Price (1985) found a statistically significant difference between the voting behaviour of those who watched the 1979 debate and those who did not, but the direction of the difference was inconsistent with perceptions of the debate.[12] With regard to 1984, LeDuc (1990) found only one statistically significant correlation between watching a given debate and vote, and this was reduced to insignificance when controls for language were introduced.[13] In their study of the 1988 debates, LeDuc and Price (1990) found that debate watchers were more likely to vote Liberal than non-watchers, but the correlation was very weak. One recently published analysis of the 1984 debates comes to a slightly different conclusion about the impact of debates on voting behaviour. Using probit analysis, Lanoue (1991) found that people who watched a leaders debate in 1984 were significantly more likely to vote Conservative and significantly less likely to vote Liberal than were non-watchers. The effect was particularly strong among French-speaking voters.

The statistics presented in the first row of table 3.3 tend to support the conclusion that debates have little impact on how Canadians vote. When vote is cross-tabulated with a dichotomous variable measuring exposure to the debates, the two variables are found to be unrelated.[14] However, it would be unreasonable to conclude from this evidence that debates do not influence voting behaviour. The crucial question is whether debate exposure made voters more likely to *change* their vote

Table 3.3
Relationship between current vote and debate exposure, vote switching and debate exposure, 1984 and 1988

Relationship tested	1984 NES		1988 re-interview[a]	
	Lambda	N	Lambda	N
Current vote, debate exposure	.000	2 561	.000	955
Current vote, previous vote				
No controls	.273*	1 962	.418*	830
Watched at least one debate	.241*	1 430	.394*	570
Watched no debates	.351*	523	.476**	259

[a]Refers to 1988 re-interview of 1984 NES respondents.

*p < .001; **p < .01.

from one election to the next. Therefore, table 3.3 also presents the results of cross-tabulations between current vote and previous vote, controlling for debate exposure. As can be seen from this table, the relationship in 1984 between current vote and previous (1980) vote is moderate, returning a lambda of 0.273.[15] This relationship is weaker among those who watched at least one debate and stronger among those who watched no debates. Not surprisingly, the relationship between current and previous (1984) vote is stronger in 1988 than in 1984, returning a lambda of 0.418.[16] As was the case in 1984, this relationship is weaker among those who watched at least one debate and stronger among those who did not watch any debate. Of course, this does not necessarily mean that the debates caused people to change their vote. It is possible that those thinking of changing their vote are more likely to watch debates. Nevertheless, the results are interesting and worthy of further investigation.

The loglinear method of analysing contingency tables is a more powerful method of studying the relationship between leaders debates and voting behaviour. This method also provides a more refined picture of exactly how variables are related. In loglinear analysis, a model representing a hypothesized relationship between two or more categoric variables is specified. No distinction need be made between independent and dependent variables; the model must simply indicate which variables are hypothesized to be related. Expected cell frequencies are calculated and compared to observed frequencies using the likelihood-ratio chi-square.[17] The larger this statistic relative to the number of degrees of freedom, the more expected frequencies differ from observed frequencies. Thus, a large likelihood-ratio statistic means that the model does not fit the data and should be rejected. An acceptable model is one in which expected cell frequencies do not differ significantly from observed frequencies. Knoke and Burke argue that a model should be accepted if the probability of a type I error lies between .10 and .35 (1980, 31). At lower probability levels, the difference between observed and expected cell frequencies is greater than would be expected to occur by chance, and the model must be rejected as not fitting the data. At higher probability levels, the model may be "too good" a fit (i.e., it may include unnecessary parameters) and should be accepted only after simpler models have been tested and rejected.

Table 3.4 presents goodness-of-fit statistics for four sets of loglinear models relating to voting behaviour and debate exposure. Goodness-of-fit statistics are used to determine which model in a given set best fits the data. Following Knoke and Burke (1980), a model will

Table 3.4
Loglinear models of relationship between current vote and debate exposure, vote switching and debate exposure, 1984 and 1988

Model tested[a]	1984 NES			1988 re-interview[b]		
	Likelihood-ratio χ^2	Degrees of freedom	P	Likelihood-ratio χ^2	Degrees of freedom	P
{VD}[c]	.000	0	1.000	.000	0	1.000
{V}{D}[d]	2.582	2	.275[e]	4.382	2	.112[e]
{VPD}[c]	.000	0	1.000[e]	.000	0	1.000
{VP}{VD}{PD}	8.507	4	.075	5.800	4	.215[e]

[a]V = current vote; D = debate exposure; P = previous vote.
[b]Refers to 1988 re-interview of 1984 NES respondents.
[c]Saturated model.
[d]Model of independence.
[e]Model is accepted as fitting data.

be accepted if the probability of a type I error is between .10 and .35. The first panel of table 3.4 displays the statistics for two sets of models of the relationship between current vote and debate exposure: one for 1984 and one for 1988. The purpose of these models is to confirm the conclusion drawn from table 3.3 that vote is unrelated to debate exposure. The second panel of table 3.4 presents statistics for two sets of models of the relationship between vote switching and debate exposure. These models were designed to confirm the second conclusion drawn from table 3.3: that debate exposure, although unrelated to vote *direction*, is related to vote *switching*. In each panel, the first model displayed is the saturated model, so named because it contains all possible interactions among the variables. A saturated model can never be rejected because it will always predict expected values perfectly; nevertheless, the next simplest model must be tested because it might also fit the data.

The saturated model in the first panel of table 3.4 posits a relationship between current vote and debate exposure. Since this model includes only one two-way interaction, the next simplest model is the model of independence, which hypothesizes that there is no relationship between current vote and debate exposure. As can be seen from the probability levels associated with the two models of independence, these models must be accepted. This exercise confirms that vote direction in 1984 and 1988 was unrelated to debate exposure. Turning now to the 1984 data in the second panel of table 3.4, we see that the saturated model posits that the relationship between 1984 vote and previous vote (in 1980) is related to debate exposure. The next simplest model omits the three-way interaction among these variables, suggesting that there is a relationship between current and previous vote, current vote and debate exposure, and previous vote and debate exposure, but not among all three. The probability level of .075 associated with this model indicates that it must be rejected. Therefore, we must conclude that the simplest model that fits the 1984 data is the saturated model. Finally, turning to the 1988 data in the second panel of table 3.4, we can see that the model that omits the three-way interaction among the variables fits the data. As this model is simpler than the saturated model, it must be accepted as the best-fitting model. The results of our second test are thus inconclusive: vote switching appears to have been related to debate watching in 1984 but not in 1988.

Although the statistics presented in table 3.4 indicate that vote switching was related to debate exposure in 1984, they do not tell us exactly how exposure to the 1984 debates affected vote switching in that election. Table 3.5 is more informative in this regard. The statistics presented in this table are the parameter estimates for the three-way-interaction saturated models of the impact of debate exposure on vote switching in both 1984 and 1988. Parameter estimates express in logarithmic form the odds that a randomly selected case will fall into a given cell. A positive parameter estimate indicates that there are more cases in the cell in question than would be expected, given the marginal distribution of cases; a negative parameter estimate indicates the opposite. Only parameter estimates for respondents who

Table 3.5
Parameter estimates, current vote by previous vote by debate exposure, 1984 and 1988

Year and sample	Current vote	Previous vote		
		Liberal	Progressive Conservative	New Democrat
1984 NES	Liberal	-.075	+.015	+.060
	Progressive Conservative	+.204	-.084	-.120
	New Democrat	-.129	+.069	+.060
1988 re-interview[a]	Liberal	-.194	-.075	+.269
	Progressive Conservative	+.132	+.002	-.134
	New Democrat	+.062	+.073	-.135

Notes: Estimates refer to loglinear model of three-way interaction among current vote, previous vote and debate exposure. All parameter estimates are for respondents who watched at least one debate. Parameters for non-watchers may be obtained by reversing the signs.

[a]Refers to 1988 re-interview of 1984 NES respondents.

watched at least one debate are displayed in table 3.5.[18] The first panel in this table presents parameter estimates for the impact of debate exposure on vote switching in 1984. The largest parameter in this panel is +.204 for the cell containing 1980 Liberal debate watchers who voted Conservative in 1984, indicating that more of these individuals voted Conservative in 1984 than would be expected, given the marginal distribution of cases. The second panel presents parameter estimates for the saturated model of the impact of debate exposure on vote switching in 1988. Although the statistics presented in table 3.4 indicate that a simpler model also fits the 1988 data, the saturated model is nonetheless theoretically interesting and worthy of further examination. The largest parameter estimate in the lower panel of table 3.5 is +.269 for the cell containing 1984 NDP debate watchers who voted Liberal in 1988, indicating that more of these individuals voted Liberal in 1988 than would be expected, given the marginal distribution of cases.

These findings suggest that the televised leaders debates had some impact on vote in the 1984 federal election by influencing those who had voted Liberal in the previous election to switch to the Tories in 1984. Of course, given the magnitude of the Conservative victory, it is questionable whether the absence of debates would have changed the outcome of the election. On the other hand, it must be remembered that leaders debates are widely covered by the media and are watched by a large proportion of the population. Therefore, individuals who do not watch the debates are nevertheless likely to see, hear or read news reports about them. Such individuals are also likely to be aware of the assessments of journalists and others about who performed well and who performed poorly. Non-watchers may also hear friends, family members and colleagues discussing the debates. Thus, to the extent that knowledge about debates is diffused throughout the population, attempts to assess the impact of debates by examining behavioural differences between watchers and non-watchers will *underestimate* the impact they seek to detect.

For the 1988 election, watching a leaders debate appears to have made people who voted for the New Democratic Party in 1984 more likely to vote for the Liberals in 1988. Given that the Conservatives won the 1988 election, it would therefore seem that the debates were not decisive in determining the outcome of the election. However, as previously discussed, the 1988 debates did change the course of the election by giving the Liberals a major mid-campaign boost in popularity. The evidence in table 3.5 suggests that this boost came at the expense of the NDP and that the Liberals may also have benefited at NDP expense on election day itself. This is not to suggest that the debates were the only reason – or even the major reason – people who had voted NDP in 1984 chose to vote Liberal in 1988. The dynamics of the 1988 election were such that many former NDP voters may have felt that the best way to stop the Free Trade Agreement was to vote Liberal. The data presented here do, however, indicate that NDP–Liberal switching was related to watching a leaders debate in the 1988 election.

It is important to discuss the findings presented in this section in terms of the study's underlying objectives. What do these findings tell us about the value and role of leaders debates? Taken altogether, they seem to indicate that debates cause at least some people to switch their vote from one election to the next. Therefore, it would seem reasonable to conclude that these individuals learn something from debates that causes them to alter their previous vote. At this point, it is unclear what Canadians learn from leaders debates because no previous studies have examined this question. However, in one sense it does not matter what people learn. Whatever they learn, it seems to help at least some of them make up their minds about how they are going to vote. And although one might question the quality of the information conveyed in televised debates, it is surely no worse – and perhaps considerably better – than that available from other sources. As Jamieson and Birdsell point out: "In campaigns without debates, spot ads and news snippets provide most of our information about those who would lead the nation. In practical terms, this reliance on spots and snippets means that we base voting decisions on bites of information averaging a quarter of a minute to a minute in length" (1988, 123). If debates provide even a few people with more extensive information on which to base their vote decision, most people would conclude that they play a useful role in our electoral process.

THE EFFECT OF LEADERS DEBATES ON VOTER TURNOUT

American scholars have devoted little attention to the relationship between televised campaign debates and political participation. In fact, a literature search yielded only one reference. Kirkpatrick (1979) discusses the question briefly using aggregate data.[19] He argues that although both the 1960 and 1976 presidential debates drew large audiences, there was no increase in voter turnout on election day. The turnout in 1960 was 62.8 percent – 3.5 percent above 1956 and 0.9 percent above 1964.[20] The turnout in 1976 was only 54.3 percent – lower than in any election since 1948. Kirkpatrick concludes from this evidence: "It is clear that debates did not greatly stimulate interest in voting" (1979, 28–29). Although the evidence he presents – especially from 1976 –

appears to support this conclusion, it is always hazardous to draw inferences about individual behaviour from aggregate data. That turnout levels in election years featuring presidential debates are not significantly higher than average or, indeed, are lower than average does not preclude the possibility that debates could influence individual voters' decisions on whether to vote. One British study presents evidence that at least suggests a link between televised campaign debates and voter turnout. Blumler and McLeod (1974) found that several mass-communications variables were related to turnout in Great Britain, even when the effects of socio-economic status, education, age and gender were controlled. Although these researchers did not examine the impact of debates per se, such events are clearly exercises in mass communication, and so it is conceivable that debates could have a similarly positive effect on voter turnout.

Canadian researchers have shown more interest than their American counterparts in the relationship between watching televised debates and voting. LeDuc and Price (1985) found that 1974 non-voters who reported watching the 1979 leaders debate were more likely to have voted in 1979 than previous non-voters who did not watch the debate.[21] They conclude, however, that "it is unlikely that the debates themselves actually stimulated greater voting participation. Rather, it is more plausible that persons already intending to vote were more likely to have watched the debates" (ibid., 153). This conclusion seems reasonable. As LeDuc (1990) reports, debate watching is associated with many other types of political activity. According to the correlations he presents, individuals who participate in various forms of political activity (from watching political programs on television to attending political meetings) are more likely to watch televised debates. Not surprisingly, these same people are also more likely to vote. This finding suggests that the apparent relationship between debate exposure and voter turnout is spurious – the result of *both* these activities being related to political interest and involvement. In any event, the possibility of a spurious relationship cannot be ignored.

Table 3.6 presents the correlations between voter turnout and debate exposure in both 1984 and 1988 with and without controls for the respondent's level of interest in the election.[22] Interest in the election was chosen as the control variable because it was more strongly associated with turnout than any of the political participation variables in 1984 and because 1988 re-interview respondents were not asked about their participation in political activities other than voting.[23] As can be seen from this table, the association between turnout and debate exposure is statistically significant but fairly weak, in both 1984 and 1988.

Table 3.6
Relationship between voter turnout and debate exposure, with and without controls for level of interest in election, 1984 and 1988

Relationship tested	1984 NES		1988 re-interview[a]	
	Pearson's r	N	Pearson's r	N
Voter turnout, debate exposure				
No controls	.183*	3 357	.129*	1 195
Very interested in election	.029	1 138	.087***	631
Fairly interested in election	.039	1 297	-.009	390
Slightly interested in election	.127**	663	.262**	124
Not at all interested in election	.168**	279	.267	49

[a]Refers to 1988 re-interview of 1984 NES respondents.

*$p < .001$; **$p < .01$; ***$p < .05$.

Furthermore, when level of interest in the election is controlled for, the correlations tend to get weaker in each of the partial tables – an indication that the observed association between voter exposure and debate exposure is spurious. The partial correlations are, however, rather interesting in that they seem to indicate that there may be some relationship between debate exposure and voter turnout among those who are less interested in the election. This conclusion is based on the fact that the largest partial correlations are for those who were slightly interested or not at all interested in the election at hand. This effect is particularly strong in 1988.[24]

The correlations presented in table 3.6 are not overly encouraging with regard to the capacity of debates to affect voter turnout. Nevertheless, the persistence of a relationship between turnout and debate exposure among individuals who express little interest in the election is intriguing because it suggests that debates may help motivate these people to vote. The loglinear goodness-of-fit statistics displayed in table 3.7 provide a more sophisticated test of the relationship between turnout and debate exposure. The two sets of models presented in the first panel of this table test the hypothesis that voter turnout in 1984 and 1988 was related to debate exposure. The probability levels of the models of independence indicate that these models do not fit the data in either 1984 or 1988. Therefore, we must conclude that voter turnout was indeed related to debate exposure. However, the question of whether this relationship is spurious remains to be addressed.

The issue of spuriousness is dealt with in the second panel of table 3.7, which presents several models designed to test the hypothesis that

Table 3.7
Loglinear models of relationship between voter turnout and debate exposure, 1984 and 1988

Model tested[a]	1984 NES			1988 re-interview[b]		
	Likelihood-ratio χ^2	Degrees of freedom	P	Likelihood-ratio χ^2	Degrees of freedom	P
{TD}[c]	0.000	0	1.000[e]	.000	0	1.000[e]
{T}{D}[d]	106.542	1	.000	18.919	1	.000
{TDI}[c]	0.000	0	1.000	.000	0	1.000[e]
{TI}{TD}{ID}	2.856	3	.414[e]	8.271	3	.041
{TD}{TI}	215.727	6	.000			
{TD}{ID}	374.694	6	.000			
{TI}{ID}	21.292	4	.000			

[a]T = voter turnout; D = debate exposure; I = interest in election.
[b]Refers to 1988 re-interview of 1984 NES respondents.
[c]Saturated model.
[d]Model of independence.
[e]Model is accepted as fitting data.

the association between voter turnout and debate exposure is related to political interest. The saturated model for both 1984 and 1988 assumes a three-way interaction among these variables. The next-simplest model states that turnout is related to interest and debate exposure, and interest is related to debate exposure, but there is no three-way interaction. In 1988, the probability level of the model that omits the three-way interaction is .041, which means that the model does not fit the data. Therefore, the saturated model must be accepted as the best-fitting model. In 1984, however, the probability level of the model that omits the three-way interaction is .414. Therefore, the model cannot be rejected; however, an even simpler model might also fit the data. To test this possibility, three additional models – each omitting one of the two-way interactions – were tested, and all were rejected. Therefore, we must conclude that in 1984 voter turnout was related to both interest and debate exposure, and that interest and debate exposure were also related, but that there was no three-way interaction among these variables.

The parameter estimates for the three-way-interaction saturated models of turnout in both elections are presented in table 3.8. Only the parameter estimates for respondents who watched at least one debate are displayed in this table. Looking at these estimates, we can see that there were more slightly interested and uninterested debate watchers who voted in both 1984 and 1988 than would be expected on the basis

Table 3.8
Parameter estimates, voter turnout by interest in election by debate exposure, 1984 and 1988

Year and sample	Very interested	Fairly interested	Slightly interested	Not at all interested
1984 NES	-.039	-.053	+.033	+.059
1988 re-inteview[a]	-.040	-.235	+.195	+.080

Notes: Estimates refer to loglinear model of three-way interaction among voter turnout, interest in the election and debate exposure. All parameter estimates are for respondents who both voted and watched at least one debate. Parameters for non-voters and non-watchers may be obtained by reversing the signs.

[a]Refers to 1988 re-interview of 1984 NES respondents.

of the marginal distribution of cases in these tables. Although most of the estimates are small, the direction of the signs is consistent with the notion that the debates may have had some influence on voter turnout among those with low levels of interest in the 1984 and 1988 elections.

The goodness-of-fit statistics, combined with the weak parameter estimates presented in table 3.8, indicate that there is little relationship between debate exposure and voter turnout that cannot be accounted for by the association of both these variables with political interest. Nevertheless, the findings presented in this section suggest that debate exposure may have some effect on voter turnout among people with little or no interest in the campaign at hand. The relationship is not strong, but its implications are important enough that the question warrants further investigation. Even if debates play only a small role in encouraging people to vote who would otherwise be unlikely to do so, they perform a worthwhile function. Voting is the most basic means of political participation in a representative democracy. If we value democracy, we must value participation in the democratic process and, by extension, any mechanism that increases participation.

THE EFFECT OF LEADERS DEBATES ON ATTITUDES TOWARD PARTY LEADERS

As mentioned above, most researchers who studied the 1960 American presidential debates were interested in whether the debates influenced individual vote decisions or the outcome of the election. Many researchers, however, were also interested in whether the debates had changed voters' attitudes toward the candidates. One of the most extensive studies of the impact of the 1960 debates on candidate image was conducted by Tannenbaum et al. (1962). These researchers asked respondents to rate Kennedy and Nixon before and after the first debate and then again following the fourth debate, using a series of semantic differential scales. After comparing candidate images before and after the first debate among respondents who watched the debate, to before and after images among those who did not watch, Tannenbaum et al. concluded: "There were substantial and significant differences in the direction and magnitude of image change *as a result of the first debate* between those respondents who viewed it on TV and those who were not exposed at all" (ibid., 285; italics in original). When exposure to all four debates was considered, however, degree of exposure had little effect on image change. This finding led the researchers to conclude that *direct* exposure may not have been necessary for an individual to be influenced by the debates: "The video clashes were an integral and vital part of the 1960 campaign – not only as TV events, but also in terms of widespread reports in the press and radio, as topics of face-to-face discussion, and as the focal point for much commentary by political pundits and the like. This very pervasiveness of the debates throughout the contest implies that they may have exerted an impact quite independent of actual TV exposure" (ibid., 288).

Findings from other studies of the 1960 presidential debates support the conclusion that at least the first debate influenced attitudes toward Kennedy and Nixon (e.g., Ben-Zeev and White 1962; Carter 1962; Kraus and Smith 1962; Lang and Lang 1962). The attitude changes found in most studies of the 1960 debates were not large, but researchers studying the 1976 debates found even smaller changes. In fact, most evidence suggests that the 1976 debates had very little impact on voters' images of Ford and Carter. After reviewing 44 studies of the 1976 debates, Sears and Chaffee concluded that "there was little lasting impact of the debates on evaluations of the candidates, preferences between them, or perceptions of candidates' attributes" (1979, 244). The apparent insignificant effect of debates on attitudes toward political leaders – like their lack of influence on voting behaviour – is generally attributed to the process of selective perception. This explanation is not without empirical support. Several studies have found that party identification, as well as pre-debate candidate preferences and evaluations, have a strong influence on how debaters are perceived and evaluated (e.g., Hagner and Rieselbach 1978; Kraus and Smith 1962; Lang and Lang 1962; Sigelman and Sigelman 1984).

LeDuc and Price (1990) examined the correlations between debate exposure and overall evaluations of party leaders in the 1979, 1984 and 1988 Canadian elections. Their findings relating to 1979 indicate no statistically significant difference between debate watchers and non-watchers on evaluations of Clark; English-speaking watchers evaluated Trudeau slightly more highly than English-speaking non-watchers;

and whether all respondents or only English-speaking respondents were considered, Broadbent was evaluated more highly by those who watched the debate than by those who did not. On the impact of the 1984 debates on overall evaluations of Turner, Mulroney and Broadbent, it was found that people with differing levels of exposure to the debates had significantly different evaluations of all three leaders. Surprisingly, however, all leaders appear to have benefited from the debates – even John Turner, whose performance in the 1984 debates was rated so poorly. In 1988, the only significant correlations were for Turner, who was rated significantly higher by debate watchers than non-watchers. LeDuc and Price conclude: "In virtually every instance where a difference between watchers and non-watchers of a debate can be discerned, the effect is that watchers tend to be more positive in their attitudes toward particular leaders than are non-watchers" (1990, 16).

Respondents to the 1984 and 1988 NESs were asked to evaluate the leaders of the Liberal, Progressive Conservative and New Democratic parties using what is known as a "feeling thermometer." On a feeling thermometer, scores above 50 degrees indicate warm or favourable feelings toward the person being evaluated; scores below 50 degrees indicate cool or unfavourable feelings. Because the feeling thermometer is a summary of an individual's feelings, differences between ratings of debate watchers and non-watchers provide information about the impact of debates on overall evaluations of party leaders. A comparison of the mean thermometer ratings of the party leaders for those who watched and those who did not watch a leaders debate in 1984 and 1988 is displayed in table 3.9. As can be seen from this table, those who watched at least one debate felt warmer toward all three party leaders than those who watched no debates. In 1984, the difference between watchers and non-watchers is greatest for evaluations of Broadbent and smallest for evaluations of Turner. This suggests that, at least in terms of personal image, Broadbent benefited most from the 1984 leaders debates and Turner benefited least. In 1988, results were reversed: Broadbent benefited least and Turner most. The differences between the leaders, however, are not very large, and the more important conclusion is that all leaders were evaluated more highly by debate watchers than by non-watchers.

Summary measures such as feeling thermometers give us some idea of the impact of televised debates on attitudes toward party leaders. They do not, however, provide any details about the impact of debates on specific components of a leader's image. An extensive body of research indicates that voters' images of political leaders are overwhelmingly dominated by personal characteristics.[25] Television is par-

Table 3.9
Overall evaluation of leaders, 1984 and 1988

Year and sample	Turner	Mulroney	Broadbent
1984 NES			
Watchers	51.81	63.72	58.48
Non-watchers	49.29**	60.04*	54.47*
1988 NES			
Watchers	48.89	56.44	52.41
Non-watchers	45.04*	54.09**	50.34***

Notes: Evaluation measured as the mean value of a leader's scores on feeling thermometer.
*p < .001; **p < .01; ***p < .05.

ticularly well suited for conveying such information. Therefore, we might expect televised debates to influence voters' judgements about the personality traits of party leaders, although research on selective perception would lead us to assume that this influence would be modest. Fortunately, respondents to the 1984 and the 1988 NESs were not only asked to evaluate party leaders using the feeling thermometer, they were also asked for their impressions of the leaders using semantic differential scales designed to measure their views about specific personal characteristics of the leaders.

Respondents to the 1984 NES were asked to give their impressions of the three leaders on 14 dimensions: arrogant, competent, ruthless, commands respect, nervous, decent, slick, sincere, shallow, sure of himself, dull, warm, represents change and listens to the views of people in this province. Opinions on each dimension were measured using semantic differential scales on which 1 meant that the word or phrase in question did not describe a leader and 7 meant that it did.[26] Respondents to the post-election wave of the 1988 NES were asked for their impressions of each leader on 4 dimensions: intelligent, trustworthy, provides strong leadership and really cares about people like you. In this case, opinions on each dimension were measured using five-point semantic differential scales, on which 1 indicated that the relevant word or phrase fit a leader "a great deal" and 5 indicated that the term fit "not at all."[27] Comparing the mean ratings given by respondents who did and did not watch the leaders debates provides us with information about the impact of the debates on specific components of the leaders' images. For 1984, this information is presented in table 3.10; for 1988, it is displayed in table 3.11.

Looking first at impressions of Liberal leader John Turner, we see that in 1984 the difference between the ratings of watchers and non-watchers is statistically significant for 5 of the 14 dimensions. Individuals who watched at least one of the 1984 leaders debates felt that Turner was more nervous and less sure of himself than did those who watched no debates. On the positive side, debate watchers felt that Turner was more decent and sincere. Watchers were also more likely than non-watchers to feel that Turner commanded respect, which

Table 3.10
Judgement of leaders' personal characteristics, 1984

Characteristics	Respondents	Turner	Mulroney	Broadbent
Arrogant	Debate watchers	3.91	3.87	2.96
	Non-watchers	3.82	3.79	3.09
Competent	Debate watchers	4.19	5.36	4.73
	Non-watchers	4.21	5.10*	4.51**
Ruthless	Debate watchers	3.53	3.86	3.06
	Non-watchers	3.49	3.69***	3.17
Commands respect	Debate watchers	4.32	5.32	4.86
	Non-watchers	4.12**	5.10*	4.57*
Nervous	Debate watchers	5.16	2.89	2.96
	Non-watchers	4.54*	2.92	3.00
Decent	Debate watchers	5.11	5.36	5.48
	Non-watchers	4.94**	5.17**	5.24*
Slick	Debate watchers	4.07	5.11	3.68
	Non-watchers	4.07	4.74*	3.46**
Sincere	Debate watchers	4.54	4.83	5.30
	Non-watchers	4.31**	4.71	5.01*
Shallow	Debate watchers	3.73	3.38	2.86
	Non-watchers	3.76	3.40	3.05***
Sure of himself	Debate watchers	4.08	5.96	5.25
	Non-watchers	4.30**	5.75*	5.09**
Dull	Debate watchers	4.08	3.09	3.51
	Non-watchers	3.99	3.24***	3.47
Warm	Debate watchers	3.89	4.89	4.92
	Non-watchers	3.82	4.74***	4.55*
Represents change	Debate watchers	3.58	5.60	4.93
	Non-watchers	3.55	5.27*	4.86
Listens to views	Debate watchers	3.90	4.84	4.64
	Non-watchers	3.83	4.60*	4.48***

Notes: Judgement measured as mean value of respondents' evaluation of each leader on given personal characteristics. Data are derived from the 1984 NES.

*$p < .001$; **$p < .01$; ***$p < .05$.

Table 3.11
Judgement of leaders' personal characteristics, 1988

Characteristics	Respondents	Turner	Mulroney	Broadbent
Intelligent	Debate watchers	2.22	1.80	1.89
	Non-watchers	2.49*	2.01*	2.04*
Trustworthy	Debate watchers	2.81	2.80	2.07
	Non-watchers	3.09*	2.89	2.30*
Strong leadership	Debate watchers	3.25	1.84	2.35
	Non-watchers	3.42**	2.10*	2.54*
Really cares	Debate watchers	2.95	2.95	2.13
	Non-watchers	3.25*	3.16*	2.36*

Notes: Judgement measured as mean value of respondents' evaluation of each leader on given personal characteristics. Data are derived from the 1988 NES.

*$p < .001$; **$p < .01$.

seems contradictory because watchers were also more likely to feel that Turner was nervous and lacked confidence – traits that do not usually command much respect. The 1984 debates appear to have had the most influence on opinions about Turner's nervousness. In fact, the largest difference between watchers and non-watchers in table 3.10 is on this trait. On the whole, however, the 1984 debates seem to have had only a minimal impact on judgements about most aspects of Turner's image – on nine dimensions, there is no statistically significant difference between the views of watchers and non-watchers. For 1988, the differences between watchers' evaluations of Turner and non-watchers' evaluations are statistically significant on all four dimensions. In all cases, however, non-watchers evaluated the Liberal leader more highly than watchers, although the differences are not large.

Turning now to impressions of Brian Mulroney, we find that in 1984 debate watchers held opinions about the Conservative leader that were significantly different from the opinions of non-watchers on 10 of the 14 dimensions. Compared with non-watchers, debate watchers felt that Mulroney was more competent, decent and warm, and that he commanded more respect, was more sure of himself and less dull. Watchers were also more likely to believe that Mulroney represented change and listened to the views of people in their province. On the negative side, debate watchers felt that Mulroney was more ruthless and slick than did non-watchers. On the basis of the evidence presented in table 3.10, it appears that the effect of the 1984 debates on attitudes toward Mulroney was mixed. On the one hand, individuals who watched at least one debate were more positive toward Mulroney on many characteristics. On the other hand, the largest single difference between the views of watchers and non-watchers was Mulroney's slickness, and in this case debate watchers had the more unfavourable impression. For 1988, the results for Mulroney are similar to those for Turner: the difference between the evaluation of watchers and non-watchers is statistically significant on three out of four dimensions, and in all cases non-watchers evaluated Mulroney more highly than watchers. As with Turner, however, the differences are minor.

Finally, an examination of impressions of NDP leader Ed Broadbent reveals that in 1984 the difference between watchers and non-watchers was statistically significant for nine dimensions. Debate watchers were more inclined to feel that Broadbent was competent, decent, sincere, sure of himself and warm, and that he commanded respect and listened to the views of people in their province. They were less likely to believe he was shallow but more likely to believe he was slick – another apparent contradiction. With the exception of perceptions about his slickness, the 1984 debates appear to have resulted in more positive attitudes toward Broadbent on most characteristics. Interestingly, the debates' greatest effect on evaluations of Broadbent was on opinions about his warmth. This may indicate that debate watchers responded to Broadbent on a more personal level than they responded to either Turner or Mulroney. For the Liberal and Conservative leaders, the greatest impact of the debates was on judgements of their nervousness and slickness – characteristics that refer more to manner and style than to enduring personal attributes. Turning to images of Broadbent in 1988, we find the differences between watchers and non-watchers were statistically significant for all dimensions, but again it was the non-watchers who evaluated Broadbent more highly. Given the poor evaluation of Broadbent's 1988 debate performance by the media and the public, this result is not very surprising.

Several conclusions can be drawn from the above findings about the impact of televised debates on attitudes toward party leaders. First, debates appear to have a positive effect on voters' overall evaluations of all leaders but are also capable of creating negative impressions of particular aspects of their personalities. With respect to the specific components of leader image examined here, no single picture emerges as to which trait judgements are most likely to be affected by televised debates. The debates influenced – for better or worse – the image of each leader in a unique way. It must be noted, however, that the differences between the evaluations of watchers and non-watchers were not great. In no case did they exceed 5 degrees on the 100-degree feeling thermometer or 1 unit on the semantic differential scales. On the other hand, comparing the judgements of watchers and non-watchers may not be a very effective means of assessing the true impact of debates. Because information about leaders debate performances is widely disseminated, non-watchers may come to hold views of the leaders that are very similar to the views of those who saw the debates. For example, the 1984 debate viewer saw John Turner appearing nervous during the debates. The non-viewer saw him being nervous on a clip of the debates shown during the evening news; or heard or read assessments of the debates indicating that Turner was nervous; or was told by friends, relatives or colleagues that Turner was nervous. To the extent that this process occurs, the analysis presented above compares the trait judgements of those with *direct* debate exposure to the judgements of those with *indirect* exposure. Given this perspective, we should not expect large differences between debate watchers and non-watchers.

So what does this tell us about the value of leaders debates and the role they play in our electoral process? Two major conclusions may be drawn from the findings in this section. First, given the current cynicism of the Canadian public about politics and politicians, televised debates may be an important means of increasing the esteem in which party leaders are held by the population. Although a certain amount of scepticism about political leaders is healthy in a democratic society, widespread contempt and disdain for those who seek our highest political office is not. Therefore, to the extent that they improve viewers' images of the party leaders, debates may increase support for the political system and reduce feelings of alienation. Second, there are indications that debates help viewers to assess the personal characteristics of the party leaders and to compare their individual strengths and weaknesses. Since many Canadians base their voting decisions on such assessments, it would seem that debates are fulfilling a useful function by providing this information.

THE EFFECT OF LEADERS DEBATES ON POLITICAL KNOWLEDGE

Up to this point, we have been examining the *persuasive* capacity of televised debates: their ability to change individual vote decisions, stimulate turnout and change attitudes toward party leaders. Virtually all empirical studies of the Kennedy–Nixon debates focused on their impact on behaviour and attitudes, as did most studies of the Carter–Ford debates. As has been noted, most of these studies concluded that the impact of debates is limited because viewers come to them with pre-existing attitudes that colour their perceptions. Both the direction of this research and its conclusions were in line with the "limited effects" and "minimal consequences" theories popular among mass communications researchers in the 1960s. In the 1970s, however, some scholars began to question both the preoccupation with persuasion effects and the conclusion that the media had little impact. These researchers argued that although unable to persuade people to change their behaviour or attitudes, the media transmitted information effectively and thereby influenced levels of knowledge. According to this view, conclusions about the limited effects of the media were at least partially a result of researchers concentrating on persuasion effects rather than transmission effects.[28]

A few studies of the Carter–Ford debates reflected the emerging interest in political knowledge and information transmission. The conclusion of most of these studies was that televised debates increased the level of knowledge people had about the candidates and the issues of a given election. In their study of the 1976 debates, Becker et al. (1978) found that following the first Carter–Ford debate more people could describe the candidates "to a friend who was unfamiliar" with them than had been able to do so before the debate, and that the increase was greatest for those who actually saw the debate. These researchers also found that more people knew the stands of the candidates on specific policy issues after the first debate than knew this information before the debate; again, the increase was greatest for those who saw the debate. Evidence presented by Miller and MacKuen (1979) is even more supportive of the notion that debates contribute to political learning. These researchers found that the amount of information an individual had about the candidates increased with the number of debates watched. Moreover, the 1976 debates had a strong independent impact on knowledge about the candidates even in the presence of controls for education, strength of partisanship, frequency of newspaper reading and exposure to television news. These researchers also found that debate watching led to perceptions of greater differences between the candidates and the parties on several policy issues.

No data on the contribution of televised debates to the political knowledge of the Canadian electorate have been published. The issue, however, is important. Most previous studies have concluded that debates have little influence either on the political behaviour of Canadians or on their attitudes toward party leaders. Although the findings presented in this study represent a modest challenge to this conclusion, the debate effects documented thus far are not large. As discussed above, however, the potential impact of debates is not limited to persuasion effects. Debates may fail to change political attitudes or behaviour but still transmit political information. It is necessary, therefore, to investigate possible transmission effects before drawing any final conclusions about the impact of debates. The capacity of televised debates to increase political knowledge is also important from the perspective of democratic theory. The ability of the people to make informed electoral choices is essential to the success of a democracy. If debates increase the amount of information Canadians have about the leaders from whom they must (indirectly) choose a prime minister, about the parties from which they must select a government or about the issues with which that government must deal, then it would seem that debates serve a very useful purpose indeed.

The impact of the 1984 leaders debates on the political knowledge of Canadians is examined in two ways: first, by exploring voters' own subjective assessments of what they learned from the debates and, second, by assessing the impact of the debates on several objective measures of political knowledge. The 1984 NES included an open-ended question asking all respondents who reported viewing at least one debate what they learned about the party leaders from the debates that they did not already know.[29] Of the 2246 respondents who watched at least one debate, only 930, or 41 percent, reported learning anything new about the party leaders; the rest said they had learned nothing new or they didn't know what they had learned. The 930 people who said that they did learn something new gave almost 1400 responses, and approximately 500 *different* responses, to the question. All substantive responses – that is, all responses other than "nothing" and "don't know" – were grouped into 12 categories. The categories are listed in table 3.12, along with the percentage of all substantive responses in each category and the percentage of references to each leader in each category.

The first three categories listed in table 3.12 – competence, character and leadership qualities – refer to enduring personality traits. Included in the competence category are traits such as capable, thoughtful, serious, intelligent and experienced, as well as the negative counterparts of these traits. The character category includes references to traits such as honest, sincere, direct, humble and compassionate, and on the negative side, evasive, sleazy, superficial and dishonest. Examples of traits in the leadership qualities category include charismatic, statesmanlike, strong, confident, decisive and their negative counterparts. The fourth category – image – includes references to style and manner: good communicator, entertaining, rusty, effective speaker, nervous, poised, articulate and bumbling. The performance judgements category is reserved for explicit judgements about the debate performances of the party leaders. Some comments in this category are: expected more of him, stronger than expected, met my expectations, best of a bad lot, influenced me most. The background facts category includes

Table 3.12
Respondents' assessments of what they learned from the 1984 debate
(percentages)

Category	All references[a]	References to Turner	References to Mulroney	References to Broadbent
Competence	12.3 (171)	15.6 (76)	12.7 (48)	9.7 (16)
Character	9.4 (131)	6.4 (32)	10.7 (41)	18.1 (31)
Leadership qualities	12.6 (175)	19.4 (95)	13.5 (52)	9.7 (16)
Image	24.4 (340)	33.8 (165)	28.8 (110)	20.8 (35)
Performance judgements	6.9 (96)	10.7 (52)	6.4 (25)	7.6 (13)
Background facts	1.7 (24)	0.6 (3)	4.6 (18)	— —
Language skills	1.6 (22)	1.3 (6)	0.9 (3)	4.8 (8)
General comments	8.4 (118)	4.7 (23)	5.1 (19)	1.9 (3)
Party references	2.9 (41)	1.4 (7)	5.2 (20)	5.4 (9)
Issue learning	11.1 (155)	3.0 (15)	6.5 (25)	11.4 (19)
Policy evaluations	7.0 (98)	2.6 (12)	5.3 (20)	9.9 (17)
Unclassified	1.7 (24)	0.6 (3)	0.2 (1)	0.8 (1)
Total responses	1 396	489	382	169
Total respondents	930	418	338	149

Notes: Cell entries are the percentages of substantive responses that fit the stated category. Numbers in parentheses are cell *N*s. Data are derived from the 1984 NES.

[a]Includes responses that were not leader-specific.

all references to specific information about the family and ethnic backgrounds, occupations and career paths of the leaders. The language skills category includes all references to the ability or inability of the leaders to communicate in a specific language; most references in this category refer to facility in French.

The final five categories listed in table 3.12 are less personal than the first seven categories. General comments is a catch-all category for non-specific comments such as: learned what he's like, learned more about him, learned I like/dislike him and got to know him. The party references category includes all comments referring to political parties rather than party leaders. Comments about issues are divided into two categories: issue learning and policy evaluations. The issue learning category is reserved for references to learning about campaign issues from the debates. Some of these comments specify particular issues such as inflation, unemployment, abortion, pensions and women's issues; others are more general (e.g., learned his stand on issues, learned about his promises and learned about his policies). The policy evaluations category includes all issue references that are evaluative in nature, for example: had no answers, not informative, had solutions, clarified issues, thinks the treasury is bottomless, didn't agree with his policies and made a lot of promises. Finally, the unclassified category contains a few comments that could not be placed in any of the other 11 categories. Responses included: they tended to confuse me, learned we need some new politicians in this country and exceedingly boring debates.

As can be seen from table 3.12, the most frequently mentioned category was image; 24 percent of all responses to the open-ended learning question referred to the leaders' images. Although image comments especially dominated references to Turner (fully 34 percent of the comments about Turner fell into this category), they were the most frequent type of comment for all three leaders. This evidence is not very encouraging in terms of the quality of information learned from televised debates, since comments in the image category tend to refer to superficial things like mannerisms and speaking style. The evidence is even more discouraging if comments about the leaders' debate performances are added to image comments. These two categories account for 31 percent of all comments, 45 percent of all references to Turner, 35 percent of all references to Mulroney and 28 percent of all references to Broadbent. The conclusions from table 3.12 are not, however, all negative. If the responses in the first three categories – competence, character and leadership qualities – are combined, they account for 34 percent of all responses, 41 percent of all references to Turner, 37 percent of all references to Mulroney and 38 percent of all references to Broadbent. Knowledge about leaders' competence, character and leadership qualities is clearly important for assessing ability and fitness to become prime minister of Canada, and the debates appear to have contributed to the public's knowledge about these traits. In addition, 11 percent of all responses refer to learning about the issues of the campaign and another 7 percent to issues in an evaluative context.

Although the typology presented in table 3.12 is a useful summary of what individuals think they learned from the 1984 debates, it is probably not a good measure of actual learning. Self-reported information is notoriously unreliable – especially when respondents are questioned many months after the event has occurred, as was the case with the 1984 NES. The problem, of course, is that we have no idea if the information respondents *say* they learned from the debates was *actually* learned from the debates or some other source. A more objective measure of political knowledge – and of the impact of debate exposure on that knowledge – is therefore required before any firm conclusions can be drawn.

Table 3.13 presents the results of five multiple regression analyses, each designed to determine the impact of watching the 1984 leaders debates on a different measure of political knowledge. Five independent variables are included in each regression equation: debate exposure, measured by the number of debates watched (0 to 3); education; political interest; media use; and political involvement.[30] The last four variables are included because studies have indicated that they are important determinants of political knowledge (e.g., Lambert et al. 1988; Miller and MacKuen 1979). Thus, their influence must be accounted for if we are to obtain an accurate assessment of the *independent* impact of the debates.

The five measures of political knowledge used in this analysis assess the *amount* of information an individual has about a given topic. The only question in the 1984 NES that could reasonably be used to assess the *accuracy* of political knowledge asks respondents to name the provincial premiers. This question is not used in this analysis because information of this nature is not likely to be conveyed in debates involving federal party leaders. The first measure of political knowledge is the number of responses to an open-ended question about the most important issue in the 1984 election.[31] The second refers to the number of responses to a closed-ended question asking which of the three major parties would do the best job and which would do the worst job of handling several important tasks of government.[32] The third measures the number of non-neutral assessments respondents could make about the personality traits of the party leaders. This variable was developed from the responses to the closed-ended question, discussed earlier in this study, that asked respondents how well or poorly a list of personality traits fit each party leader.[33] The fourth measure refers to the number of responses volunteered when respondents were asked what they liked and disliked about each of the federal party leaders.[34] The fifth measure of political knowledge is the number of responses volunteered

Table 3.13
Determinants of political knowledge, 1984

Predictors and summary statistics	Measures of political knowledge				
	Most important issue	Best & worst party	Personality trait judgements	Leader likes & dislikes	Party likes & dislikes
Predictors[a]					
Education	.145*	.100*	.119*	.202*	.189*
Political interest	.222*	.158*	.175*	.185*	.160*
Media use	.198*	.109*	.139*	.137*	.159*
Political involvement	.043***	.093*	.058**	.062*	.112*
Debate exposure	.056*	.063*	.117*	.136*	.075*
Summary statistics					
Total adjusted R^2	.239	.141	.187	.250	.237
R^2 change due to debate exposure	.003*	.003*	.011*	.015*	.005*
Proportion of total R^2 due to debate exposure	.013	.021	.059	.060	.021

Notes: Data are derived from the 1984 NES.

[a]Numbers in this part of the table are standardized regression coefficients. For all equations $N = 3\,374$.

*$p < .001$; **$p < .01$; ***$p < .05$.

when respondents were asked what they liked and disliked about the three major federal political parties.[35]

As can be seen from the standardized regression coefficients displayed in table 3.13, debate exposure had a statistically significant positive impact on all five measures of political knowledge even after the effects of education, political interest, media use and political involvement were accounted for. The greater the number of debates watched, the more issues could be named as important election issues, the more times one party could be named as the best or worst to handle certain tasks, the more non-neutral assessments could be made of the leaders' personality traits, and the more reasons could be given for liking and disliking the parties and party leaders. The clearest indication of the impact of the debates on political knowledge is the proportion of the total R^2 for each regression equation that can be attributed to debate exposure. R^2 is a measure of the variance in a dependent variable that can be explained by the combined effects of the independent variables. Thus, the proportion of R^2 due to debate exposure is a measure of how much of the variance in political knowledge can be explained by the fact that a respondent watched a leaders debate. This figure ranges from 1 percent for the most important issue in the election to 6 percent for personality trait judgements and leader likes and dislikes; for the best/worst party equation and the party likes and dislikes equation, this figure is 2 percent.

The statistics presented in table 3.13 suggest that the most important effect of debate exposure on political knowledge is to increase the amount of information individuals have about the party leaders. Strong independent debate effects were found for both measures of this type of information. Debate exposure, however, also increased the amount of information individuals had about the parties, as well as their ability to choose which party could best deal with certain important government tasks. Debate exposure had the smallest impact on the number of issues that could be named as the most important in the election. Perhaps this information is more widely available from other sources than are the other types of information. The strong beta coefficients for political interest and media use in this equation support this conclusion.

Before concluding our analysis of the effect of the 1984 debates on political knowledge, we must test one remaining hypothesis. Miller and MacKuen found that the impact of debate exposure on knowledge about presidential candidates was greatest for those with low levels of political attentiveness. They argued that this finding confirmed the "uses and gratifications" model of media effects: "Basically this model assumes that individuals have different motivations and media usage habits and that media effects on voters depend upon these motivations to follow the campaign. The highly attentive are likely to be informed about politics even without presidential debates; thus for them the debates may not be as crucial an information source as for the less attentive" (1979, 329). Similarly, Patterson found that debate exposure had the most influence on issue awareness among those with low levels of interest in politics. He provided an explanation similar to that offered by Miller and MacKuen (1979): "The contribution of these telecasts, it would appear, depends on whether the issue information they provide is already possessed by the voter or is likely to be obtained from another source. High interest voters were more highly informed about the candidates' positions before the ... debates, and most of them followed a newspaper regularly; consequently, these telecasts' information was somewhat redundant" (Patterson 1980, 165).

For our purposes, the major hypothesis generated by the uses and gratifications model is that televised debates have a greater effect on the political knowledge of people with few other sources of political information than on the knowledge levels of those who have other means of finding out what they need to know. This hypothesis was tested by combining the five measures of political knowledge already discussed into a summary measure of political knowledge.[36] This summary measure was regressed on the five independent variables discussed above: education, political interest, media use, political involvement and debate exposure. The media use variable was then removed from the analysis, and the equations were rerun separately for those with low and high levels of media use.[37] The results of this analysis – displayed in table 3.14 – strongly support the hypothesis that the impact of televised debates on political knowledge is greatest for those with few other sources of political information. The regression coefficient for the debate exposure variable is more than twice as large for low media users as for high users. Among low media users, debate exposure was a stronger predictor of political knowledge than education, political interest or involvement; among high media users, the impact of debate exposure was weaker than the impact of other predictors. Finally, the proportion of the total explained variance in political knowledge due to debate exposure was 21 percent among low media users and only 4 percent for high media users.

It is not possible to carry out the above analysis for the 1988 election because comparable questions were not asked in either the 1988 reinterview or the 1988 NES. Other types of analysis, however, can assess the impact of the 1988 debates on political knowledge. Because the 1988 NES included a campaign-period survey, it is possible to look at the immediate impact of the 1988 debates on the knowledge levels of the Canadian electorate. Three scales designed to measure levels of political knowledge were created using 1988 NES data. The first scale measures subjective knowledge of the major party leaders; that is, it measures how much respondents felt they knew about the leaders.[38] The second scale measures knowledge of party positions on three major issues: promotion of French, relations with the United States and levels of taxes and services.[39] The third scale measures knowledge of the party leaders' positions on the same three issues.[40] Figure 3.3 tracks levels of knowledge throughout the 1988 campaign, as measured by these three scales. As this figure illustrates, knowledge levels are noticeably higher in the post-debate period (intervals 8 through 16) than in the pre-debate period. Although one would expect knowledge levels to increase as the campaign progressed, the interval in which the debates were held

Table 3.14
Determinants of political knowledge for all respondents, and for selected media users, 1984

Predictors and summary statistics	All respondents	Low media users	High media users
Predictors[a]			
Education	.168*	.135*	.223*
Political interest	.216*	.194*	.242*
Political involvement	.094*	.149*	.107*
Debate exposure	.122*	.205*	.100*
Media use	.169*	—	—
Summary statistics			
Total adjusted R^2	.296	.182	.206
R^2 change due to debate exposure	.012*	.039*	.009*
Proportion of total R^2 due to debate exposure	.085	.214	.044
N	(3 374)	(1 214)	(2 160)

Notes: Data are derived from the 1984 NES.
[a]Numbers in this part of the table are standardized regression coefficients.
*$p < .001$.

(interval 7) seems to mark the shift to higher knowledge levels – especially about the parties' and leaders' positions on issues. These results would seem to indicate that the 1988 leaders debates had a modest but immediate impact on levels of political knowledge.

Taken altogether, the findings presented in this section lead to the conclusion that televised debates transmit information to the public and, in this manner, contribute to a more informed Canadian electorate. Analysis of the 1988 election indicated that political knowledge increased following the leaders debates. Analysis of the 1984 election also indicated that debate exposure increased political knowledge. The debate effects documented in the multiple regression analyses were not powerful; indeed, the debate exposure variable produced the weakest or second-weakest coefficients of the five independent variables. It can be argued, however, that finding debate exposure to have *any* impact on political knowledge independent of "heavy-hitting" predictors such as education, political interest, media use and political involvement is notable; a stringent test was applied and passed. Moreover, it should be noted that all the questions used to measure political knowledge for

Figure 3.3
Respondents' scores on three knowledge scales, 1988

Mean score on scale

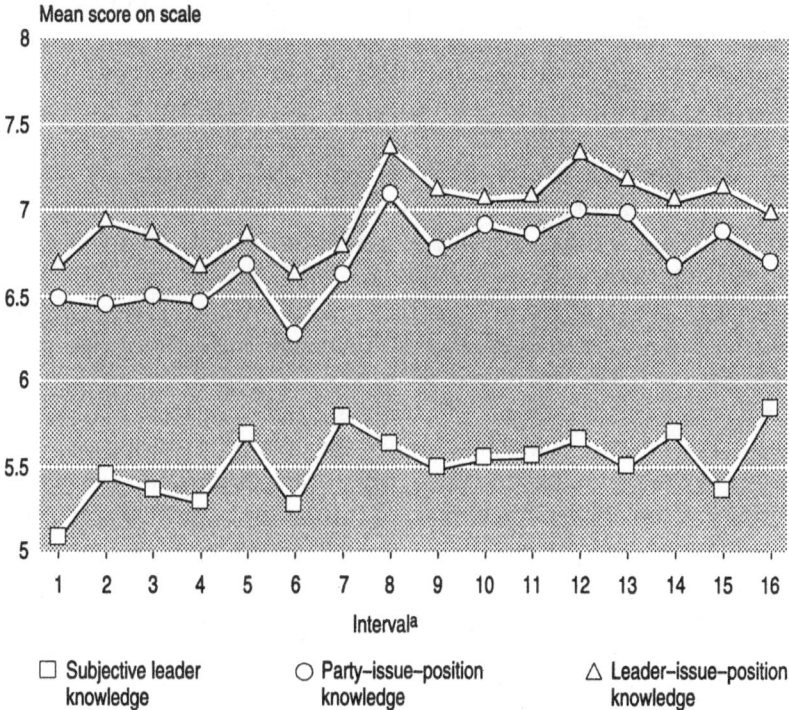

Interval[a]

☐ Subjective leader   ○ Party–issue–position   △ Leader–issue–position
   knowledge   knowledge   knowledge

Notes: Data are derived from the 1988 NES.

[a]Intervals start on 4 October and end on 20 November. All but the sixteenth are three-day intervals; the sixteenth is a two-day interval. No data were gathered on 10 October. The average sample size of the intervals is 226 respondents. The debates occurred during the seventh interval.

the 1984 analysis were asked many months after the debates. It would appear, therefore, that the information learned from the debates is retained long after the events themselves have faded from the public eye. Probably the most important finding presented here – indeed, probably the most important finding in the entire study – is that debates are an especially significant source of political information among those members of the electorate who have few other information sources. Given this fact, it seems clear that televised leaders debates play a crucial role in our electoral process.

CONCLUSIONS AND RECOMMENDATIONS

This study has examined the impact of the 1984 and 1988 Canadian federal party leaders debates on individual vote decisions, voter turnout, attitudes toward the party leaders and political knowledge. With regard to vote decisions, it was concluded that the 1984 debates had some impact by apparently influencing individuals who voted Liberal in 1980 to vote Conservative in 1984. Whether this impact was sufficient to determine the outcome of the 1984 election is unknown; however, given the size of the Conservative victory, it is unlikely that any single event was decisive. More likely, many factors all pointing in the same direction combined to produce the victory, although the debates were, undoubtedly, one of those factors. Analysis of the 1988 election revealed that watching a debate appears to have made people who voted for the New Democratic Party in 1984 more likely to vote Liberal in 1988. Since the Conservatives won the 1988 election, it would seem that the debates did not greatly influence the outcome. The debates did, however, change the course of the 1988 election by increasing support for the Liberals and thus making the campaign a much closer fight in the post-debate period than it had been in the pre-debate period.

For voter turnout, a statistically significant relationship was found between debate watching and voter turnout in both 1984 and 1988. However, further analysis led to the conclusion that this relationship was spurious – both debate watching and turnout were related to the respondent's level of interest in the campaign. Interesting but statistically inconclusive results pointed to the possibility that watching televised debates may have encouraged individuals with little interest in the election to vote.

The most important conclusion drawn from examining the impact of debates on attitudes toward the party leaders was that debates have a positive influence on voters' overall evaluations of party leaders. In both 1984 and 1988, debate watchers evaluated all three party leaders significantly more positively than non-watchers. The debates also influenced voters' judgements about the personal characteristics of the party leaders. With regard to specific traits, however, debates appear to be capable of creating negative impressions as well as positive impressions. No single picture emerged as to which trait judgements debates are most likely to affect; the debates influenced the image of each leader differently. The differences between debate watchers and non-watchers were not very large, but since information about the debates is widely diffused throughout the population, analyses that compare watchers and non-watchers may be comparing only the impact of direct versus indirect debate exposure.

When respondents to the 1984 NES were asked what they learned from the debates, the most frequent responses were about the images and performances of the leaders. A high percentage of responses also dealt with learning about the leaders' competence, character and leadership qualities, and a smaller proportion focused on policy issues. When gains in political knowledge were assessed by more objective means, it was found that debate exposure had a statistically significant positive impact on several types of knowledge, independent of the impact of education, political interest, political involvement and media use. The effect was particularly strong for people who rarely or never use other sources of information. Analysis of political knowledge carried out using 1988 NES data indicated that debates had a small but immediate impact on knowledge levels.

The aim of this study was to examine the impact of televised leaders debates and to assess the value of these events and the role they play in the Canadian electoral process. Taken altogether, the findings presented in this study strongly suggest that televised debates play a valuable role in Canadian election campaigns. Although this research did not uncover massive debate effects, it did reveal that debates have a discernible influence on the Canadian electorate and that this influence is overwhelmingly positive. First, since vote switching is related to debate exposure, it would appear that debates are capable of aiding the vote decision of at least some of the people some of the time. Second, debates may encourage people who are less interested in politics to vote, although the findings on this issue were not conclusive. Third, debates appear to aid voters in assessing the personal characteristics of the party leaders and to enhance their overall evaluations of those leaders. Finally, and most important, it seems clear that debates contribute to the political information on which voters – especially low media users – base their decisions.

As to whether debates should be a mandatory part of Canadian elections, I would have to agree with those who support such a move. Although debates appear on their way to becoming a regular feature of federal election campaigns in this country, their presence is not assured. The political interests of an individual party leader might well intervene at some point to prevent a debate. This should not be allowed to happen. Televised debates are the only opportunity – except for party ads and 30-second news bites – that most voters have to see and hear the party leaders. And, as the evidence presented in this study demonstrates, voters use this opportunity in a variety of ways that enhance the quality of the democratic process. No individual should have the right to obstruct this process by scuttling a televised debate. This is particularly true given that the individual most likely to refuse to debate is the one who already has the most control over the electoral process – the prime minister.

Not surprisingly, many people disagree with the notion of mandatory debates. Some opponents argue that the media should not be forced to carry any particular content. Others argue that party leaders should not be required to debate because the principle of freedom of speech implies the freedom to remain silent. These arguments, however, should not be allowed to prevent the institutionalization of debates. Although it would be improper to require the media to cover any particular event, I would argue that debates are more akin to public-service broadcasting than to conventional news. Therefore, it would be neither improper nor unprecedented to require the television networks to carry debates, since broadcasting during election periods is already regulated and broadcasters are already required to provide free time to the political parties. As to the argument that politicians have the right to remain silent, it seems to me that this right should not and need not prevent debates from taking place. Party leaders could be required to be present for a debate, while retaining the right not to speak. Of course, any leader exercising this right might well be penalized by the voters, but that is preferable to allowing the voters to be penalized by the politicians. I believe that the evidence presented in this study on the positive impact of debates on the Canadian electorate is sufficient to warrant the institutionalization of debates. Such a move might well infringe on the rights of the media and the political parties. However, whenever the interests of the media, the parties and the voters conflict, the interests of the voters should prevail.

NOTES

1. For further discussion of the factors politicians consider in deciding whether to participate in televised debates, see Cheney (1979), Kirkpatrick (1979), LeDuc (1990) and Martel (1983).

2. See, for example, Bishop et al. (1978), Bitzer and Rueter (1980), Jamieson and Birdsell (1988), Kraus (1962, 1979, 1988), Martel (1983) and Ranney (1979).

3. Some findings regarding the effects of Canadian campaign debates are presented by Lanoue (1991), LeDuc (1990) and LeDuc and Price (1985, 1990).

4. The tendency of the North American media to cover the "horse-race" aspects of televised debates and of election campaigns in general is well documented. See, for example, Frizzell and Westell (1985), Frizzell et al. (1989), Kraus (1988), Patterson (1980) and Robinson and Sheehan (1983).

5. For an examination of the factors influencing the vote decision in Canada, see Clarke et al. (1979, 1984, 1991).

6. The 1984 NES was conducted by R.D. Lambert, S.D. Brown, J.E. Curtis, B.J. Kay and J.M. Wilson. The face-to-face interviews for this study were car-

ried out by Canadian Facts Ltd. The 1988 re-interview of 1984 NES respondents was conducted by R.D. Lambert, S.D. Brown, J.E. Curtis, B.J. Kay, L. LeDuc and J.H. Pammett. The telephone interviews for this study were carried out by the Carleton University Journalism Survey Centre. The 1988 NES was conducted by R. Johnston, A. Blais, H.E. Brady and J. Crête. The telephone interviews for this study were conducted by the Institute for Social Research, York University. All of these studies were funded by the Social Sciences and Humanities Research Council of Canada (SSHRCC). The principal investigators, SSHRCC and those responsible for collecting the data bear no responsibility for the analysis and interpretations presented here.

7. The 1984 NES and the 1988 re-interview did not ask respondents which leader had won the debates. Respondents were, however, asked the following question: "In your opinion, how well did each of the leaders perform in the debates that you saw? The closer to '10', the better you think a leader did, the closer to '0', the poorer you think he did." For the purposes of this study, a respondent is considered to have felt a given leader won the debate if he or she rated that leader's performance more favourably than the performances of his opponents. Respondents in the post-election wave of the 1988 NES were asked: "Which leader performed BEST in the debate?" The almost identical results from the two 1988 election studies indicate that the performance evaluation questions are an adequate measure of which leader was felt to have won the debates.

8. For a summary of the results of public opinion polls conducted during the 1984 election, see Frizzell and Westell (1985, 82). Polls taken before the first two debates gave the Conservatives between 39 percent and 43 percent of the decided vote, the Liberals 45 percent to 49 percent. The CTV poll conducted immediately following these debates placed the Conservatives at 45 percent and the Liberals at 36 percent.

9. The data in figure 3.1 are derived from the campaign-period survey of the 1988 NES. The average daily sample from 25 October to 20 November was 80 respondents. The figures for 25 October give Mulroney a slight edge over his opponents. These figures, however, are based on only 19 respondents whose assessment could be based only on the 24 October French debate.

10. For a summary of the results of public opinion polls conducted during the 1988 election, see Frizzell et al. (1989, 95).

11. The vote intention question in the 1988 NES is worded as follows: "Which party do you think you will vote for: the Conservative Party, the Liberal Party, the New Democratic Party, or another party?" Respondents who said they didn't know how they were going to vote were asked: "Perhaps you have not yet made up your mind. But which party are you leaning towards now?" The results of these two questions were combined to produce the data displayed in figure 3.2. The x-axis of figure 3.2 groups the interview dates into 16 intervals, as follows:

Interval 1: October 4–6   Interval 9: October 29–31
Interval 2: October 7–9   Interval 10: November 1–3
Interval 3: October 11–13   Interval 11: November 4–6
Interval 4: October 14–16   Interval 12: November 7–9
Interval 5: October 17–19   Interval 13: November 10–12
Interval 6: October 20–22   Interval 14: November 13–15
Interval 7: October 23–25   Interval 15: November 16–18
Interval 8: October 26–28   Interval 16: November 19–20

No interviews were conducted on 10 October. The average sample size of these intervals is 226 respondents.

12. In their paper, LeDuc and Price present data indicating that impressions of Progressive Conservative leader Joe Clark's debate performance were less positive than impressions of his opponents' performances. Debate watchers, however, were more likely than non-watchers to vote Conservative. Therefore, LeDuc and Price conclude that "watchers of the debates were not more likely to have voted Conservative, but Conservatives were more likely to have watched the debates" (1985, 150).

13. The correlation in question is between watching the English debate and *not* voting for the New Democratic Party.

14. Since the debates involved only the leaders of the Liberal, Progressive Conservative and New Democratic parties, respondents who voted for other parties are excluded from the analysis. The 1988 data presented in tables 3.3 to 3.8 are from the re-interview of 1984 NES respondents. The question regarding debate exposure in both the 1984 NES and the 1988 re-interview is worded as follows: "Did you see any of the debates among the federal party leaders on television?"

15. 1980 vote was measured in 1984 and is, therefore, subject to recall error. However, to the extent that respondents tend to report past behaviour that is consistent with current behaviour, vote switching will be underestimated rather than overestimated, and there is no reason to suspect that debate watchers will recall their vote in 1980 any more or less accurately than non-watchers. For a discussion of the problems of recall data, see MacDermid (1987) and Wiseman (1987).

16. Since the 1984 NES and 1988 re-interview constitute a panel, actual 1984 vote was used to measure previous vote in 1988.

17. The likelihood-ratio chi-square is similar to the traditional chi-square statistic, but is calculated using maximum-likelihood methods. Knoke and Burke argue that the likelihood-ratio statistic is preferable to the chi-square (1980, 30).

18. Since the debate exposure variable is dichotomous, the parameters for non-watchers can be obtained simply by reversing the signs.

19. The absence of individual-level information on the impact of debates on voter turnout in the United States is probably due, at least in part, to the tend-

ency of American debate researchers to employ experimental research designs or multiple-wave surveys administered at various times during the campaign. Information on whether respondents voted cannot be obtained in most of these studies because the data are collected before election day.

20. Although Kirkpatrick (1979) does not make the point, the slightly higher turnout in 1960 can presumably be attributed to the public's heightened interest in the close campaign.

21. The difference between the groups was statistically significant and persisted in the presence of controls for language and socio-economic status. Language is an important control in any analysis of the 1979 debate because the debate was in English only.

22. As with the previous analyses, the debate exposure variable is dichotomous. The turnout question in both the 1984 NES and the 1988 re-interview is worded as follows: "Now, thinking about this year's federal election, we find that a lot of people weren't able to vote because they were sick, or didn't have time, or had some other reasons for not voting. How about you? Did you vote this time, or did something happen to keep you away from voting?" The election interest question is worded as follows: "We have found that people sometimes don't pay too much attention to elections. How about yourself? Were you very interested in the recent federal election, fairly interested, slightly interested, or not at all interested in it?"

23. The correlation (Pearson's r) between turnout and interest was .372 in 1984. The correlations between turnout and various other forms of participation ranged from .241 for reading about politics to .121 for trying to convince friends how to vote.

24. The correlation for those who were not at all interested in the 1988 election is not statistically significant, but this can be attributed to the small number of respondents in this category.

25. For analyses of the content of leader images in the United States since 1952, see Miller et al. (1986), Nie et al. (1979) and Shabad and Anderson (1979). For an analysis of the content of leader images in Canada from 1974 to 1984, see Brown et al. (1988).

26. The 1984 NES scales were introduced as follows: "Now we'd like to know your impressions of what certain political leaders are like. I'll read a word or phrase, and I'd like you to tell me how well it fits or describes each of the three leaders shown on this card. The more you think the word or phrase describes a leader, the closer your answer should be to '7'. The less it fits, the closer your answer should be to '1'. If you have no idea at all about how a word or phrase fits a leader, tell me and we'll go on to the next one."

27. The 1988 NES scales were introduced as follows: "Now, we'd like to know about your impressions of the party leaders. I am going to read a list of words and phrases people use to describe political figures. After each one, I would like you to tell me how much the word or phrase fits your impressions."

28. For debates research, the pivotal articles on these issues appear to be Becker et al. (1975), McCombs (1972) and Robinson (1972). For a recent, brief review of research in the field of political communications, see Iyengar and Lenart (1989).

29. The exact wording of this question is: "What did you learn, if anything, that you didn't already know about the leaders from the televised debates?" Up to two responses were recorded for each respondent.

30. The wording of the education question is: "What is the highest grade or level of school you reached?" The responses are: no formal education, some elementary, elementary graduate, some high school, high school graduate, some college or technical school, college or technical school graduate, some university, bachelor's degree and graduate/professional degree. The political interest variable is a 0–5 scale created by summing the responses to two questions: one on interest in the 1984 election and one on attention to politics generally. The wording for the interest question is given in note 22. The wording of the attention question is: "Do you pay much attention to politics generally – that is, from day to day, when there isn't a big election campaign going on? Would you say that you follow politics very closely, fairly closely, or not much at all?" The media use variable is a 0–6 scale created by summing the responses to the following two questions: "How often do you read about politics in the newspapers and magazines?" and "How often do you watch programs about politics on television?" The responses to these two questions, as well as to the other questions included in the traditional political participation battery, are: often, sometimes, seldom and never. The political involvement variable is a 0–18 scale created by summing the responses to the remaining six political participation questions, which ask respondents how often they discuss politics with other people, try to convince friends to vote the same as themselves, attend a political meeting or rally, contact public officials or politicians, spend time working for a political party or a candidate, and contribute money to a political party or candidate.

31. The most important issue question is: "Now, I would like to ask you some questions about the 1984 federal election. What, in your opinion, was the most important issue in that election? Was there any other issue that you think was important in the 1984 federal election? What was it?" The most important issue scale runs from 0 to 2. If no substantive response was given, the respondent scored 0; two substantive responses scored 2. All responses other than "nothing" and "don't know" were considered substantive.

32. The best/worst party question is: "Now, I'm going to ask you about a number of tasks that the federal government has to deal with. Forget for a moment the likelihood of each party getting elected to government. I'd like you to tell me which of the *three* major federal parties would probably do the *best* job and which would probably do the *worst* job on each task *if it were the government*." Inquiries were made about 12 tasks: controlling infla-

tion, dealing with the provincial governments, dealing with the United States, handling relations with Quebec, running the government competently, dealing with unemployment, providing social welfare measures, protecting the environment, limiting the size of government, dealing with women's issues, working for world peace and handling the deficit. Responding Liberal, Conservative or NDP for a given task resulted in a score of 1. Saying that there is no difference among the three parties, that more than one party is the best or worst, or that you don't know which party would do the best or worst job was scored 0. Therefore, the best/worst party scale is a measure of the number of times a respondent named *one* of the three major parties as the best or worst to deal with a given task. This scale runs from 0 to 24.

33. The wording for the trait judgement question is given in note 26, and the list of traits is presented in table 3.10. Neutral responses (4 on the 1–7 scales) were coded 0, as were the responses "don't know" and "refused"; all other responses were coded 1. The personality trait judgement scale is 0–42.

34. The leader like/dislike question is: "Now, we would like to ask you about your impressions of the various leaders of the federal political parties. Is there anything in particular you like/dislike about Mr. _____? Anything else?" Up to three likes and three dislikes were coded for each leader, resulting in a scale that could run from 0 to 18 but in reality runs from 0 to 16.

35. The party like/dislike question is: "Now, I would like to ask you what you personally think are the good and bad points about the political parties at the federal level in Canada. Is there anything in particular that you like/dislike about the federal Liberal/PC/NDP? Anything else?" Up to two likes and two dislikes were coded for each party, resulting in a 0–12 scale.

36. Summing all five measures results in a 93-point scale.

37. Low level of media use was defined as a score between 0 and 3 on the 7-point media use scale described in note 30. High level of media use was defined as a score between 4 and 7.

38. The 1988 NES subjective leader knowledge question is: "First I'm going to read a list of names of people in politics. For each name, please tell me whether you know quite a lot, a fair amount, just a little, or nothing at all about the person." Respondents who said they knew nothing at all about a leader were given a score of 0; those who said they knew quite a lot were given a score of 3. The subjective leader knowledge scale runs from 0 to 9.

39. The 1988 NES party issue position knowledge scale was created from nine closed-ended questions that asked survey respondents for the positions of the three major parties on three issues: (a) "Does the Federal _____ party think that much more, somewhat more, about the same as now, somewhat less, or much less should be done to promote French?" (b) "Does the Federal _____ party think that Canada should be much closer to the United States, somewhat closer, about the same as now, somewhat more distant, or much

more distant?" (c) "Does the Federal _____ party think the level of taxes and services should be much higher, somewhat higher, about the same, somewhat lower, or much lower than now?" Those who responded to these questions were given a score of 1; those who refused to answer or said they didn't know scored 0. This scale runs from 0 to 9.

40. The 1988 NES leader issue position knowledge scale was created from nine closed-ended questions that asked survey respondents for the positions of the three federal party leaders on three issues. The format of these questions and the specific issues they addressed were the same as those used to measure party positions. Responses were also coded the same way (see note 39).

REFERENCES

Becker, L.B., M.E. McCombs and J.M. McLeod. 1975. "The Development of Political Cognitions." In *Political Communication: Issues and Strategies for Research,* ed. S.H. Chaffee. Beverly Hills: Sage Publications.

Becker, L.B., I.A. Sobowale, R.E. Cobbey and C.H. Eyal. 1978. "Debates' Effects on Voters' Understanding of Candidates and Issues." In *The Presidential Debates: Media, Electoral, and Policy Perspectives,* ed. G.F. Bishop, R.G. Meadow and M. Jackson-Beeck. New York: Praeger.

Ben-Zeev, S., and I.S. White. 1962. "Effects and Implications." In *The Great Debates: Kennedy vs. Nixon, 1960,* ed. S. Kraus. Bloomington: Indiana University Press.

Berelson, B.R., P.F. Lazarsfeld and W.N. McPhee. 1954. *Voting.* Chicago: University of Chicago Press.

Bishop, G.F., R.G. Meadow and M. Jackson-Beeck, eds. 1978. *The Presidential Debates: Media, Electoral, and Policy Perspectives.* New York: Praeger.

Bitzer, L., and T. Rueter. 1980. *Carter vs Ford: The Counterfeit Debates of 1976.* Madison: University of Wisconsin Press.

Blumler, J.G., and J.M. McLeod. 1974. "Communication and Voter Turnout in Britain." In *Sociological Theory and Survey Research,* ed. T. Leggatt. Beverly Hills: Sage Publications.

Brown, S.D., R.D. Lambert, B.J. Kay and J.E. Curtis. 1988. "In the Eye of the Beholder: Leader Images in Canada." *Canadian Journal of Political Science* 21:729–55.

Campbell, A., P.E. Converse, W.E. Miller and D.E. Stokes. 1960. *The American Voter.* New York: John Wiley and Sons.

Carter, R.F. 1962. "Some Effects of the Debates." In *The Great Debates: Kennedy vs. Nixon, 1960,* ed. S. Kraus. Bloomington: Indiana University Press.

Chaffee, S.H., and S.Y. Choe. 1980. "Time of Decision and Media Use During the Ford-Carter Campaign." *Public Opinion Quarterly* 44:53–69.

Cheney, R.B. 1979. "The 1976 Presidential Debates: A Republican Perspective." In *The Past and Future of Presidential Debates*, ed. A. Ranney. Washington, DC: American Enterprise Institute for Public Policy Research.

Clarke, H.D., J. Jenson, L. LeDuc and J.H. Pammett. 1979. *Political Choice in Canada*. Toronto: McGraw-Hill Ryerson.

———. 1984. *Absent Mandate: The Politics of Discontent in Canada*. Toronto: Gage.

———. 1991. *Absent Mandate: Interpreting Change in Canadian Elections*. 2d ed. Toronto: Gage.

Davis, D.K. 1979. "Influence on Vote Decisions." In *The Great Debates: Carter vs. Ford, 1976*, ed. S. Kraus. Bloomington: Indiana University Press.

Davis, M.H. 1982. "Voting Intentions and the 1980 Carter-Reagan Debate." *Journal of Applied Social Psychology* 12:481–92.

Dennis, J., S.H. Chaffee and S.Y. Choe. 1979. "Impact on Partisan, Image, and Issue Voting." In *The Great Debates: Carter vs. Ford, 1976*, ed. S. Kraus. Bloomington: Indiana University Press.

Fletcher, F. 1988. "The Media and the 1984 Landslide." In *Canada at the Polls, 1984*, ed. H.R. Penniman. Washington, DC: American Enterprise Institute for Public Policy Research.

Frizzell, A., and A. Westell. 1985. *The Canadian General Election of 1984*. Ottawa: Carleton University Press.

Frizzell, A., J.H. Pammett and A. Westell. 1989. *The Canadian General Election of 1988*. Ottawa: Carleton University Press.

Geer, J.G. 1988. "The Effects of Presidential Debates on the Electorate's Preferences for Candidates." *American Politics Quarterly* 16:486–501.

Hagner, P.R., and L.N. Rieselbach. 1978. "The Impact of the 1976 Presidential Debates: Conversion or Reinforcement?" In *The Presidential Debates: Media, Electoral, and Policy Perspectives*, ed. G.F. Bishop, R.G. Meadow and M. Jackson-Beeck. New York: Praeger.

Iyengar, S., and S. Lenart. 1989. "Beyond 'Minimal Consequences': A Survey of Media Political Effects." In *Political Behavior Annual*. Vol. 2, ed. S. Long. Boulder: Westview.

Jamieson, K.H., and D.S. Birdsell. 1988. *Presidential Debates: The Challenge of Creating an Informed Electorate*. New York: Oxford University Press.

Johnston, R. 1990. "Do Campaigns Matter?" Paper presented at the symposium "Analyzing Democracy," York University.

Katz, E., and J.J. Feldman. 1962. "The Debates in the Light of Research: A Survey of Surveys." In *The Great Debates: Kennedy vs. Nixon, 1960*, ed. S. Kraus. Bloomington: Indiana University Press.

Kirkpatrick, E.M. 1979. "Presidential Candidate Debates: What Can We Learn from 1960?" In *The Past and Future of Presidential Debates*, ed. A. Ranney. Washington, DC: American Enterprise Institute for Public Policy Research.

Knoke, D., and P.J. Burke. 1980. *Log-linear Models*. Newbury Park: Sage Publications.

Kraus, S., ed. 1962. *The Great Debates: Kennedy vs. Nixon, 1960*. Bloomington: Indiana University Press.

———, ed. 1979. *The Great Debates: Carter vs. Ford, 1976*. Bloomington: Indiana University Press.

———. 1988. *Televised Presidential Debates and Public Policy*. Hillsdale: Lawrence Erlbaum Associates.

Kraus, S., and R.G. Smith. 1962. "Issues and Images." In *The Great Debates: Kennedy vs. Nixon, 1960*, ed. S. Kraus. Bloomington: Indiana University Press.

Krause, R. 1989. "The Parties and the Campaign – The Progressive Conservative Campaign: Mission Accomplished." In A. Frizzell, J.H. Pammett and A. Westell, *The Canadian General Election of 1988*. Ottawa: Carleton University Press.

Lambert, R.D., J.E. Curtis, B.J. Kay and S.D. Brown. 1988. "The Sources of Political Knowledge." *Canadian Journal of Political Science* 21:359–74.

Lang, K., and G.E. Lang. 1962. "Reactions of Viewers." In *The Great Debates: Kennedy vs. Nixon, 1960*, ed. S. Kraus. Bloomington: Indiana University Press.

———. 1978. "The Formation of Public Opinion: Direct and Mediated Effects of the First Debate." In *The Presidential Debates: Media, Electoral, and Policy Perspectives*, ed. G.F. Bishop, R.G. Meadow and M. Jackson-Beeck. New York: Praeger.

Lanoue, D.J. 1991. "Debates That Mattered: Voters' Reactions to the 1984 Canadian Leadership Debates." *Canadian Journal of Political Science* 24:51–65.

Lazarsfeld, P.F., B. Berelson and H. Gaudet. 1944. *The People's Choice*. 3d ed. New York: Columbia University Press.

LeDuc, L. 1990. "Party Strategies and the Use of Televised Campaign Debates." *European Journal of Political Research* 18:121–41.

LeDuc, L., and R. Price. 1985. "Great Debates: The Televised Leadership Debates of 1979." *Canadian Journal of Political Science* 18:135–53.

———. 1990. "Campaign Debates and Party Leader Images: The 'Encounter '88' Case." Paper presented at the annual meeting of the Canadian Political Science Association, Victoria.

McCombs, M.E. 1972. "Mass Communication in Political Campaigns: Information, Gratification, and Persuasion." In *Current Perspectives in Mass Communications Research,* ed. F.G. Kline and P.J. Tichenor. Beverly Hills: Sage Publications.

MacDermid, R. 1987. "The Recall of Past Partisanship: Feeble Memories or Frail Concepts." Paper presented at the annual meeting of the Canadian Political Science Association, Hamilton.

MacDonald, L.I. 1984. *Mulroney: The Making of a Prime Minister.* Toronto: McClelland and Stewart.

Martel, M. 1983. *Political Campaign Debates: Images, Strategies and Tactics.* New York: Longman.

Maser, P. 1989. "On the Hustings." In A. Frizzell, J.H. Pammett and A. Westell, *The Canadian General Election of 1988.* Ottawa: Carleton University Press.

Miller, A.H., and M. MacKuen. 1979. "Learning About the Candidates: The 1976 Presidential Debates." *Public Opinion Quarterly* 43:326–46.

Miller, A.H., M.P. Wattenberg and O. Malanchuk. 1986. "Schematic Assessments of Presidential Candidates." *American Political Science Review* 80:521–40.

Miller, A.H., W.E. Miller, A.S. Raine and T.A. Brown. 1976. "A Majority Party in Disarray: Policy Polarization in the 1972 Election." *American Political Science Review* 70:753–78.

Nie, N.H., S. Verba and J.R. Petrocik. 1979. *The Changing American Voter.* Cambridge: Harvard University Press.

Patterson, T.E. 1980. *The Mass Media Election: How Americans Choose Their President.* New York: Praeger.

Perlin, G. 1988. "Opportunity Regained: The Tory Victory in 1984." In *Canada at the Polls, 1984,* ed. H.R. Penniman. Washington, DC: American Enterprise Institute for Public Policy Research.

Ranney, A., ed. 1979. *The Past and Future of Presidential Debates.* Washington, DC: American Enterprise Institute for Public Policy Research.

Robinson, J.P. 1972. "Mass Communication and Information Diffusion." In *Current Perspectives in Mass Communications Research,* ed. F.G. Kline and P.J. Tichenor. Beverly Hills: Sage Publications.

Robinson, M.J., and M.A. Sheehan. 1983. *Over the Wire and on TV.* New York: Russell Sage.

Schrott, P.R. 1990. "Electoral Consequences of 'Winning' Televised Campaign Debates." *Public Opinion Quarterly* 54:567–85.

Sears, D.O., and S.H. Chaffee. 1979. "Uses and Effects of the 1976 Debates: An Overview of Empirical Studies." In *The Great Debates: Carter vs. Ford, 1976,* ed. S. Kraus. Bloomington: Indiana University Press.

Sears, V. 1985. "The Buttery-Smooth Conservatives." In A. Frizzell and A. Westell, *The Canadian General Election of 1984.* Ottawa: Carleton University Press.

Shabad, G., and K. Anderson. 1979. "Candidate Evaluations by Men and Women." *Public Opinion Quarterly* 43:18–35.

Sigelman, L., and C.K. Sigelman. 1984. "Judgments of the Carter-Reagan Debate: The Eyes of the Beholders." *Public Opinion Quarterly* 48:624–28.

Simpson, J. 1985. "The Vincible Liberals." In A. Frizzell and A. Westell, *The Canadian General Election of 1984.* Ottawa: Carleton University Press.

———. 1989. "The Fog Merchants." *Globe and Mail,* 1 March, A6.

Tannenbaum, P.H., B.S. Greenberg and F.R. Silverman. 1962. "Candidate Images." In *The Great Debates: Kennedy vs. Nixon, 1960,* ed. S. Kraus. Bloomington: Indiana University Press.

Wiseman, N. 1987. "The Use, Misuse, and Abuse of the National Election Studies." *Journal of Canadian Studies* 21:21–37.

4

THE ORGANIZATION OF TELEVISED LEADERS DEBATES IN THE UNITED STATES, EUROPE, AUSTRALIA AND CANADA

~

Robert Bernier
Denis Monière

INTRODUCTION

THE TELEVISION ERA has profoundly altered the political process by expanding audiences, personalizing power, reducing the role of political parties and "nationalizing" the political debate. As in most Western societies, "Television remains the primary source of news information for Canadians. In fact, the public is most likely to rank this medium first for objectivity, accuracy and in-depth reporting" (Frizzell et al. 1989, 77, citing Adams and Levitin 1988).

Fred Fletcher calculated that in the early 1980s 52 percent of voters derived their news information from television, compared with 30 percent from newspapers and 11 percent from radio (Fletcher et al. 1981, 285). In France, an IFREP (Institut français de recherche psychosociologique) poll taken on the eve of the 1988 presidential election revealed that 77 percent of French people based their impressions of the candidates on what they had seen on television (*Le Parisien libéré*, 25 March 1988). Similar results were observed in Germany where 52 percent of respondents named television as their prime source of information on political events, compared with 34 percent for daily newspapers and 10 percent for radio (Metzner 1984, 39).

Before television, citizens rarely had an opportunity to witness the political parties, and their ideas, in direct confrontation with one another. They seldom heard political speeches. Now, politicians enter our homes nightly through television news telecasts. There used to be a tradition of public debates between political candidates, but those debates usually featured local candidates, not party leaders. There were, obviously, exceptions, such as the celebrated debates between Abraham Lincoln and Stephen Douglas in the summer of 1858. In the province of Quebec, Charles-Eugène Boucher of Boucherville debated with Liberal leader Gustave-Henry Joly before an audience of 6 000 in August 1875.

Television has expanded public debate to a national forum. The leaders of the principal political parties use television to communicate instantly with the electorate. No politician today can afford to ignore this medium, because from the time television became a factor in political communication strategies, the images and personalities of the candidates, as projected on television, have been one of the leading factors in determining people's voting choices.

The Role and Importance of Debates in the Electoral Process

Because of their exceptional and spectacular nature, televised debates draw huge audiences, far larger, in fact, than any other type of political event. Katz and Feldman (1962) estimated that 60 to 65 percent of adult Americans watched the first Kennedy–Nixon debate in 1960. It has also been estimated that about 6 percent of American voters, or some four million people, made up their minds on the basis of this debate (Hellweg and Philips 1981). According to Sears and Chaffee (1979), the audience share for the first Ford–Carter debate in 1976 reached 70 percent. In 1980, 120 million people are estimated to have seen at least one of the Carter–Reagan debates. In France, the 1988 debate between François Mitterrand and Jacques Chirac attracted some 26 million viewers. In Canada, the 1988 French-language debate was seen by more than two million viewers and the English-language debate by four million. Close to 30 percent of voters said that they made up their minds on the basis of the debates (*Gallup Report* 1988).

This interest can be explained by the unpredictable and competitive nature of televised debates. Viewers' curiosity, it seems, is piqued by the debates' confrontational character. Interest is also stimulated by the fact that it is the viewers who will ultimately decide who wins and who loses.

Televised debates are helpful for voters because they provide the only opportunity for them to compare the positions, personalities and abilities of the candidates at the same time and in the same place. Voters can therefore compare the performances and policies of the candidates, and more easily evaluate the similarities and differences in the positions of the various parties. Author Antonine Maillet, who moderated the 1988 French-language debate, explained the role of the debate in the following terms: "Tonight, Canadians have a unique opportunity to experience democracy in action, for it is democracy, combined with modern technology, that enables citizens throughout the country to meet, in a single location, the leaders of the three largest parties, who have come here to personally present their visions of Canada."

The unique characteristic of televised debates is that they offer citizens an inexpensive, first-hand source of comparative information. Election campaigns have traditionally provided information sporadically and indirectly. Voters acquired their political knowledge by reading newspapers, listening to news broadcasts and watching campaign commercials. All this was second-hand information, moulded and mediated by journalists or political communication specialists. Apart from attending political meetings and reading party platforms, which few voters do, watching televised debates provides the only direct, easy and inexpensive access to political views. In addition, according to Miller and Mackuen (1979, 344), the debates serve to increase the public's knowledge of politics and politicians.

In Canada, televised debates gained prominence during the 1980s as pivotal events in election campaigns. Canada kept pace with other Western democracies in this regard, holding four federal political debates by 1989, while the United States held presidential debates in five elections and France in three. Political strategists and party leaders became convinced of the need for this media exercise as a tool to maximize their election support. There are increasing numbers of swing voters and there has been a significant decline in party loyalty. As a result, voters increasingly wait until the actual campaign before deciding which way to vote. For example, in 1984, 50 percent of Canadians had not made up their minds when the election was called (Fletcher 1988, 161). All these factors favour televised debates, especially when the party leaders are relatively unknown, as was the case in 1984.

Party leaders are willing to participate in televised debates when they believe it is to their advantage, that is, when they expect to increase their support. However, the leader of a party in power with a comfortable lead in voter support will want to find reasons for avoiding a debate. Leaders are more eager to participate if they are behind in the polls, if they are ahead but losing ground, or if the polls indicate that their level of support is fluctuating.

Although it is difficult to determine the exact effect that debates have on the final results of an election, significant shifts in voters' intentions can be seen as a result of the debates. The impact of a debate is especially significant during a tight race, and a shift of two to three percentage points in the undecided vote could mean the difference between victory and defeat. In France, for example, Valéry Giscard d'Estaing's 1974 victory over François Mitterrand has been attributed to their performances in the televised debate. Okrent described the situation as follows:

> According to a poll taken the same night, the debate changed the opinions of 10 percent of the viewers. Forty-seven percent felt that Valéry Giscard d'Estaing won the debate, and 38 percent preferred Mitterrand. The shift in votes in both directions as a result of the debates was less than 3 percent. This figure was obtained by comparing the election results with polls taken before the second round. The television debate was only marginally influential, but it was the undecided voters who determined the outcome of the election. (1988, 138)

In the end, Giscard d'Estaing's margin of victory was 424 599 votes, or 1.9 percent of the total.

In Canada, televised debates also played a key role in the 1984 and 1988 election campaigns. The 1984 debate between Brian Mulroney, John Turner and Ed Broadbent was won by the Progressive Conservative leader, according to the 78 percent of Canadians who felt that he had outperformed Turner. Subsequent opinion polls revealed large shifts in voters' intentions: "The 1984 shift was the largest since the beginning of national polling in Canada, a period spanning 13 previous federal elections. The polls showed the Liberals with 49 percent of the decided vote in early July 1984, a 10 percent lead over the Conservatives. Within three weeks of the election call on July 9, Liberal support had dropped to 39 percent, ending up at 28 percent on election day" (Fletcher 1988, 161).

Analysts agree that this shift was the result of the leaders' performances during the televised debates. Poll results in Quebec after the French debate indicated a 10 to 12 percent shift in voter intentions away from the Liberals and toward the Progressive Conservatives (Fletcher 1988, 181). It was noted, as well, that commentaries by journalists after the debate influenced voters' choices. The same phenomenon occurred in 1988 when the debate enabled John Turner, whose party was in third position in the polls before the debate, to make a spectacular comeback and preserve the Liberals' status as the official opposition.

Although controversy still surrounds the effect that televised debates have, and the findings of the main studies are inconclusive, political communication specialists have identified eight effects of televised political debates (Trent and Friedenburg 1983, 263–73):

1. By their dramatic nature, debates help stimulate interest in politics and attract very large audiences.
2. They reinforce the partisan views of those who have already decided to support a particular party, that is, they have a confirming effect.
3. Debates may make it easier to recruit campaign workers.
4. Debates result in few conversions or significant shifts in voters' intentions; however, they may be a deciding factor in a tight race, making the difference between election victory and defeat, as was the case in the election of U.S. President Kennedy in 1960.
5. Debates help voters determine what is important and what the basic issues are.
6. Debates raise the level of awareness and understanding of problems and party policies.
7. They enable candidates to make themselves more widely known or to correct negative aspects of their public image.
8. Debates help legitimize political institutions and encourage the political involvement of young people.

Despite these significant contributions to the democratic process, televised debates are not unanimously applauded. They have been criticized for emphasizing image and favouring appearance at the expense of substance, and for failing to provide voters with added information. They are said to help the most superficial candidates and prevent thinking candidates from winning elections. They tend to relate political success to candidates' abilities as performers rather than to their wisdom or the correctness of their judgement. In the early 1960s, when André Laurendeau pondered the value of this innovation in the democratic process, he decided that "qualities that make a good performer on television are not necessarily qualities that make a good politician" (1962). However, in the era of "new politics," surely communication skills are an essential aspect of political skills. There are also those who deplore the fact that the media spend too much time covering the negotiations surrounding the debate format, to the detriment of more pressing issues (Swerdlow 1984, 11).

Research Objectives

This study compares televised debate practices in several democracies to clarify the relationship between the debate's format, its internal dynamics, its content and its impact. By analysing the way debates are organized in the United States, Europe (France, the Netherlands, Germany and Scandinavia), Australia and Canada, we hope to answer the following questions: Who should organize debates? Who should be allowed to participate? How many debates should there be? How long should they last? When should they take place? What role should journalists play?

The debate format greatly affects the dynamics of the interaction between leaders, as well as the content, and we will see that the formats vary considerably from one country to another. Historically, there have been three basic models: the parallel news conference format used in Sweden and the United States; the direct confrontation format used primarily in Europe; and finally, the mixed format, which includes both direct interaction between the candidates and an active role for journalists.

TELEVISED DEBATES IN THE UNITED STATES

In the United States, the process of negotiating the organization and formats of televised presidential election debates has gone through several variations since 1960.

The four debates held in 1960 were preceded by a series of 12 negotiating sessions between the television networks and the candidates' representatives. The networks preferred a direct confrontation between the candidates, while the candidates' advisers insisted that a number of journalists participate in the debate together with a moderator. The candidates' advisers won the struggle, setting the stage for their continued domination of the format negotiating process (Kraus 1988, 38).

Between late 1960 and 1976, no debates were held during the three presidential elections, apparently because the candidates declined to participate. This was largely because of the political climate created by the Vietnam War and, later, the Watergate affair.

When President Gerald Ford expressed an interest in meeting Jimmy Carter in a televised debate in the fall of 1976, a new group entered the negotiation process. The League of Women Voters Education Fund, a nonprofit organization with no ties to the government or political parties, became the debate organizer. Their involvement permitted broadcasters to cover the debates as news events. It should be remembered that a special Act of Congress was required in 1960, setting aside the equal time provisions in section 315 of the *Communications Act of 1934*, to permit broadcasting of the Kennedy–Nixon debates. Without that resolution, broadcasters would have had to provide equal time to the many minor party presidential candidates, which would have effectively prevented broadcasting of the debates (Kraus 1988, 40).

In 1976, however, Congress refused to set aside the Act to permit the televising of debates between the major presidential candidates. Instead, a complex series of legal manoeuvres was undertaken to allow the networks to cover the debates as "bona fide media events" sponsored by a nonpartisan group (in this case, the League of Women Voters). News coverage is exempt from the equal time provisions. The resulting body of legal opinion influenced the course of the negotiations surrounding the 1976 debates. There was much criticism and bitter discussion over the participation of candidates from smaller parties, the selection of journalists, and the roles of the television networks and the organizer. Candidates from smaller parties sued the League of Women Voters and the television networks in an attempt to be allowed to participate in the debates but the two-way debates prevailed (Kraus 1988, 40–41).

In the fall of 1976, Republican President Gerald Ford faced Democratic challenger Jimmy Carter in three campaign debates, while Republican vice-presidential candidate Robert Dole faced Democrat Walter Mondale in another. The formats were similar to those established in 1960 in that, in some of the debates, the candidates were allowed to make opening and closing remarks, and the debates included a moderator and a panel of journalists who posed questions to the candidates. The candidates were also given time to refute their opponents' remarks.

In contrast to the 1960 debates, however, the televised debates of 1976 took place before a live audience. This innovation prompted objections from President Ford's political advisers and was the subject of its own debate. The President's legal advisers pointed out that a live audience was needed to lend credibility to the argument that the debate was a bona fide media event and, therefore, not subject to the equal time requirement. However, the candidates' representatives, with the consent of the League, succeeded in preventing the networks from showing audience reaction. The only shots of the audience permitted in 1976 were those taken before and after the debates, much to the displeasure of network management (Kraus 1988, 42–44).

During the 1980 presidential campaign, there were two televised debates, one between Republican candidate Ronald Reagan and John B. Anderson, a minor party candidate, and the other between Reagan and Democrat Jimmy Carter, the incumbent president.

In the spring of 1979, the League of Women Voters was assured by the Republican and Democratic national committees that it would be allowed to sponsor and organize a series of televised debates to be held during the presidential election campaign that was to take place in the fall of 1980. In March 1980, the Federal Election Commission authorized groups like the League to collect funds from business, labour and charitable foundations to finance events such as debates between presidential candidates. In July 1980, League representatives asked journalists' associations to provide a list of eminent journalists to participate in the debates as representatives of the media (Martel 1983, 7–8).

On 19 August, the League invited Reagan and Carter to take part in a series of four televised debates, the first of which would be held in Baltimore on 18 September, the second in Louisville on 2 October, the third in Portland on 13 October and the fourth in Cleveland on 27 October 1980.

According to Ruth Hinerfeld, president of the League at that time, the idea of having four debates was based on the 1976 experience, and the locations were selected based on geographic diversity and facilities that were available to the League (Martel 1983, 8).

In addition, as a token of its neutrality, the League insisted on allowing a minor party candidate to participate. To qualify, such a candidate would have to receive at least 15 percent in the polls by 10 September 1980. That candidate was John Anderson, who ran as a Republican in the primaries but as an Independent in the general election.

President Carter and his advisers refused to participate in the debate held in Baltimore on 21 September 1980 (it had originally been scheduled for 18 September) because the polls showed that Anderson's entry into the race would draw votes away from the Democrats. The Democrats attacked the League's credibility, implying that the debate between Anderson and Reagan was really a debate between two Republicans. This strategy on the part of the Democrats was designed to cast doubt on the neutrality of the League and the value of the debate (Martel 1983, 9).

In the fall of 1980, the American economy was stagnating and inflation was high. The American hostage situation in Iran was also doing nothing to improve President Carter's standing in the polls. He therefore was not eager to meet Anderson and Reagan in a three-way debate.

In the days preceding the Baltimore debate, the League invited Carter and Reagan to a two-way debate to be held in the Public Music Hall in Cleveland, Ohio, on 28 October. After lengthy negotiations over a format that would satisfy the strategic interests of both candidates in a volatile political atmosphere, Carter agreed to debate with Reagan. The use of questions from journalists in the first half of the debate favoured Carter, who was better informed than Reagan, while holding the debate one week before the election favoured Reagan, who had a better television presence. Reagan's ensuing victory in the televised debate was crowned by such rhetorical tactics as the use of "There you go again" when Carter tried to attack him. ABC took a telephone poll after the debate and confirmed the success of the California governor's performance (Martel 1983, 27–28).

In 1984, the League of Women Voters again sponsored presidential debates and was heavily criticized, especially on the process for selecting journalists to make up the panel. Three debates were presented: the first took place on 7 October in Louisville, Kentucky, and dealt with economic and domestic political issues; the second, held in Philadelphia on 11 October, dealt with general topics; and the third, held in Kansas City on 21 October, dealt with foreign affairs and defence. Two of these debates were between incumbent President Reagan and Walter Mondale, while the Philadelphia debate pitted vice-presidential incumbent George Bush against Geraldine Ferraro.

The format of these debates was similar to that of previous debates: a moderator and a panel of journalists took turns asking questions of the candidates. Candidates were also given opportunities to refute their opponent's answer.

When the debate format was under negotiation, the League submitted the names of 100 journalists from which the candidates' representatives could select the panel. Despite their credentials, this list of journalists was rejected by the candidates' representatives, who chose Barbara Walters of ABC as moderator for the Louisville debate and Diane Sawyer of CBS, Fred Barnes of the *Baltimore Sun* and James Wilghart of the Scripps Howard news service as panelists. For the vice-presidential debate held in Philadelphia on 11 October, the candidates' representatives chose Sander Vanocur of ABC as moderator, and Robert Boyd of the *Philadelphia Inquirer*, Jack White of *Time* magazine and John Mashek of *U.S. News and World Report* as the panelists. For the final debate between Mondale and Reagan in Kansas City, Edwin Newman of PBS was moderator, and the panel consisted of Morton Kondracke of the *New Republic*, Georgie Ann Geyer of Universal Press Syndicate, Henry Trewhitt of the *Baltimore Sun* and Marvin Kalb of NBC.

For the first time, the League's panelist selection process had been categorically rejected by the candidates' representatives. The list of journalists submitted in 1976 by the League had been accepted by the candidates' advisers as an inventory from which to make their selections; in 1980, the names of some journalists had been rejected, but the selection had been made from the list submitted by the League (Kraus 1988, 56–57).

Immediately after the 1984 presidential election, the two principal American parties declared that they were unhappy with the way the League of Women Voters had handled the debates, and decided in 1986 to create the Commission on Presidential Debates. This nonprofit organization, with a legal status similar to that of the League, included the heads of the Republican and Democratic national committees. In the two years leading up to the 1988 presidential election, the League of Women Voters attempted to argue that it was best suited to sponsor the debates because of its experience and nonpartisan nature. In the period preceding the negotiations for the 1988 presidential debates, representatives of the Republican and Democratic candidates presented a 16-page document establishing the rules, including such details as where the cameras could be placed and what portions of the stage could be shot. This document prompted such dissension among the members of the new Commission on Presidential Debates, the League of Women Voters and the television networks that the League was eventually replaced as the debate sponsor by the Commission on Presidential Debates (Interview, Sidney Kraus, 1991). Two debates were held in 1988 as part of the presidential election campaign.

According to Kraus, the negotiations surrounding televised debates in the United States are controlled by the candidates, who do not hesitate to threaten to pull out of the debates as an intimidation technique or to publicly embarrass the sponsors or the television networks when this type of tactic suits their purposes. Kraus, an expert on political debates in the United States, says that the candidates' control over the negotiations enables them to shape the format in their favour, thereby projecting a more positive image of themselves and increasing their chances of winning the election (Kraus 1988, 64). He concludes that politicians should be removed from the debate negotiating process (Interview, Sidney Kraus, 1991).

In the United States, journalists play a major role in televised debates. Many experts believe that this limits the likelihood of direct confrontation between the candidates, who can simply confine themselves to answering the journalists' questions. Some observers, such as Ranney (1979) and Salent (1979), have characterized the debates as "televised joint appearances" or joint news conferences at which the candidates simply answer questions from a panel of journalists. A study by Tiemens et al. (1985) showed a low level of conflict and contradiction between Carter and Reagan during the 1980 debate. According to the study, this lacklustre performance resulted from the debate format, which deprived the encounter of spontaneity and condemned it to sterility. However, the candidates prefer this format because it reduces the risk of direct confrontation, since there is always a danger that an aggressive approach will reflect negatively on the aggressor.

According to Kraus, debates could be made a regular feature of U.S. elections by amending the *Federal Election Campaign Act of 1971* to require a candidate to participate in the candidates' debate to qualify for the tax credits allowed under the Act. Candidates who refused to debate would thus be denied public funding (Kraus 1988, 154).

TELEVISED DEBATES IN EUROPE AND AUSTRALIA

Debates in France

The French televised debate format most closely approximates a duel or a direct confrontation. Journalists had little to do with two of the three debates between presidential candidates (1974 and 1988). They were therefore characterized as "stopwatch journalists" (Okrent 1988, 42) because they simply kept time and signalled changes in topics. Okrent notes that when journalists moderate and structure the debate, as was the case in 1981, more topics are covered than in the direct confrontation format where the candidates select the topics for discussion. However, in France, 69 percent of voters prefer a direct confrontation between the two candidates to a debate moderated by journalists (ibid., 41).

Under section 16 of the *loi du 30 septembre 1986* (Act of 30 September 1986), the Commission nationale de la communication et des libertés (CNCL) is responsible for regulating the scheduling and broadcasting of election debates in France. This board has full powers to regulate radio, television and telecommunications, as well as advertising, including political advertisements. The CNCL was replaced on 17 January 1989 by the Conseil supérieur de l'audiovisuel (CSA), which retained the same powers except for telecommunications, which were removed from its jurisdiction.

These regulatory bodies were established to guarantee pluralism on the airwaves and ensure that all currents of opinion had access to the electronic media. Their mandate was to ensure balanced treatment of information by the electronic media, whether public or private. To this end, two principles have been established: before an election campaign, the Commission ensures that the principle of "equitable" access is adhered to following the "three-thirds" rule – one-third of air time goes to the government, one-third to the parliamentary majority and one-third to the parliamentary opposition. During the official campaign in the electronic media, which lasts two weeks, candidates must be treated equally. This equal-treatment principle takes priority over the editorial freedom of the electronic media. During the election campaign, the government agency determines the number and length of broadcasts and the scheduling of candidates on the publicly owned networks (Interviews, Francis Balle and Béatrice Jacomet, 1991). The CSA's authority extends to presidential and legislative elections in France as well as to European elections.

In a decision made on 10 March 1988 (decision no. 88-73), the CNCL confirmed the established practice by limiting televised debates to the second round of presidential elections: "It [the televised debate] can take place only in the second round, providing both candidates agree. Half the total debate time is allocated to the time allowed each candidate" (France 1988, 3915).

Holding a televised debate before the first round of elections would be impractical, given the large number of candidates involved and the fact that the law requires that all candidates be treated equally. Therefore, televised debates in France are always held between the first and second rounds. This avoids the thorny issue of how many and which candidates will be allowed to take part in the debate because, under the French electoral system, only two candidates can be left by the second round.

In 1988, the televised debate was held on 28 April, 10 days before the vote on 8 May. It was telecast live over the national public networks TF1 and Antenne 2, and recorded for telecast over those private networks that opted to carry it. The moderators for the debate were the news directors of the two networks, Michèle Cotta and Elie Vannier. The debate was originally scheduled to last one hour and 50 minutes, but was extended by 30 minutes to comply with the rule guaranteeing the candidates equal speaking time, since one of the candidates had used more time.

According to a SOFRES (Société française d'études et de sondages) poll of 1 000 people taken immediately after the debate, François Mitterrand was the winner: 42 percent of the respondents thought that he had come out ahead, compared with 33 percent for Jacques Chirac. Eighteen percent felt it was a tie. A PSOS poll taken the day after the debate indicated that 55 percent intended to vote for Mitterrand, versus 45 percent for Chirac. A poll taken by the same firm on 24 April, four days before the debate, revealed that 53 percent intended to vote for Mitterrand and 47 percent for Chirac. The audience for the debate was estimated at 25 million, out of a total of 29 million eligible voters, making the election debate the most watched television show of the year. One can therefore conclude that the debate had some influence on voter intentions. Two important events occurred after the debate that also may have influenced the final result, namely, the release of three French hostages held in Lebanon and the violent resolution of a hostage-taking incident in New Caledonia. When the election was held, Mitterrand received 54.02 percent of the vote and Chirac 45.97 percent.

Two other televised debates in France, in 1974 and 1981, both featured Valéry Giscard d'Estaing and François Mitterrand. The first of these debates was televised on 10 May 1974. The rules for both debates were established by the Commission nationale de contrôle, which determined the permitted backdrops and camera angles. The latter were limited to long shots, medium shots and close-ups of each candidate. Cut-aways to show someone reacting or listening were not allowed.

In 1974, the two candidates agreed to a direct-confrontation format in front of two journalists, Jacqueline Baudrier and Alain Duhamel, who watched the dialogue between the two party leaders without asking any questions. Their role was simply to keep track of the amount of time each candidate spoke, using the two clocks in front of them with the candidates' names on them. The topics for discussion and the order in which they would be discussed were not established in advance. The candidates alone controlled the debate.

The scheduled length of the debate was one hour and 30 minutes but was extended to one hour and 45 minutes as a result of the equal-time rule, since François Mitterrand had exhausted his time before Giscard d'Estaing. The ORTF (Office de radiodiffusion télévision française) estimated the audience at 23 million and noted a very high level of public interest (Cazeneuve 1974, 196; Nel 1990, 31).

In 1981, in an unusual step, the incumbent president sent a written invitation to debate to his challenger. Giscard d'Estaing evidently thought he had done well in the 1974 debate and wanted to repeat his strong showing. However, the invitation gave his opponent, Mitterrand, an opportunity to set the conditions. Mitterrand had not been well served by the 1974 debate format, which he described as a kind of political dogfight that was ill-suited to dialogue with the French people. For the first time in France, therefore, technical questions regarding the televised images were negotiated in order to bring the visual aspect of the debate under the equality principle as well. Restrictions were placed on the shooting and framing of images. For example, only medium shots and close-ups were allowed, while cut-aways and reaction shots were expressly prohibited: "Only the candidate who is speaking can be shown, and no cut-away shots or shots of the reaction of the opponent or of the referee will be permitted" (Nel 1990, 34). In this way, there is a sense of direct interaction with the public. Mitterrand understood that, in a televised debate, you have to convince not the opponent opposite you but the television viewer, who is not even present in the studio.

In his reply to Giscard d'Estaing, Mitterrand also objected to the 1974 debate format and demanded that journalists be present:

> The key responses by each of the candidates, who may debate as much as they want in equal amounts of time, can only be given in answer to specific questions from competent observers in an atmosphere from which any element of sensationalism has been removed. I therefore tell you absolutely that either journalists and an independent producer will conduct the debate or there will be no debate. (Okrent 1988, 62)

The two representatives of the candidates and Jacques Boutet, the chairman of the Commission nationale de contrôle, negotiated the debate format. The one that was finally agreed on provided for a debate of one hour and 40 minutes on three topics: institutions and liberties, domestic policy, and foreign policy. The debate would be moderated by two journalists who would ask questions and control the amount of time allowed each candidate. The President of France was allowed to choose the journalists from a list of four names submitted by François Mitterrand. The two journalists selected, Jean Boissonnet of Europe 1 and Michèle Cotta of RTL, were chosen alphabetically, according to the President.

Both candidates based their communication strategy on the viewer. For Giscard d'Estaing, the purpose of the debate was to shed light on the choice that the French people were about to make, while Mitterrand suggested that it was to inform, to help people understand and to engage in dialogue with the nation.

The debate took place on 5 May 1981 as part of the official campaign, five days before the vote. It lasted 110 minutes, with each candidate allotted 55 minutes. According to Okrent, in 1981, 64 percent of the French public felt that the debate was the best way to learn about the candidates' positions (1988, 139).

In France, there have also been televised debates between party leaders outside election campaigns. Raymond Barre met François Mitterrand on 12 May 1977 (Tarnowski 1988), Lionel Jospin met Simone Weil on 21 May 1984, and most recently, Prime Minister Laurent Fabius met RPR (Rassemblement pour la République) leader Jacques Chirac on 27 October 1985 (Champagne 1990, 169–91). Since these debates took place outside election periods, they were not subject to the equality rule and it was left to the discretion of the political parties and the networks to invite whomever they wished. The idea for the 1985 debate came from Laurent Fabius while appearing on the TF1 television program "L'heure de vérité." These debates mainly serve the personal ambitions of the political leaders involved by increasing their popularity and improving their positions within their own parties (ibid., 185).

Debates in the Netherlands

Televised debates were introduced into Dutch political life in 1977, and were part of the 1981, 1982, 1986 and 1989 election campaigns. Debates are not governed by the electoral laws, but are handled instead by broadcasting associations, a type of viewer association peculiar to the Netherlands. Membership in these associations ranges from 100 000 to 500 000 people, and they are usually partisan (that is, they have a party affiliation). For example, there is VARA, an amateur radio association affiliated with the Labour party, and KRO, a Catholic broadcasting association linked to the Christian Democrat party. Protestants have an association, as do the Greens. Even apolitical viewers have an association, known as TROS. These organizations negotiate with the parties to determine a debate format. In practice, the liberal-minded associations representing the large Dutch political parties – PvdA (Partij van de Arbeid), CDA (Christen Demokratische) and VVD (Volspartij voor Vryheid en Demokratie) – cooperate in organizing the debate or debates and deciding who will participate. In this respect, the parties are not treated equally in the Netherlands since the large parties are able to take advantage of the situation and control the process at election time, at least for televised debates. As a result, there is a tendency to exclude the small parties on the extreme left or right. In addition, the debate format changes from election to election, depending on the balance of power among the parties.

In the first debate, in which Prime Minister Joop Den Uyl (PvdA) faced opposition leader Hans Wiegel (VVD), the two parties agreed to a format based on the American model. This agreement resulted in the following rules:

1. The debate was to cover six predetermined general topics, namely, unemployment, foreign policy, public security, education, housing and revenue policy.
2. The choice of the specific questions to be asked on each topic was to be left to a panel of three journalists, on whom the two parties agreed.
3. The speaker of the House of Representatives would act as moderator.

4. Unlike the American model, direct exchanges would be permitted between the two leaders. When a journalist asked the first question, the leader who had been selected in a draw to answer first would give his response. His opponent would then be allowed to respond, and so forth, with the questions being asked alternately of the leaders.

5. The debate was scheduled to last one hour and 40 minutes. (It actually lasted 11 minutes longer because the moderator showed some flexibility and allowed exchanges to run their course.)

The debate took place one week before voting day, 25 May 1977, and was seen by three million viewers out of a total population of 13 million.

A study of the impact of the debate compared the pre- and post-debate voting intentions of a small sample of people (312 before the debate and 280 after, including 235 who had been questioned before the debate). The study concluded that the debate had served primarily to reinforce partisan predispositions (De Bock 1978). Thus, 46 percent of the respondents felt that the PvdA (Labour party) representative had won, 26 percent felt that the representative of the right-wing VVD had won, and 6 percent had no opinion. The study noted that these results were highly partisan because 71 percent of the respondents who identified ideologically with the left thought that Den Uyl had won, while 69 percent of the supporters of the right thought that Wiegel had won. The debate, therefore, did not significantly influence the outcome of the election because only 2 percent of respondents said that the debate was the deciding factor in determining their vote, while 14 percent said that the debate had helped them decide. The debate seemed primarily to reduce the number of undecided voters, since the number who had no opinion about their attitude toward the government fell from 7 percent before the debate to 1 percent after, while the number who had no opinion about the opposition fell from 19 percent to 2 percent.

A large majority of respondents felt that the debate did not enlighten them significantly about party platforms (73 percent) or the leaders (69 percent). Paradoxically, however, 72 percent of respondents thought that holding the debate was a good idea.

Because the Netherlands has many political parties, a reflection in part of its electoral system of proportional representation, a single debate involving only the leaders of the two largest parties was seen as unfair to the smaller parties. The Dutch therefore experimented in the 1980s, holding several televised debates to allow all the parties represented in Parliament to take advantage of these opportunities. In 1981, there were three debates: one large debate on the eve of the election involving representatives of four parties (CDA, PvdA, VVD and D66, which is a left-liberal party), preceded by two other debates, one between the leaders of D66 and VVD, and the other between the leaders of CDA and PvdA. This format was repeated for the 1982 election.

During the 1986 election as well, several debates were held. The largest debate was televised on the eve of the election and involved the leaders of three parties: CDA, PvdA and VVD. Five days before the vote, two more debates were held, and these were organized along religious lines, since religion plays an important role in Dutch politics. Here, the representative of the Christian Democrat party faced first the leader of GPV and then the leader of RPF, both Protestant parties.

In 1989, only two debates were held. One featured the leaders of the two largest parties, CDA and PvdA, and was televised four days before the vote. The other, held on the eve of the election, featured the leaders of five parties – CDA, PvdA, VVD, D66 and the leftist Green party.

Journalists in the Netherlands play a role similar to that of their French colleagues. They moderate the candidates' exchanges when necessary, apportion the amount of speaking time and introduce the topics for discussion. They rarely ask questions; the candidates pose most of the questions themselves.

The length of the debates varies. The major debates involving more than two leaders normally last two hours, while the smaller ones last 40 minutes. The candidates generally make a few opening remarks in which they outline their positions on issues that have been established in advance. Then they interact directly with one another. This format is similar to a round-table discussion.

The audiences for these debates in the Netherlands are small, compared with those in North America and France, where debates garner the attention of at least 50 percent of the electorate. According to polls taken in the Netherlands in 1981, only 25 percent of the respondents had seen the debates. This proportion rose in 1982 to 30 percent before falling again in 1986 to 25 percent for the major debate.

To gauge the impact of these debates, we consulted van der Eijk and van Praag (1987), who wrote the only book on this subject that has been published in Dutch. This study deals with the 1986 election and is based on a sample of 600 people living in the town of OuderAmstel, south of Amsterdam. The respondents were questioned twice, the first time 10 days before the vote and the second on voting day, before the results were known. The study concluded that the debates were not the reason for the victory of the Christian Democrats, who gained nine extra seats, increasing from 44 to 53 seats out of 150. There was no discernible difference in attitude between those who had seen the debate and those who had not. The authors discovered that the leader of the Liberal party, who was thought by most respondents to have won the debate, actually suffered the greatest losses for his party in the election. This study ran counter to the opinion expressed in most of the media that it was the performances of the leaders in the debate that explained the Christian Democrat victory.

Debates in Germany

In the Federal Republic of Germany, there were five consecutive debates before the Bundestag elections of 1972, 1976, 1980, 1983 and 1987. Paradoxically, the reunification of Germany prevented the holding of a televised debate before the last Bundestag election on 2 December 1990 because of the increased number of parties that could claim the right to participate in what is known as the "elephant round" of debates. The former Communist party, the East German PDS and the Alternative party (Alternative Liste) would have joined SPD (Sozialdemokratische Partei Deutschlands), CSU (Christlich Soziale Union), CDU (Christlich Demokratische Union Deutschlands), FDP (Freie Demokratische Partei) and the Green party in the debates. However, the main reason for not holding the debate was the popularity of the CDU-CSU coalition led by Chancellor Helmut Kohl. Moreover, Kohl had been annoyed during the 1987 debate by the Greens, whose representative, Ms. Ditfurth, had broken the rules of the debate by addressing her adversaries directly and had been particularly aggressive toward Chancellor Kohl. The official explanation advanced by journalist H.D. Lueg of the ARD network was that Chancellor Kohl wanted to stand in personally for cabinet minister Schaeuble at an election rally to be held on the day the debate was scheduled because Schaeuble had been the victim of a terrorist attack, which had caused an outpouring of emotion and compassion within the CDU (Interview, H.D. Lueg, 1991).

In Germany, the national television networks take the initiative in inviting the parties to a televised debate. Since the electoral laws do not require the electronic media to treat all the parties equally, the networks invite only representatives of parties with seats in the Bundestag, thereby giving them a degree of public legitimacy.

The first German experience with televised debates came in 1972 when, following the American model, three debates were organized and broadcast by the ARD network on 18 October, the ZDF network on 2 November, and by both networks on 15 November, four days before the election. The format for these debates varied. The first two debates lasted one hour each and journalists played a major role, asking questions of the party representatives and following up with additional questions. Thus the interaction was primarily between the journalists and the leaders, rather than between the leaders themselves. The third debate was different, first because it lasted two hours and second because the exchanges were solely between the leaders, since the moderators (W. Hubner of ARD and R. Woller of ZDF) confined themselves to apportioning the time equally between the leaders.

In subsequent elections, the format was again changed to provide for only one debate, to be held on the Thursday preceding election day. This makes it possible for voters to recall their impressions of the debate when they go to vote; in addition, there is little time for media pronouncements on the leaders' performances to influence voters' choices. The debates are televised by both national networks, ARD and ZDF. Some have lasted three hours or more, with the 1976 debate continuing for three hours and 45 minutes. Since 1983, however, the debates have been limited to two hours. The debates are hosted by journalists who act as moderators, guiding the discussion by asking questions and sometimes calming the participants. Neither the questions nor the topics for discussion are determined in advance, which leaves room for spontaneity. The editors-in-chief of the ZDF and ARD networks act as moderators. Except for the Greens, who have adopted a very aggressive stance, the party representatives are content to answer journalists' questions without interrupting or attacking one another.

Unlike France, therefore, the debates in Germany do not resemble a televised duel. The party leaders have always been opposed to the French format, claiming that German elections are parliamentary in nature, not presidential, and that it is the parties that are being elected, not the chancellor. In addition, the existence of party coalitions, which are an integral part of the German political system in both the government and the opposition, would make it difficult to stage direct confrontations between the chancellor and the leader of the opposition party. However, the direct confrontation format is used in some of the Länder or German states. All parties with seats in the Bundestag are represented in the debates, so there were five participants in 1987. It is not necessarily the party leaders who participate in the debates, because sometimes a party's candidate for chancellor is not the party leader, as was the case with Helmut Schmidt in the 1976 election. The Greens designated two representatives in 1987, a man and a woman, leaving it up to the networks to decide randomly who would participate.

Interest in televised debates is declining in Germany, judging by the percentage of eligible voters who watch them. This proportion fell from 84 percent in 1972 to 75 percent in 1976, 68 percent in 1980, 56 percent in 1983 and 46 percent in 1987. Despite this decline in voter interest, the debates remain major political events that are viewed by around half the German electorate. This audience still surpasses those for soccer games, which are extremely popular in Germany. The declining interest in the 1980s can be explained by the introduction of cable television and the proliferation of private channels competing with the public networks and depriving them of their monopoly. By the end of 1990, 4.5 million or 60 percent of West German homes were equipped with cable television.

In Germany, the debates influence voter attitudes. In a study comparing the responses of people who had seen televised debates with those who had not, Schrott (1990) showed that the debates affected how the public viewed the participants. He observed that people who had seen the debates had a more positive view of politicians. The debates also tended to work in favour of the incumbent chancellor, who was given a more positive rating than his opponent by those who watched the debate than by those who did not. "In West Germany ... it is the challenger who constantly loses ground and the chancellor who appears to gain" (ibid.). German voters seem to give greater credibility to positive arguments than to critical attacks on an adversary (Baker et al. 1981, 541). The same phenomenon has been observed in some American debates (Stewart 1975).

Schrott also observed that being considered the winner of a debate had an influence on the subsequent vote and that this effect did not depend on one's position (candidate for chancellor or simply an allied candidate): "Not only the chancellor and his challenger, but other participants too are likely to gain votes for their parties if judged as the winner. This indicates that the debates in West Germany are not simply a contest between the chancellor and his challenger but involve the other two participants equally strongly. A small party such as the FDP might gain substantially from its leader being the winner of the debate ... No doubt, debates matter for vote choice in West Germany" (Schrott 1990).

Debates in Scandinavia

Televised debates in Scandinavian countries are part of political life, although their format varies from one country to another.

In Denmark, a three-hour debate among the leaders of all the political parties is broadcast on radio and television two days before election day. The event takes the form of a news conference with a time period allotted for the presentation of each candidate's election platform.

According to Siune (1991), when the television broadcasting monopoly was broken in Denmark with the arrival of channel TV2, the rules of the game guaranteeing the presence of all the parties at the event were changed. The new channel held the debate the day before the election and invited representatives of only the most popular parties.

The Norwegian format differs from the Danish model, as the debate takes place in front of journalists or a group of voters who ask the candidates questions. For a Norwegian political candidate to participate in the televised debate, his or her party is expected to meet the following criteria: the party must already have been represented in the Norwegian Parliament during one of the last two mandates, must have fielded candidates in a majority of electoral districts and must have a national organization. An exception, however, is that a minority party that is a member of a coalition in power or that represents a credible alternative to the government may participate in the debate (Siune 1991).

In the parallel news conference format used in Sweden, party representatives meet two journalists 48 hours before the vote; the journalists take turns questioning the representatives on their policies. This approach is similar to an oral examination before the public, which acts as the jury. Any direct confrontation between the participants is avoided, with the result that these debates more closely resemble a news conference than a traditional debate. The event is televised in prime time on all the networks, which in Sweden are publicly owned.

In theory, only parties represented in the Swedish Parliament have access to the televised debates. Two minority parties not represented in the Parliament participated in the debates held during the 1988 election campaign, however, only because the Swedish broadcasting organization deemed that some of the issues in their election platforms were priorities for the election. Swedish radio and television broadcasting law gives broadcasting organizations the authority to decide who will participate in the televised debates (Siune 1991).

Debates in Australia

Televised debates in Australia are a recent innovation, with only two debates held so far during general elections. The first was in 1984, pitting Prime Minister Bob Hawke against the Liberal leader, Andrew Peacock. The two leaders met again in a debate during the 1990 election. According to Warhurst (1991), the 1984 debate was broadcast on all the stations in the country, while the 1990 debate was broadcast only on the Australian Broadcasting Corporation, Special Broadcasting Service and only one of the three private television networks. One study revealed that 56 percent of the Australian electorate listened to the 1990 debate (Lloyd 1990, 97). According to Lloyd, the impact of this event on voters was significant during the 1990 election campaign. Lasting

60 minutes, the 1990 debate had opening and closing remarks by the candidates and included a panel of journalists who asked the candidates questions. In addition, the leaders discussed election issues during part of this time, thus provoking heated exchanges (ibid., 5).

TELEVISED DEBATES IN CANADA

Debates during Federal Elections

In Canada, debates were held during the 1968, 1979, 1984 and 1988 elections, with a different format for each.

The 1968 Debate Format

The 1968 debate copied the parallel press conference format used in the United States. That year, the media took the initiative, calling for a televised debate when the election campaign was launched. Circumstances favoured the holding of such a historic event because both major party leaders were running for the first time in their new positions: Robert Stanfield of the Progressive Conservatives and Pierre Trudeau of the Liberals had been chosen leaders of their parties in the previous few months. They were therefore both eager to take up the challenge to make themselves better known to the Canadian public. Pierre Trudeau was considered the more telegenic of the two and was the object of a craze unique in Canadian politics, which journalists dubbed Trudeaumania. Stanfield had a less flamboyant style but was seen as a serious, honest politician.

The Progressive Conservative leader was the first to accept the debate proposal by the CTV and CBC networks on the condition that Prime Minister Trudeau not be accorded any special treatment. The debate had to be on equal terms. Stanfield had much to gain from a televised debate, which would attract a far larger audience than he could otherwise hope to reach.

Liberal strategists, on the other hand, were not so eager for a debate, feeling that the prime minister had the most to lose because he already enjoyed a strong lead in the polls. The May Gallup poll showed that 50 percent of decided voters intended to vote Liberal, 29 percent Conservative, 16 percent NDP and 5 percent for other parties (*Gallup Report* 1968). The negotiations were therefore difficult and dragged on from 30 April to 29 May 1968.

The Liberals faced a dilemma. How could they minimize the negative impact of a refusal to debate, or, if they ultimately felt obliged to agree to a debate, how could they minimize its risks? They therefore insisted on several conditions: the debate had to be carried by all the networks, it had to include the leaders of all five parties with seats in the House of Commons and it had to be bilingual.

CTV originally wanted a debate involving only the leaders of the two largest parties. There was little enthusiasm for handing the NDP a platform, not to mention the Ralliement créditiste. Also, the debate was to be in English only. This proposed format provided Trudeau with an opportunity to have his conditions accepted and thereby resolve his dilemma. He was adamant that all parties be included. This condition served two purposes: it reinforced his image as a democrat and, if his conditions were rejected, he could withdraw without losing face. Also, if smaller parties were allowed to participate, they would serve to divert attention, to dilute the confrontation between Trudeau and Stanfield, and lessen the risks of a poor performance. The prime minister also insisted that the debate be bilingual, because this was part of his vision of Canada and because it would distinguish him from his adversaries; the leaders of the Progressive Conservatives and NDP did not speak French.

The Progressive Conservative and NDP leaders, unable publicly to refuse a bilingual debate, demanded that simultaneous interpretation be available. Liberal strategists did not like this solution because it deprived Trudeau of the advantage of his bilingualism and could even detract from a clear understanding of his message. It seemed absurd to have his English-language statements repeated in French by an interpreter when he could do a better job himself in his own native tongue. Similarly, the Liberal leader could express himself in English far better than any interpreter. The cause of bilingualism was nonetheless deemed worthy of a concession to the Liberals' political opponents and they finally agreed to a bilingual debate with simultaneous interpretation, in which each leader expressed himself in the language of his choice. However, party leaders were provided with a button which they could push to block the interpretation of their own statements in case they wanted to speak for themselves in both languages. Canada therefore innovated in the area of televised debates, not only by holding a bilingual debate but also by including four party leaders, the Liberals having dropped their initial demand for a round table of five leaders.

This left the thorny issue of the allocation of speaking time. For this first debate, it was decided that time would not be allocated equally. The Social Credit leader would be allowed to speak only in the final 40 minutes of the debate, giving the other leaders 80 additional minutes. However, what seemed to be a handicap turned out to be an advantage for Réal Caouette, who caught the interest of the viewers by enlivening the end of what had been a rather dull and tedious debate.

With his fiery style and colourful language, the Créditiste leader breathed new life into the debate (*La Presse* 1968).

The debate was televised from 9:00 PM to 11:00 PM on Sunday, 9 June, two weeks before voting day. To lend weight to the event, the studio was set up in the Confederation Room in the Parliament buildings where federal-provincial conferences were normally held. The co-producers of the telecast were Don Macpherson of CTV and Jim Shaw of CBC. The co-hosts were Pierre Nadeau and Charles Templeton, and the journalists were Jean-Marc Poliquin of Radio-Canada, Ron Collister of CBC and Tom Gould of CTV. Each leader was allowed three minutes for opening remarks. Each then had two minutes to answer a question from a journalist, which each of the other leaders was allowed to rebut for 90 seconds. A small light on each leader's desk, which was also visible on television screens, came on 30 seconds before the end of his allotted time and began to blink when the time had expired. The moderator was responsible for allocating speaking time, taking into account interruptions caused by interpretation, which delayed the next speaker and slowed the pace of the debate.

The 1979 Debate Format

In contrast to the usual scenario, in which the leader of the opposition eagerly calls for a televised debate as soon as an election is called, it was he who was most reluctant in 1979. The Progressive Conservative leader, Joe Clark, had the most to lose under the circumstances because he had everything to prove, while the Liberal leader, Pierre Trudeau, had little to lose and the NDP could only gain from a television appearance by its leader, Ed Broadbent.

The Progressive Conservatives therefore would have preferred no debate at all. They dragged their feet during the negotiations and rejected the proposal of the three television networks for a 90-minute telecast involving the leaders of the Liberal, Progressive Conservative and New Democratic parties. The networks had decided to exclude Fabien Roy, the leader of the Ralliement créditiste, on the grounds that his party was running candidates only in Quebec and therefore had no chance of forming the next government. In addition, the Créditiste leader did not speak English, and no one seemed eager to repeat the 1968 experience of a bilingual debate.

To resolve the bilingualism problem and the unfairness of an English-only debate, Radio-Canada suggested that all the leaders, including Fabien Roy, participate in a round table where they would respond to successive questions in French from two journalists, without any direct exchanges between the leaders. The Liberals rejected this format, thereby depriving the French-speaking audience of a debate and prompting some political commentators to say that the Canadian duality was indeed two solitudes (Décary 1979).

At the outset of the negotiations, the Progressive Conservative strategists demanded that the debate take the form of a direct confrontation between Pierre Trudeau and Joe Clark, thereby excluding both the NDP leader and journalists. They hoped to capitalize on the debating skills of their leader, Joe Clark, who had succeeded in scoring points off the prime minister several times in the House. In the end, though, the Conservatives had to bow to the rules established by the networks because a refusal to participate in the debate would have lent credibility to the contention that their leader, who was already under attack from the media and the other parties, was a coward.

The CTV, CBC and Global networks had demands of their own, particularly regarding a livelier format allowing as many direct exchanges between the leaders as possible, which in turn would maintain audience interest. In the end a compromise was agreed on that, although not a direct confrontation between the two leaders, allowed more latitude than in 1968 when the leaders were confined to answering the journalists' questions and were not allowed to address each other directly. It was decided to hold three direct confrontations in which the leaders would alternately face one another for 30 minutes, in the hope that this would lead to a livelier debate. The parties agreed as well that each leader would make brief introductory remarks for three minutes and concluding remarks lasting no longer than four minutes. The order of speakers was determined by a draw: Joe Clark was to start, followed by Pierre Trudeau and then Ed Broadbent. The reverse order would be followed for the concluding remarks.

David Johnston who, at age 37, had just been appointed President of McGill University, was chosen as moderator for his mediation abilities and political neutrality. To ease the formal structure of the debate, the moderator was given additional responsibility and room to exercise judgement. However, this new format made the journalists' task more difficult because it was more ambiguous. Peter Desbarats, representing the Global network, expressed his confusion: "I'm a bit vague. I don't think we'll have the opportunity to ask anything very penetrating. The restrictions of format bother all of us. It's not really a press conference kind of a thing" (*The Gazette*, 11 May 1979). The journalists, who considered themselves the representatives of the public, felt entitled to ask all the questions they wanted and even to contradict a leader if they believed he was wrong. Normally, journalists adopt a distant or critical stance toward politicians, based on the belief that their credibility will be damaged if they appear as mere sounding boards. However, the party representatives insisted that the journalists be limited to introducing the debate and that it was not their role to trade arguments with the leaders, since the leaders could do that among themselves. This approach was finally adopted, although in practice the moderator allowed several follow-up questions from the journalists and even had to reprimand them when they became too aggressive. Peter Desbarats, for instance, engaged in a lively exchange with the prime minister, who had accused the journalist of having misquoted him as saying that it was treasonous to support Quebec separatists. Desbarats replied, "He did use the word 'treason.' I was there. I heard it." The prime minister also had a run-in with David Halton, who reminded him of a statement in Vancouver accusing the unemployed of being lazy.

The choice of political correspondents from the three networks for the debate (Bruce Phillips from CTV, Peter Desbarats from Global and David Halton from CBC) was accepted by all the participants, but was attacked by the National Action Committee on the Status of Women (NAC), which decried the lack of women on the panel. NAC also criticized the dearth of questions on issues of particular importance to women. To make up for this deficiency, NAC invited the three party leaders to take part in a forum on women's issues, but the leaders declined (Rex 1979).

The 1984 Debate Format
The 1984 election marked a turning point in Canadian politics because the two largest parties had new leaders, each claiming to represent new directions, and because the election resulted in a political realignment that saw the Progressive Conservatives return to power after 20 years of Liberal rule. The Liberals had been returned to power in February 1980, after defeating the Progressive Conservatives in the House with the support of the New Democrats and the abstention of the Créditistes. (There were no televised debates in 1980 because Pierre Trudeau had refused to participate.)

The situation in 1984 was favourable, therefore, for the holding of a debate because there were two new party leaders who were interested in maximizing their media exposure. Further, the election was to take place in the summer and special events were needed to attract the attention of voters, since most would be on vacation during much of the election campaign.

As was to be expected, the Progressive Conservative leader took advantage of his first news conference after the election was called to challenge his opponents to a televised debate. In so doing, he took the wind out of the sails of NDP leader Ed Broadbent, who had been advised to take the initiative (MacDonald 1984, 287). Brian Mulroney was extremely eager to confront John Turner before the television cameras. "Just wait till I get Turner into a television studio," he liked to say. "The voters will be able to see the difference for themselves" (ibid., 290). The Conservatives needed a debate at any cost to strengthen the image of Brian Mulroney, who was seen by the electorate, according to the Conservatives' own polls, as less competent than the Liberal leader (Hay 1984, 13). Having thus taken the initiative, the Conservative strategists had no manoeuvring room and had to accept whatever conditions were laid down by the Liberal strategists.

A debate was also likely to benefit Ed Broadbent, even though there was a strong possibility that one would be held in French, because the leader of a smaller party always benefits from a televised debate in which he is treated as the equal of the other leaders and a credible alternative to the two major parties. Broadbent therefore declared that he was prepared to debate "any time, any place" (*Globe and Mail* 1984).

For the Liberal leader, the risks were greater than the potential benefits. First, his party enjoyed a 10 percent opinion-poll lead over the Conservatives. In addition, John Turner was ill at ease before the cameras after an extended absence from politics. During the leadership race he had seemed nervous and hesitant in answering journalists' questions. His ticks, dry throat and rapid eye movements worried his advisers, who feared he might commit a serious blunder. He was, they thought, too "hot" for television (MacDonald 1984, 287). Finally, his French was still laboured and could place him at a disadvantage in a debate with the Progressive Conservative leader. It would be difficult for Turner to refuse to debate, however, without running the risk of even harsher criticism from the media and his political opponents, who would accuse him of disregard for the voters and a lack of leadership. Turner therefore agreed in principle to a debate to be held on 14 July, but the Liberals were then able to impose their conditions because the other two parties had already agreed to participate.

The Progressive Conservatives suggested five regional debates followed by a national debate. The Liberals rejected this format as too onerous for their leader, who was still the head of government running the daily business of the nation. It was therefore agreed to hold two national debates of two hours each, one in French and the other in English. The risks would therefore be reduced, because a poor performance by the Liberal leader in French could be offset later in the English debate.

The television network executives wanted a debate at the end of the campaign on 26 August, after vacationers had returned home and the

audiences would be larger. The Progressive Conservative and NDP negotiators, Michael Meighen and Gerald Caplan, also wanted the debate
to be held at the end of the election campaign, because the issues would
then be known. The Liberal strategists rejected this argument, however,
and insisted that the debates take place before 26 July, that is, early in
the campaign, so that a possible poor performance by their leader would
have less impact. At least this was the explanation offered by Gerald
Caplan for the choices of 24 July for the debate in French and 25 July
for the debate in English (Rusk 1984).

The parties agreed to return to the tried-and-true 1979 format,
which included three direct confrontations of 30 minutes each in which
each leader debated directly with the other two. Each leader would
also have three minutes to make opening remarks and four minutes
to sum up.

Lots were drawn to determine the speaking order. Brian Mulroney
would open the French debate, followed by Ed Broadbent and John
Turner, with the reverse order for the summation. For the English debate,
Broadbent drew the opening position, followed by Turner and Mulroney.
The order for the one-on-one confrontations was the following:
in French, Turner and Mulroney would face each other first, followed
by Turner and Broadbent, then, finally, Mulroney and Broadbent. In
the English debate, suspense would be maintained until the end, because
the first half-hour featured the Broadbent–Turner debate, the second
round the Broadbent–Mulroney debate, and it was not until the final
round that Mulroney would meet Turner.

The choice of moderators and journalists did not pose any particular problems. For the former, well-known academics were selected to
ensure a serious, objective, credible telecast. David Johnston, President
of McGill University and moderator of the 1979 debate, was chosen
to moderate the English debate. It was agreed that Raymond Landry,
Dean of the Faculty of Civil Law at the University of Ottawa, would
moderate the French debate. The English networks selected David
Halton of the CBC, Bruce Phillips of CTV and Peter Trueman of Global
to ask questions, while the French networks chose Jean Paré, editor of
the newsmagazine l'Actualité, Luc Lavoie of TVA and Louis Martin of
Radio-Canada.

The debates were to be taped at the studios of CJOH in Ottawa using
the same set that had been used in the 1979 debate. For the French
debate, Turner would stand in the middle, flanked by Mulroney on the
right of the television screen and Broadbent on the left. In English,
Broadbent would stand in the middle, with Mulroney on the right and
Turner on the left. The French debate would be televised on 24 July

from 8:00 PM to 10:00 PM, and the English debate, the next day from 9:00 PM to 11:00 PM.

In addition to these negotiations, NAC demanded that a third debate be held on women's issues. Once again, the leaders of the two opposition parties agreed without hesitation, while the prime minister took several days to respond. Turner had an image problem with women voters as a result of the "tactile politics" incident in which he patted the posterior of the female party president, and he would have only aggravated the situation by avoiding questions on women's issues. He agreed, even though he had said earlier that his schedule would enable him to participate in a maximum of two debates.

The debate on women's issues took place in Toronto on 15 August. In contrast to the format for the national debates, this event more closely resembled a parallel press conference than a true debate. There was also a live audience that openly demonstrated its reactions, usually in support of the NDP leader. The debate was chaired by another academic, Dr. Caroline Andrew, Professor of Political Science at the University of Ottawa.

The 1988 Debate Format

Since the *Canada Elections Act* does not cover the organization of debates, the political parties and television network executives renegotiate for each election the format to be used. This process gives rise to a lively debate about the debates, with each party trying to outdo the others in issuing statements and blaming the other side for holding up negotiations over various aspects of the debates: dates, length, number and format.

It is not surprising, therefore, that discussions surrounding the format of the 1988 debates were soon overshadowed by a dispute between the party strategists, trying to take advantage of the media interest to curry favour with the public. These rivalries would not exist if the parties were not convinced that voters are extremely interested in the debates as an instrument of democracy and that there is a political price to be paid for being perceived as reluctant to debate. Martel calls this the "meta-debate" period and considers it to be a psychological war involving candidates and party strategists before the televised debates are held (Martel 1983, 151–65; Bernier 1991, 140–42).

In 1988, neither the leader of the party in power nor the leaders of the opposition parties rejected out-of-hand the idea of holding a televised debate. The precedent set by the 1984 debate in which the leaders all recognized the importance of a debate for the democratic process could not be ignored. In addition, despite the Progressive Conservatives' comfortable lead in the polls, the volatility of the Canadian electorate was such that all parties could reasonably expect to make gains. Most important, there was the question of free trade, which deeply divided the Canadian electorate and was serious enough to warrant a public debate of its own. In an election that had the aura of a referendum and was crucial to Canada's future, a leader's refusal to debate would have had disastrous consequences for his party.

A few weeks before the campaign began, Brian Mulroney had said that he would be willing to participate in a televised debate under two conditions: that there be only two debates and that they take place early in the campaign, on 15 and 16 October. These types of demands seem to be a constant for the leader of the party in power, because Turner had adopted the same position in 1984. In addition, the Conservative leader did not want to repeat the experience of a single-issue debate, like the 1984 debate on women's issues, and he steadfastly refused any suggestion of a debate devoted solely to free trade.

The leaders of the Liberals and NDP continually badgered Mulroney about the number of debates, insisting on the need for a debate on free trade. John Turner denounced the obstinate refusal of the Conservatives as cowardice, and suggested that Mulroney was refusing because he did not have any confidence in the agreement and did not want the Canadian people to gain a better understanding of its implications (Howard and Waddell 1988). The two opposition-party leaders also proposed a debate devoted exclusively to women's issues. Ed Broadbent wanted four debates of 90 minutes each, claiming that the three-hour format suggested by the Conservatives would be too long for Canadians.

Another player in these negotiations, the television networks, had interests that were not necessarily consistent with those of the political parties – namely, profitability. To televise debates, the networks would have to cancel their regular programming, suffering heavy advertising losses, because the debates would take place in prime time. According to Tim Kotcheff, vice-president of programming at CTV in Toronto, a three-hour prime-time debate causes a relative loss of advertising revenues of between $600 000 and $750 000 for a network like CTV. To this must be added a relative loss of $100 000 for each affiliated station that carries the debate (Interview, Tim Kotcheff, 1991). Generally, therefore, networks do not favour a series of debates, and prefer that debates be held toward the end of an election campaign so that they draw as many viewers as possible.

Because of this, in 1988, an alliance was formed between the Progressive Conservatives and the television networks to call for only two debates, one in English and one in French, each lasting three hours.

The second hour would deal with issues of particular importance to women, while the first and third hours would deal with subjects of general interest, including the Free Trade Agreement, which could be discussed at length. The media representatives rejected the NDP argument, claiming that it was an insult to Canadians to say that they were unable to concentrate on public affairs for three hours in a row. On 11 October, the two opposition parties, unwilling to bear the blame for cancelling the debates, reluctantly accepted the media's offer to hold the debates on 24 and 25 October. This was better than no debate at all, in their view.

The 1988 debates had a different format from that of the 1984 debates, which consisted of three successive direct confrontations. Because of the length of the debates, the pace was increased and lengthy sequences involving the same leaders were avoided. The format adopted by the party strategists called for a series of nine exchanges lasting 16 to 17 minutes each and involving two leaders at a time. In each round of approximately one hour, the French debate saw Mulroney facing Broadbent first, Broadbent facing Turner second, and finally Turner facing Mulroney. This order was reversed for the English debate. A change in 1988 allowed the leader who was not involved in a particular segment to leave the set. Each leader had a trailer outside the studio where he could rest and consult with his strategists during these segments. The order in which the three candidates presented their opening and closing remarks was determined by a draw.

"Face à face 88" was televised on 24 October from 8:00 PM to 11:00 PM on the TVA, Radio-Canada and Quatre-Saisons networks, and the next day "Encounter 88" was televised in the same time slot by CBC, CTV and Global.

Two women were asked to host the debates to uphold the principle of gender equality, probably because there was no debate devoted exclusively to women's issues. They were Antonine Maillet, an author, and Rosalie Silberman Abella, who chaired the Ontario Labour Relations Board. In Quebec, there was considerable surprise and a short-lived controversy surrounding the choice of a literary personality to host a political debate. However the striking "deprofessionalization" of the job attracted public attention to the debate. The choice of Maillet was defended on the grounds that the public, which was in a strongly apolitical mood, would identify more easily with someone who was well known but never involved in politics.

The French-speaking panel of journalists included Daniel Lessard (Radio-Canada), Hélène Fouquet (TQS) and Guy Gendron (TVA), while David Halton (CBC), Pamela Wallin (CTV) and Doug Small (Global) made up the English-speaking panel.

An analysis of the distribution of questions shows that the French debate was very orderly and methodical. Each journalist in turn was called upon to ask a question of the leaders. The journalists adhered scrupulously to the principle of equal treatment, asking each leader a total of 10 questions. Broadbent and Turner received one joint question. With one exception, therefore, each direct confrontation saw the two leaders questioned alternately. The debate format was therefore highly impartial, with an equitable distribution of speaking time.

During the English debate, the journalists posed fewer questions – 24 in comparison with 31 during the French debate. They also used a different approach, putting nine questions to two leaders at the same time. The Conservative leader was asked more individual questions than his opponents, seven in comparison with five for Broadbent and three for Turner.

There was also a problem with the management of the debate when David Halton asked a question on defence policy during the segment devoted to women's issues. Broadbent protested that the question was irrelevant to the topic at hand and asked that he be allowed to put off his answer until later so as not to infringe on the time set aside for women's issues. Turner was also interrupted at one point by a technical glitch when the CBC's theme music was played inadvertently.

The leaders were not asked the same questions during the two debates. There was more uniformity in the French debate, where all three leaders were asked the same questions on the main issues. In English, however, the broader range of questions asked reduced the opportunity to compare the leaders' responses. The French-speaking journalists focused more on constitutional and environmental issues, while their English-speaking colleagues asked questions on the GST (Goods and Services Tax), interest rates and native rights, but none on the debt, drugs, pornography, old-age pensions or the location of the space agency, which was a regional issue.

Close to two million Quebec residents and more than four million people in the rest of Canada watched all or some of the televised French and English debates. Table 4.1 shows the composition of the audience, by age group and sex, during the broadcasts of the French and English debates, as measured by the Bureau of Broadcast Measurement (BBM) and Nielsen. Subtracting the figures in the 18- to 49-year-old viewer columns (W18–49 and M18–49) from those of viewers 18 and older (W18+ and M18+) gives the number of viewers aged 50 and over. This calculation reveals that 73 percent of viewers during the French debate and 65 percent of viewers during the English debate were 50 years of age and older (Bernier 1991, 173).

Table 4.1
Viewer ratings during the leaders debates, as measured by BBM and Nielsen

Encounter 88	Viewers (in thousands)						
A.C. Nielsen NTI	V2+	W18+	W18–49	W25–54	M18+	M18–49	M25–54
CTV	1 308	672	285	297	573	263	274
CBC	2 493	1 151	328	266	1 300	625	635
Global	244	111	43	59	104	61	61
Total	4 045	1 934	656	722	11 977	949	970
BBM	V2+	W18+	W18–49	W25–54	M18+	M18–49	M25–54
CTV	1 509	722	249	277	712	359	345
CBC	2 238	1 087	407	475	1 066	468	476
Global	279	119	107	95	144	117	85
Total	4 026	1 928	763	847	1 922	944	906
Face à face 88							
A.C. Nielsen NTI	V2+	W18+	W18–49	W25–54	M18+	M18–49	M25–54
TVA	597	313	153	132	261	175	145
Radio-Canada	1 260	626	269	294	610	304	366
Total	1 857	939	422	426	871	479	511
BBM	V2+	W18+	W18–49	W25–54	M18+	M18–49	M25–54
TVA	778	382	236	233	346	211	212
Radio-Canada	1 387	710	294	292	610	289	270
Total	2 165	1 092	530	525	956	500	482

Source: Bernier 1991, 174.

Note: V = viewers; W = women; M = men. The figures accompanying these letters represent the age groups.

Debates in Ontario

Four televised debates have taken place during Ontario provincial elections. The first was produced in 1971 by the Ontario network of the CBC and CFTO, the Toronto CTV affiliate. The second took place during the 1975 campaign and was produced by CFTO. In 1987 and 1990, the debates were produced by stations of the CBC network, Global and CFTO.

Ontario's first televised election debate, in the fall of 1971, was taped in the studio and telecast several days later. The debate lasted one hour and included two segments: one 45-minute segment in which the three candidates answered questions put to them by journalists Larry Solway and Fraser Kelly, and another 15-minute segment that was less structured. The three candidates (Conservative Premier William Davis, Liberal leader Robert Nixon and NDP leader Stephen Lewis) complained about the format, which they found frustrating because it prevented any direct confrontation between them.

The format provided for a series of questions, alternating among the leaders, on the economy, unemployment, taxes and the funding of separate schools, an issue that prompted bitter attacks on Davis's government by the opposition party leaders.

For the 1975 provincial election, two separate debates were pre-recorded a week apart, one between Premier William Davis and the NDP leader, Stephen Lewis, and the other between the premier and the Liberal leader, Robert Nixon. The second debate degenerated into a stormy confrontation when Nixon accused the premier of misrepresenting and distorting the facts surrounding the budget deficit, government advertising and patronage.

The 1987 debate involved the new premier, David Peterson, NDP leader Bob Rae and Conservative leader Larry Grossman. The debate format was negotiated in a single day by representatives of the parties and the television stations. The debate, which lasted 90 minutes, was broadcast live from the CFTO studios. It was produced by Tim Kotcheff and Ted Stuebing. The moderator was David Johnston of McGill University, and the panel consisted of journalists Tom Clark from CFTO, Robert Fisher from the CBC and Leslie Jones from Global.

The leaders discussed such topics as free trade, education, the economy and bilingualism. According to Maurice Girard (1987) of the Canadian Press, the leaders only repeated what they had been saying throughout the campaign. The debate was televised live to an estimated audience of 1.4 million (Christie 1987). The next day, the *Globe and Mail* and the *Toronto Star* reported that Conservative leader Larry Grossman and NDP leader Bob Rae had attacked Premier Peterson, accusing him of waffling on free trade.

The fourth televised debate in an Ontario provincial election took place on 20 August 1990, in the middle of the summer election campaign, after several days of negotiations between representatives of the candidates and the television networks.

The debate was broadcast live and produced in the CBC's Toronto studios by Bill Kendrick and Blair Harley. The moderator was Peter Desbarats, Dean of Journalism at the University of Western Ontario, and the panelists were Robert Fisher from Global, Tom Clark from CFTO-TV and Lyn Whitham from the CBC. The format was changed from previous debates. At the end of each of the six rounds, the candidates were allowed three minutes to debate among themselves a topic or issue of general interest. The 90-minute debate proved difficult for the premier, who was attacked over the Patti Starr scandal. Starr was the Ontario Liberal party fund-raiser who had been charged with fraud and violation of the Ontario *Election Act*. Although the Liberal government was defeated in the election three weeks later, David Peterson did manage to improve on his poor performance in the 1987 debate. The 1990 debate was broadcast simultaneously throughout the province by Global, CTV and the CBC and nationally by CBC Newsworld.

Debates in Quebec

Quebec's First Televised Debate
After the inception of televised debates in the United States with the Kennedy–Nixon confrontation in 1960, Quebec was the first Canadian province to hold a political debate. It followed a long and difficult negotiating process involving all the issues that arise when a debate is organized: the choice of date, moderator, format, journalists and so forth. The negotiators for the two parties, Marcel Gagnon for the Liberals and Jean Beaulieu for the Union nationale, had only the American precedent to guide them. Theodore H. White's book, *The Making of the President 1960* (1961), became very popular in Quebec in the fall of 1962 as each party pored over it to learn the techniques of televised debating.

The Debate Format
Radio-Canada suggested that Daniel Johnson meet Jean Lesage on 11 November 1962, three days before the vote. However, the leader of the Union nationale understood the risk in holding such an event on the eve of an election and proposed 31 October instead. The Liberals, however, would agree only to 11 November and rejected any other date, while Jean Lesage busily denounced his opponent for cowardice and trying to dodge a debate.

The dispute was finally resolved on 5 November when Johnson agreed to the date proposed by the Liberals, no doubt concluding that it was better to risk a debate than to have no debate at all and bear the blame. Other disagreements remained to be settled, however, including the choice of a moderator and journalists. Daniel Johnson had eliminated Gérard Pelletier and André Laurendeau in advance, casting doubt on their impartiality. Three names were accepted by the parties for the position of moderator: Raymond Charette, Roland Lelièvre and Paul-Émile Tremblay. The final choice was made by Radio-Canada news director Marc Thibeault, who settled on Raymond Charette. With regard to choosing journalists, it was not until the last minute that the parties agreed to name three each: the Liberals chose Gérard Pelletier of *La Presse*, Paul Sauriol of *Le Devoir* and Jean-V. Dufresne of *Maclean's*, while the Union nationale selected Bill Bantey of the Montreal *Gazette* and Clément Brown and Lucien Langlois of *Montréal-Matin*.

The format that had been chosen prevented any direct confrontation between the two leaders. The debate was divided into four segments during which the leaders would discuss the following issues: the nationalization of electricity, the natural gas affair, party platforms and the Liberal government's record. The leaders would each have seven minutes to discuss each topic before answering questions from the journalists. Johnson and Lesage would then be given five minutes each at the end to summarize and make concluding remarks.

A host of technical details was also raised in the discussions. The parties agreed that the debate would last one hour and 45 minutes and would be broadcast between 8:30 PM and 10:15 PM. The order of speakers and questions would be determined in a draw. Finally, to avoid strong contrasts in the television images favouring one candidate over the other, as had happened in the Kennedy–Nixon debate, it was agreed that both leaders would have their television make-up applied by the same person.

To prepare for the debate, the Union nationale leader retained the services of Paul Langlais, vice-president of Télé-Métropole, who was assisted by Paul Gros d'Aillon, Jean Blanchet, René Caron, Paul Levert and Jean-Paul Cardinal. Jean Lesage's technical adviser was Maurice Leroux, a former producer for Radio-Canada, who was assisted by a team of experts that included Guy Gagnon, Gérard Brady, François Nobert, Claude Morin, Jean Morin and Pierre Chaput. Maurice Leroux even travelled to Washington to view the American debate and meet with the people who had advised President Kennedy in 1960.

The Liberal advisers understood the importance of physical and mental preparation for such an event. They had the premier interrupt his campaigning and take a two-day rest in the Windsor Hotel (O'Neill and Benjamin 1978, 39–40). Lesage also planned to borrow the Kennedy technique of talking directly to the viewers rather than to his opponent, and to try to provoke Johnson into losing his temper.

Johnson did not make any special preparations for the debate, relying on his ability to improvise to carry the day. He continued to talk himself hoarse on the campaign trail, like an old-style politician, and on the Saturday before the debate he attended his brother's wedding and made a campaign stop in Sorel. On the day of the debate, he even agreed to attend a public meeting in Saint-Hyacinthe. When he finally reached studio 42 at Radio-Canada, he was tired and tense. He did not allow himself time to review and assimilate the notes prepared for him by his advisers. This lack of preparation proved fatal. When Jean Lesage arrived at the studio, he was greeted by about a hundred Liberal party supporters who applauded him warmly; when Daniel Johnson arrived, he was accompanied only by two advisers.

Despite the moderator's impartiality, the debaters were not allowed equal time. The Union nationale leader spoke for 51 minutes while the Liberal leader spoke for only 40 minutes because the journalists asked nine questions of Johnson and only four of Lesage. This was perhaps indicative of a positive bias in favour of the Liberal leader, whose modern approach appealed to the intellectual class.

The two leaders were different in their demeanour. Lesage was calm and smiling, in full control of his faculties. Johnson, however, appeared nervous, constantly taking his glasses off and putting them in his coat pocket, and referring to his notes before answering a question.

The first televised debate in Quebec aroused considerable interest across Canada and inspired other politicians to demand similar events. Only three days later, Lester Pearson challenged Prime Minister John Diefenbaker to a televised debate, referring explicitly to the Quebec experience (*Le Devoir* 1962). An election campaign was also underway in Newfoundland and James J. Greene, the leader of the opposition, challenged Joey Smallwood to such a debate. Smallwood declined.

The Effect of the Election Act *on Televised Debates in Quebec*

Quebec's new *Election Act* came into effect on 21 December 1984. When an election was called for the fall of 1985, Radio-Canada and TVA attempted to organize a televised debate between Premier Pierre-Marc Johnson and the leader of the Liberal party, Robert Bourassa. However, section 427 of the Quebec *Election Act* required that televised debates held during an election campaign must include "all the leaders of the parties represented in the National Assembly or which have obtained at least 3 percent of the valid votes at the last general election" (*Election Act*, 1984, c. 51, s. 427).

Quebec's director-general of elections, Pierre Côté, therefore declared that:

1. Section 427 of the *Election Act* governs debates between leaders;
2. A serious violation of its provisions could result in the application of sections 501 and 510 concerning corrupt election practices, with all the disastrous consequences this would entail for successful candidates;
3. I therefore believe that, in order to be fair, a leaders debate should include four leaders at the same time under the circumstances prevailing for this election, namely you [Mr. Bourassa], Mr. Johnson, Mr. Léveillé and Mr. Monière, in keeping with fair principles yet to be established. (Côté 1985)

In response to a legal opinion requested by the director-general of elections during the campaign, the legal firm of Tremblay, Bertrand, Morisset, Bois and Migneault of Sainte-Foy stated:

> Any debate carried on radio or television is covered by the principle set forth in section 405, namely that the expenses incurred shall be considered election campaign expenses, unless the debate is held under section 427, which constitutes the sole exception in this regard.
>
> However, there is nothing in the *Election Act* to prevent two party leaders from agreeing to share the cost of a radio or television broadcast, during which they may hold a debate or do whatever else they see fit. This then would be considered an election expense to be handled in accordance with Title VIII, Chapter III, including especially being accounted for as such by both participants and prorated to the time actually used. (Tremblay et al. 1985, 8 and 11)

However, the presentation of televised debates by the two major parties using their own funds creates an ethical dilemma for anyone asked to act as moderator or panelist, as well as a problem of fairness toward the candidates who are excluded.

The two leading candidates eventually refused the various debate formats proposed by the television networks for different and strategic reasons. Robert Bourassa demanded a one-hour debate with no marginal candidates, while Pierre-Marc Johnson insisted that the debate comply with the guidelines laid down by the director-general of elections. The Quebec press was infuriated and questioned whether there had been a violation of the public's right to know.

According to editorialist Lysiane Gagnon, "Issues related to the question of fair play are too important to be left in the hands of a man for whom the letter of the law is more important than common sense and the free flow of information" (1985). A few years later, the president of the Quebec Federation of Professional Journalists (FPJQ) asked the Commission parlementaire des institutions to "amend the Quebec *Election Act* to remove televised debates from its scope, since they have become an essential part of election campaigns." According to him, "the director general of elections has interpreted section 427 of the *Election Act* in such a way that many see it as an obstacle to freedom of the press" (Barnabé 1988). The FPJQ asked that sections 407 and 427 of the *Election Act* be amended so that debates between party leaders would not be considered an election expense and would be excluded from section 427.

On 20 September 1988, the director-general of elections told the

Commission: "I agree totally that the Act should be amended. I would not want to repeat the experience we had in 1985." He also added: "New CRTC regulations suggest that all political parties should have an opportunity to participate in televised debates, but not necessarily in the same debate ... I also like the fact that it is the CRTC that is moving in this direction rather than having it in our Act" (Quebec, National Assembly 1988). The Quebec *Election Act* was accordingly amended on 22 March 1989 to exclude from its provisions debates between party leaders (1989, c. 1, s. 88).

When Radio-Canada or the CBC televises debates during a federal election campaign, they are considered public affairs programming and not free time provided to political parties. It would be interesting to examine the possibility of institutionalizing debates through an agency such as the Canadian Radio-television and Telecommunications Commission (CRTC). In a directive issued on 2 September 1988, the CRTC announced: "In the case of the so-called 'debates,' it may not be practical to include all rival parties or candidates in one program. However, if this type of broadcast takes place, all parties and candidates should be accommodated, even if doing so requires that more than one program be broadcast" (CRTC 1988, 13).

Debates in Other Provinces

Televised debates are more popular in Atlantic Canada than in the West. In Newfoundland, the two most recent provincial election debates were held in 1985 and 1989.

The debate on 27 March 1985 lasted 90 minutes and was produced by the CBC. It employed a parallel news conference format, although one section allowed a 20-minute direct confrontation between the candidates. The moderator was the well-known businessperson Bill Wells and the panelists were journalists Rick Seaward and Bill Gillespie from the CBC and Greg Stamp. The candidates were Conservative Premier Brian Peckford, NDP leader Peter Fenwick, and Liberal leader Leo Barry. In a post-mortem on the election and the debate, the organizers and some Newfoundland journalists concluded that it would have been preferable if the final speeches had been two minutes long instead of three and if the direct confrontation between the leaders had lasted only 15 minutes.

The 1989 debate was produced by NTV and the format was similar to that used for the federal election debate held in the fall of 1988. The moderator was an academic, Douglas House, and two of the three panelists were journalists from NTV. According to some, the CBC had originally offered to organize and televise a debate close to election day, but the candidates' representatives declined the offer, giving NTV an opportunity to jump in and organize the 1989 event. The candidates involved were Liberal leader Clyde Wells, Conservative leader Tom Rideout and NDP leader Peter Fenwick. During the debate itself, the candidates broke what few rules there were by interrupting one another during heated exchanges.

In Nova Scotia, there were televised debates in the 1981, 1984 and 1988 provincial election campaigns. Each debate lasted 90 minutes and was produced by the Atlantic Television System (ATV). The three debates also had the same format: a moderator and three journalists asked questions of the candidates, and the candidates were also given brief periods in which to rebut the answers of their opponents. Further, the candidates were allowed to make opening and closing statements. For the debate of 3 October 1981, Bruce Graham of ATV acted as moderator and the panelists were journalists Rick Grant, Blain Henshaw and Ian Morrison, all of ATV. For the November 1984 debate, Bruce Graham was again moderator, while journalists Robert Rankin (ATV), Steve Murphy (CJCH Radio) and Harold Shea (*Halifax Herald*) were panelists. The third debate, held on 3 September 1988, was moderated by David Wright of ATV, while Heather Proudfoot and Steve Murphy of ATV, and Allan Jeffers of the *Halifax Herald* constituted the panel. The producer for the last two debates was Ian Morrison, a panelist for the 1981 debate. The 1988 debate was described by some as a parallel news conference at which the journalists' questions and the candidates' answers failed to generate much heat. The participants in the debate in the fall of 1988 were the Conservative premier, John Buchanan, New Democrat Alexa McDonough and Liberal Vince MacLean.

In New Brunswick, televised leaders debates were held in 1987 and 1991. The election debate in the fall of 1987 was organized and produced by the CBC. With only a few exceptions, the format was similar to that of the 1988 federal election debate and there were no direct confrontations between the candidates. Terry Séguin of the CBC moderated the debate, and journalists André Vignault and Lynda Boyle of the CBC were panelists. The participants were the incumbent premier, Richard Hatfield, Liberal leader Frank McKenna and New Democrat George Little. (The 1991 debate took place after this study was completed.)

In British Columbia, the opposition and the media made numerous unsuccessful attempts to organize a leaders debate. Premier Bill Bennett agreed during the 1983 campaign to participate in a televised debate with the leaders of the opposition parties, but his representatives wanted to confine the debate to such a limited number of topics that the opposition parties felt compelled to decline the offer. As soon as the election writs were issued in 1986, the CBC wrote to Bill Vander Zalm inviting him to participate in a televised debate with the other party leaders. At the same time, NDP leader Bob Skelly challenged Vander Zalm to debate the issues on television. Premier Vander Zalm was apparently prepared to participate with the other party leaders in a public discussion of the issues, but refused to do so within the framework of a debate. The project was therefore dropped.

British Columbia voters were finally able to view their first televised provincial leaders debate in 1991. The debate in British Columbia, on 8 October, was important because the organizers – the CBC – were persuaded to include Liberal leader Gordon Wilson, though his party was not considered a significant competitor in the election. In the event, he won press and public support in the debate against the incumbent Social Credit premier, Rita Johnston, and the NDP leader, Mike Harcourt, and, as a direct consequence, was able to increase the Liberal vote substantially.

There has been no recent leaders debate in Alberta, though one was held there in the 1970s; Saskatchewan, like British Columbia, held its first in 1991. In Manitoba, a debate was held on 30 August 1990 between Conservative premier Gary Filmon, Liberal leader Sharon Carstairs and NDP leader Gary Doer. The proceedings were organized and broadcast simultaneously by the CBC, CKY, CKND and MTN. The parallel news conference format provided for opening and closing statements by the three leaders as well as direct confrontations between two leaders at a time, all under the guidance of a moderator but without a panel of journalists. The debate lasted one hour. During the direct confrontations, the candidates discussed Manitoba's future, the economy and health insurance.

CONCLUSION AND RECOMMENDATIONS

A review of various debate formats used in Canada shows that, after some experimentation, a mix of the American and French models seems to have been adopted, that is, a combination of parallel news conference and direct confrontation. Journalists play an active role, introducing topics for discussion, but the candidates also have an opportunity for direct exchanges with one another and these can sometimes be quite heated.

The Canadian format is also distinguished from the French, Australian and American models by the presence of a third participant, which makes the debate a three-sided one. There was even a four-way debate in 1968. Canada is also the only country among those considered in this study where debates are held in two languages.

The *Canada Elections Act* (1988) does not explicitly mention televised debates. Section 317, which governs political broadcasts, deals with the allocation of paid and free time among the registered parties. All parties have access to air time, but not on an equal footing. Under section 307, all broadcasters are required to make available 6.5 hours of prime time for purchase by registered parties. The distribution of this time is determined by the percentage of seats each registered party holds in the House of Commons, the percentage of votes it obtained in the previous election, and the number of candidates it fielded in the previous election (CRTC 1988, 10; *Canada Elections Act*, s. 310). The same rules apply to the distribution of free time, which must be equal to or greater than that made available in the previous general election. In 1988, the total amount of free air time that radio and television networks were required to make available to registered parties was 6 hours of radio and 11.5 hours of television. The distribution of free time by network and type of electronic medium is presented in table 4.2. The formula for the allocation of free time is similar to that for allocating paid time under the *Canada Elections Act*. Both provide little time for smaller parties.

These regulations, however, do not apply to debates. The resulting legal void favours the prime minister, who in the end decides whether a debate will be held. Refusals to participate in televised debates have always come from incumbent prime ministers and rarely from opposition leaders. As far as we know, Pierre Trudeau is the only opposition leader who ever refused to debate. He did this in 1980 for strategic reasons. Under our parliamentary system, the prime minister has

Table 4.2
Free air time

Radio	
CBC AM English	2 hours
CBC AM French	2 hours
Radiomutuel	1 hour
Télémédia	1 hour
Television	
CBC English	3 hours 30 minutes
CBC French	3 hours 30 minutes
CTV	3 hours 30 minutes
TVA	1 hour

Source: Canada, Elections Canada (1988, 9).

Note: In addition to the time made available for purchase, the radio and television networks listed provided the amounts of free air time shown above.

considerable control over the election process because he or she can also decide the date of the election.

The absence of any legislation also favours the larger parties because the networks invite only the leaders of parties with seats in the House, thereby eliminating the smaller parties. Being excluded from this national forum serves to marginalize the small parties by undermining their credibility. However, this imbalance in the democratic process seems unavoidable because voters would probably lose interest if all parties were represented in debates at the same time. Also, the larger parties would no doubt refuse to participate in an event that placed them on the same footing as smaller parties representing only a fraction of the population. In the United States, it is for this reason that, in 1975, Congress suspended section 315 of the *Communications Act* requiring "equal time access" for presidential campaigns to eliminate claims of marginal candidates and clear the way for two-way debates. However, this measure provoked the anger of both the smaller parties and the media.

In Canada, smaller parties have challenged their treatment by broadcasters in the courts, on seven different occasions since 1981, but the courts have always refused to force broadcasters to give them more time. In 1988, the Green Party of Ontario sought an injunction to block the leaders debate. The party leader, Seymour Trieger, unsuccessfully sought compensation because he was excluded from the debate and prevented from putting the party's ecological views before the public. Trieger based his case on the *Canadian Charter of Rights and Freedoms* guarantee of freedom of expression and association. However, Mr. Justice Archie Campbell of the Supreme Court of Ontario ruled that the application for an injunction was unjustified because it conflicted with two other rights, namely, the right of the other leaders to debate with whomever they wished and the right of a free press to publish whatever it wanted: "The right to free speech does not necessarily mean the right to make someone else listen or the right to have someone else carry that message to the public" (Sheppard 1988). According to the decision, the courts should not interfere in the operation of the media, although the issue did raise the question of the public interest.

The lawyer for CTV pointed out that the media could not force the leaders of the other parties to participate in a debate with the leader of the Green party. Thus, the legal void made it impossible for the courts to take a firm stand where there were conflicting rights.

In Quebec, the National Assembly amended the *Election Act* in 1989 to permit televised debates solely between the leaders of the two largest parties. Previously, the Act required broadcasters to invite the leaders of all parties that held seats or had received at least 3 percent of the vote in the last general election. As a result, the director-general of elections required the television networks in 1985 to invite the leaders of the Union nationale and the Parti indépendantiste along with the leaders of the Liberal party and the Parti québécois. Since the strategists for the latter two parties rejected such a format, plans for a televised debate were dropped. There is therefore an obvious trend, at least in North America, to restrict the political rights of the smaller parties. All parties are not equal before the media, which hampers the emergence of new political forces.

The Institutionalization of Debates

As long as party leaders are allowed to decide for themselves whether or not they participate in a televised debate, they will be able to make the rules work to their political advantage and not necessarily in favour of a better-informed public. It is paradoxical that in a democratic society the refusal of a single individual to debate can deprive all voters of information they need to decide how to vote. It is astounding to think that the law of the land has nothing at all to say about televised debates, which have profoundly changed election campaigns but are nevertheless left entirely to the discretion of the parties and the television networks. Should voters' interests be subordinated to those of television networks and political parties?

To create an atmosphere of openness and improve the flow of information that voters need to make an informed choice, we believe that televised debates should be institutionalized and should be held at every election. Public opinion also supports televised debates and, compared with other sources, debates provide the greatest amount of useful information. This is shown by polls in several countries, including France, the Netherlands and the United States. A Gallup poll taken in the United States in 1980 showed that 70 percent of respondents were in favour of debates (Swerdlow 1984, 13; Riley and Hollihan 1981).

We believe the democratic process would be better served by a discussion of political issues, by the clash of ideas and the people embodying them than by no debate at all. The conflicting interests of the parties and the voters must be resolved: the former wanting above all to win the election and therefore control the campaign as much as possible, while the latter need comparative information for making an informed choice. Since these two interests cannot always be reconciled, a mechanism should be established to ensure that the public interest takes precedence over the interests of the political parties.

What can be done to ensure that at each election the public interest takes priority over the strategic interests of the parties or the economic interests of the television networks? How can party leaders be forced to submit to a debate to allow voters an opportunity to compare them?

The problems experienced in Quebec with that province's *Election Act* and televised debates should not obscure the fact that elections are held for the benefit of voters and that party interests should be subordinated to the public interest. It is therefore with the public interest in mind that we recommend to the Commission that it include leaders debates in the sections of the *Broadcasting Act* dealing with election campaigns, which fall under the jurisdiction of the Canadian Radio-television and Telecommunications Commission. To reinforce the soundness of such a section in the *Broadcasting Act*, it should be accompanied by a section in the *Canada Elections Act* requiring the electronic media to make available a certain amount of additional time for such debates and link the allotment of air time to the parties for their political messages to their participation in the leaders debates. The broadcasting arbitrator could monitor the parties to ensure that they comply with this new provision of the *Canada Elections Act* concerning debates.

Making debates compulsory would certainly infringe on the freedom of the party leaders and the media, but such debates permit an essential confrontation of political ideas and social visions. Legal writers have commented explicitly on this point: "The absence of spending limits gives an unfair advantage to those who have access to large campaign funds. Therefore, it can be argued that the facilitating of more candidates or parties to be heard effectively is more protective of the rights of free expression than giving a free rein to those with access to large amounts of money" (Beckton 1982, 114).

Finally, the vast majority of people who were interviewed during our research for this study favoured compulsory debates.

Who Should Organize Televised Debates?

In other countries, such as the United States and the Netherlands, debates are arranged by outside organizations such as the League of Women Voters Education Fund, the Commission on Presidential Debates and the television viewer associations in the Netherlands. In Canada, the organization of debates has historically been left to the parties and the media, which have set the rules.

The presence of an outside observer at debate negotiations would make the process public, thereby moderating the demands of the parties and facilitating an agreement. Since the actual holding of the debate would no longer be the subject of these negotiations, they could focus

on the technical aspects of the proceedings. For example: Will the
leaders be allowed to address each other directly? Should journalists
be involved? Who will ask the questions? Who will be the moderator?
Should there be a live studio audience? What camera shots will
be allowed?

There would no longer be difficult negotiations about the organization of debates, and these discussions would no longer be election
issues, as in the past. The parties would adopt a less acrimonious attitude because of the moderating effect of an outside observer. This
observer could be a representative of a legally recognized university
or professional association.

Who Should Participate?

If a clause requiring televised debates were written into the *Broadcasting
Act*, all parties running candidates in the election would presumably
have access to a portion of the air time. In this case, would all parties
then be treated equally?

In countries where debates are held, the equality principle usually
applies only to parties with seats in Parliament. This limits the number
of participants in the debate. However, the principle of equality is reinforced by the principle of equity, which gives parties that do not have
seats an opportunity to air their views in a similar framework. This
implies the recognition of two classes of parties and therefore the holding
of two types of debates because it is impossible, for practical reasons,
to have representatives from all parties on the set at the same time.

The approach that is eventually chosen needs to be as fair as possible
to everyone. Therefore, instead of simply excluding the smaller parties
from the debates, which tends to marginalize and discredit them, a
round table could be organized to include all parties fielding candidates in at least 50 ridings, as is done in the Netherlands. Another solution would be to add to the free air time made available to each party
an additional amount equivalent to the ratio of free time received by the
large parties for the televised debates. The ultimate aim of these measures
would be to enable the public to become better acquainted with all
options available in the political market-place.

How Many Debates Should There Be?

In light of the official languages policy, there would have to be at least
two televised debates for parties with seats in the House of Commons.
The 1968 experiment (a bilingual debate with simultaneous interpretation) was not very successful because the delay caused by
interpretation slowed the pace of the debate and, in practical terms,

prevented direct exchanges between the leaders. Someone who does not have an excellent command of French is obviously disadvantaged in a French debate, but this is the price of a bilingual country whose aspiring leaders should be able to address both linguistic communities.

This language requirement would not apply to the round table for the smaller parties, since a parallel news conference format lends itself well to simultaneous interpretation. In addition, this debate should take place after the debates involving the larger parties, to allow the smaller parties to react to the issues that were discussed and to the policies that were proposed.

In our view, single-issue debates should be discarded because a debate focused on one question or issue is likely to be less interesting and to attract a smaller audience than an open debate in which the leaders can set their own priorities. However, in some cases, when a particular issue dominates public interest even before the writs are issued, as with free trade in September 1988, the force of circumstances can make a single-issue debate essential. For example, in the run-up to the last federal election, Canadians believed that free trade should be the central issue in the election campaign (*Decima Quarterly* 1988, 21, table 7). However, the Nielsen surveys showed that the French debate in 1984 was seen by 956 000 on Radio-Canada and 617 000 on TVA, while the debate on women's issues was seen by only 553 000 on Radio-Canada and 459 000 on TVA. This suggests that the public is less interested in single-issue debates than in more wide-ranging debates. The potential audience for the French debates was three million.

The single-issue format would also vastly increase the number of debates needed, since there are always several major issues in an election, and all these debates would need to be held in both English and French. If debates became too frequent, however, they would no longer be seen as special events and the audience would likely lose interest.

How Long Should the Debates Last?

In most countries that we studied, debates last less than two hours (90 minutes). The 1988 debates in Canada lasting three hours are the exception, although some debates in Germany and Denmark have lasted three hours or more.

The length of the debates depends on the number held during the election campaign. In Canada, for linguistic reasons, no more than four debates would be appropriate, two in each language, because voters would probably not tune in to any more than that. We did not find any cases in which there were more than four televised debates. A two-hour format seems the most reasonable, if the intent is to maintain viewer interest.

When Should the Debates Take Place?

The timing of the debates has been an important issue in past negotiations. In most of the cases we studied – France, Germany, Denmark and the Netherlands – the debates take place at the end of the election campaign, for the following reasons:

1. At the end of an election campaign all the issues are known, and the debate provides as much information as possible because none of the parties is still attempting, for strategic reasons, to hold back some of its positions or intentions. A debate is likely to be more substantive at the end of a campaign than at the beginning because party leaders can no longer put off answers to certain questions, such as the cost of their campaign promises.
2. Public interest in a campaign reaches its height toward the end, thereby maximizing the size of the audience for the debate.
3. If a debate is held close to voting day, people are able to recall more of what they saw and heard; it helps them make an informed decision.
4. If a debate takes place at the very end of the campaign, public perceptions of the parties and leaders are less likely to be affected by post-debate comments by journalists about who won and lost. Post-debate analysis can have considerable influence on certain classes of voters. A debate held at the end of the campaign limits the impact of media analysis and also prevents the parties from exploiting the performances of the leaders, negatively or positively, in their advertising and public comments.

Party leaders and strategists are not always willing to have the debate at the end of the campaign, especially if they are convinced that they have more to lose than to gain from a debate. This reluctance is motivated by a fear of performing poorly in the debate, and the resulting negative impact this would have on the vote. Parties are reluctant to have the success or failure of an entire campaign determined by their performance in a single television program, where random events can play an enormous role. They also feel that a leader who is unjustly accused of something may not have enough time to set the record straight. If a debate is held early in the campaign, parties have time to correct any blunders leaders may make and to try to induce the electorate to forget any negative impressions that the debate may have left.

It is therefore in the parties' interest to hold the debate early in a campaign, but in the voters' interest to schedule the debate at the end of a campaign.

The ideal system would therefore be to have one debate at the beginning of the campaign, to grab the attention of the electorate, and then another at the end, to summarize the parties' positions. The second debate could take place one week before voting day.

What Role Should Journalists Play?

The presence of journalists influences the dynamics of a debate because the journalists determine, through their questions, the topics for discussion and bring forward information that influences the judgement of voters. Do the topics and questions selected by journalists reflect what the public wants to know? Is their perception of the major issues relevant?

The journalists' professional duty is to inform the public, and for this reason they are considered an appropriate choice to moderate the debates. However, they have their own strategic interests because their participation in such an event raises their profile and credibility. Journalists have a delicate and uncomfortable role to play, because they have to strike a proper balance between being too aggressive and too compliant.

Having examined various formats, we believe that the presence of journalists is desirable because they tend to ensure a more substantive debate by forcing the leaders to address a wider variety of issues than they would if left to debate among themselves. The presence of journalists can pose a problem, however, if there are differences between the public's perception of the main issues and the journalists' perception.

Even though they claim to represent public opinion, journalists sometimes become caught up in their personal preoccupations. They may be tempted to ask questions that will make headlines the following day (Jamieson and Birdsell 1988, 168). Our research into Canadian debates (Monière 1992) convinces us that journalists have occasionally emphasized peripheral issues relating to election tactics or power politics, such as the place of the NDP in the party system or the positions the leaders would adopt if a minority government were returned, neglecting such major issues as unemployment, housing, labour relations and so forth. Further, the concerns of French-speaking and English-speaking journalists differ; the latter, for instance, usually pay little attention to constitutional matters, bilingualism or federal-provincial relations.

Finally, we must consider the similarity of the questions put to the leaders in a debate. Here, too, important differences emerged in the debates we studied, since the leaders were not all required to answer the same questions. For example, in the 1984 debates in both English and French, the Progressive Conservative leader was not asked to answer questions on women's issues, which were addressed exclusively to the Liberal and NDP leaders. In other debates, the leaders were not all asked the same number of questions. This lack of uniformity obviously makes it more difficult for voters to compare positions during a debate.

These professional biases can be corrected through greater public participation in developing questions for the leaders. For example, a poll could be taken before the debates to determine the nature and order of questions to be asked, with journalists serving to relay the public's major concerns. The television networks could ask their viewers two days before the debates to prepare questions and submit them by telephone. The journalists would collate all this information and formulate the questions they would ask. This operation would serve two purposes: it would draw the public's attention to the debates through the added publicity and then involve the public more directly in the debates.

Regardless of the format used or the performances of the various participants in televised debates, the public always gains from a debate because debates provide a unique opportunity for effective comparisons of political positions and policies. It would be illogical to deprive voters of an event that improves the quality of the political information they need to make an informed choice. A joint poll conducted in 1983 by ABC and Harvard University revealed that respondents agreed on the value of presidential debates (Kraus 1988, 148). If and when the *Canada Elections Act* is reformed, voters' interests must be put first.

ABBREVIATIONS

c., ch.	chapter
Pub. L.	Public Law
R.S.C.	Revised Statutes of Canada
R.S.O.	Revised Statutes of Ontario
S.Q.	Statutes of Quebec
s(s).	section(s)
Stat.	United States Statutes at Large

INTERVIEWS

All interviews took place in 1991.

Balle, Francis	France
Chalmers, Jane (telephone)	Manitoba
Crocker, Ron	Toronto
Deom, Jeff (telephone)	Nova Scotia

Field, Terry (telephone)	Alberta
Furlong, John (telephone)	Newfoundland
Héroux, Michel	Montreal
Jacomet, Béatrice	France
Kendrick, Bill	Toronto
Kotcheff, Tim	Toronto
Kraus, Sidney (telephone)	United States
Lueg, H.D.	Bonn, Germany
Martel, Myles	United States
Morrison, Ian (telephone)	Nova Scotia
Pederson, Marc (telephone)	New Brunswick
Pietrus, Mike (telephone)	Saskatchewan
Rushton, Doug (telephone)	British Columbia
Schrott, Peter	Berlin
Stuebing, Ted	Toronto
van Praag, Philip	Netherlands

BIBLIOGRAPHY

This study was completed in August 1991 (with some minor additions in November 1991).

In this study, quoted material that originated in French has been translated into English.

Adams, Michael, and Jordan A. Levitin. 1988. "Media Bias as Viewed by the Canadian Public." In *Canadian Legislatures, 1987–1988*, ed. Robert J. Fleming. Ottawa: Ampersand Communications Services.

Allen, Gene, and Richard Mackie. 1990. "Peterson Faces Attack over Starr in Leaders' Debate." *Globe and Mail*, 21 August.

Baker, K.L., H. Norpoth and K. Schoenbach. 1981. "Die Fernsehdebatten der Spitzenkandidaten vor den Bundestagswahlen 1972 und 1976." *Publizistik* 26:530–44.

Barnabé, Réal. 1988. *Changer la loi pour permettre la tenue de débats télévisés entre les chefs*. Fédération professionnelle des journalistes du Québec, 18 August.

Beckton, Clare. 1982. "Freedom of Expression." In *The Canadian Charter of Rights and Freedoms*, ed. G.-A. Beaudoin and W.S. Tarnopolski. Toronto: Carswell.

Bernier, Robert. 1991. *Gérer la victoire? Organisation, communication, stratégie.* Montreal: Gaëtan Morin.

Canada, *Broadcasting Act*, R.S.C. 1985, c. B-9.

———. *Canada Elections Act*, R.S.C. 1985, c. E-2, ss. 307, 310, 317.

Canada. Elections Canada. 1988. *Broadcast Guidelines*. Ottawa.

Canadian Press. 1990. "L'opposition attaque David Peterson." *Le Droit*, 21 August.

Canadian Radio-television and Telecommunications Commission (CRTC). 1988. "A Policy with Respect to Election Campaign Broadcasting." Public Notice CRTC 1988–142. Ottawa: CRTC.

Cazeneuve, Jean. 1974. *L'homme téléspectateur*. Paris: Denoel.

Champagne, Patrick. 1990. *Faire l'opinion*. Paris: Éditions de Minuit.

Christie, Alan. 1987. "Peterson Called 'Indecisive' over Free Trade with U.S." *Toronto Star*, 18 August.

Conseil de presse du Québec. 1988. *Modifications proposées par le Conseil de presse du Québec à la Loi électorale québécoise*. 1988-08-02.

Côté, Pierre F., Directeur général des élections du Québec. 1985. Letter to Robert Bourassa, leader of the Quebec Liberal party, "The leaders' debate: the directeur général des élections answers a written question from the leader of the Liberal party of Quebec." 20 November.

De Bock, Harold. 1978. "The Influence of the Den Uyl–Wiegel Television Debate on Party Policy and Party Leadership Evaluation." Paper presented at the Amsterdam Symposium on Mass Communication, 6–9 November.

Décary, Robert. 1979. "Un pays, deux débats." *Le Devoir*, 30 April.

Decima Quarterly Report (Executive Summary). 1988. "Specific Issues." 9:19–33.

Le Devoir. 1962. "Pearson veut un débat télévisé avec Dief." 15 November.

Fisher, Douglas. 1971. "3 Capable Men in TV Debate." *Toronto Telegram*, 5 October.

Fletcher, Frederick J. 1981. "Playing the Game: The Mass Media and the 1979 Campaign." In *Canada at the Polls: 1979 and 1980*, ed. Howard Penniman. Washington, DC: American Enterprise Institute for Public Policy Research.

———. 1988. "The Media and the 1984 Landslide." In *Canada at the Polls, 1984: A Study of the Federal General Elections*, ed. Howard Penniman. Washington, DC: American Enterprise Institute for Public Policy Research.

France. *Loi du 30 septembre 1986. Journal officiel,* 1 Octobre 1986, p. 11755.

France. 1988. *Journal officiel,* 23 March.

Frizzell, Alan, Jon H. Pammett and Anthony Westell. 1989. *The Canadian General Election of 1988.* Ottawa: Carleton University Press.

Gagnon, Lysiane. 1985. "Le suspense continue." *La Presse,* 16 November.

Gallup Report. 1968. "Liberal Support Highest Since Election of 1963." 25 May.

————. 1988. "Conservatives Regain Lead, Tory Majority Foreseen." 19 November.

Girard, Maurice. 1987. "Débat à l'image de la campagne: terne et poli." *Le Droit,* 18 August.

Globe and Mail. 1984. "Liberals Dictate Rules for TV Debate: NDP." 17 July.

————. 1987. "Grossman Attacks Peterson on Trade Stand in Debate." 21 August.

Hall, Chris. 1990. "Garbage Disposal, Pay Equity Liven Up TV Election Debate." *Ottawa Citizen,* 21 August.

Hay, John. 1984. "The Battle of the Image Men." *Maclean's* (6 August): 10–13.

Hellweg, S.A., and S.L. Philips. 1981. "A Verbal and Visual Analysis of the 1980 Houston Republican Presidential Primary Debates." *Southern Speech Communication Journal* 47 (autumn): 25–38.

Howard, Ross, and Christopher Waddell. 1988. "Mulroney Begins Re-election Quest Citing Leadership." *Globe and Mail,* 3 October.

Jamieson, K.S., and D.S. Birdsell. 1988. *Presidential Debates.* New York: Oxford University Press.

Katz, E., and J. Feldman. 1962. "The Debates in the Light of Research: A Survey of Survey." In *The Great Debates: Kennedy versus Nixon 1960,* ed. S. Kraus. Bloomington: Indiana University Press.

Kennedy, Mark. 1987. "Peterson on Defensive in Debate." *Ottawa Citizen,* 18 August.

Kraus, Sidney. 1988. *Televised Presidential Debates and Public Policy.* Hillsdale: Lawrence Erlbaum Associates.

Laurendeau, André. 1962. "Chronique d'une campagne." *Le Devoir,* 7 November.

Lesage, Gilles. 1985. "Le faux débat sur le débat." *Le Devoir,* 9 November.

Lloyd, C.J. 1990. "The 1990 Media Campaign." In *The Greening of Australian Politics,* ed. C. Bean, I. McAllister and J. Warhurst. Melbourne: Longman Cheshire.

MacDonald, L. Ian. 1984. *Mulroney: The Making of the Prime Minister.* Toronto: McClelland and Stewart.

Martel, Myles. 1983. *Political Campaign Debates, Images, Strategies and Tactics.* New York: Longman.

Maychak, Matt. 1990. "Gloves Off as Party Leaders Slug It Out in TV Debate." *Toronto Star*, 21 August.

Metzner, Alfred. 1984. *Media Perspektiven.* Frankfurt.

Miller, A., and M. Mackuen. 1979. "Learning about Candidates: The 1976 Presidential Debates." *Public Opinion Quarterly* (Autumn): 326–46.

Monière, Denis. 1992. *Le combat des chefs: analyse des débats télévisés au Canada.* Montreal: Éditions Québec-Amérique.

Nel, N. 1990. *Le débat télévisé.* Paris: A. Colin.

Okrent, Christine. 1988. *Le duel.* Paris: Hachette.

O'Neill, Pierre, and Jacques Benjamin. 1978. *Les mandarins du pouvoir.* Montreal: Éditions Québec-Amérique.

Ontario. *Election Act*, R.S.O. 1980, c. 142.

La Presse. 1968. "15 millions de spectateurs témoins d'un débat sans éclat." 10 June.

Quebec. *Election Act*, S.Q. 1984, c. 51, s. 427.

———. *Election Act*, S.Q. 1989, c. 1, s. 88.

Quebec. Assemblée nationale. 1988. *Journal des Débats*, Commission permanente des institutions, 20 September. No. 25.

Quebec. Commission des droits de la personne, Commission parlementaire des institutions sur la révision de la Loi électorale. 1988. *Mémoire de la Commission des droits de la personne.* Québec.

Ranney, A. 1979. *The Past and the Future of Presidential Debates.* Washington, DC: American Enterprise Institute for Public Policy Research.

Rex, Kathleen. 1979. "CBC Ignored Women's Issues in TV Debate, NAC Says." *Globe and Mail*, 16 May.

Riley, Patricia, and Thomas A. Hollihan. 1981. "The 1980 Presidential Debates: A Content Analysis of the Issues and Arguments." *Speaker and Gavel* 18 (Winter): 48–49.

Rusk, James. 1984. "Party Leaders Agree to Twin TV Debates." *Globe and Mail*, 18 July.

Salent, R. 1979. "The Good but Not Great Non-Debates." In *The Great Debates: Carter versus Ford 1976*, ed. S. Kraus. Bloomington: Indiana University Press.

Schrott, Peter. 1990. "Electoral Consequences of 'Winning' Televised Campaign Debates." *Public Policy Quarterly* 54:567–85.

Sears, D.O., and S.H. Chaffee. 1979. "Uses and Effects of the 1976 Debate." In *The Great Debates: Carter versus Ford 1976*, ed. S. Kraus. Bloomington: Indiana University Press.

Sheppard, Robert. 1988. "Greens' Bid to Crash Debates Rejected as Rights Interference." *Globe and Mail*, 22 October.

Siune, Karen. 1991. "Campaign Communication in Scandinavia." In *Media, Elections and Democracy*, ed. Frederick J. Fletcher. Vol. 19 of the research studies of the Royal Commission on Electoral Reform and Party Financing. Ottawa and Toronto: RCERPF/Dundurn.

Smith, Michael. 1987. "Party Leaders Debate Ranges from Free Trade to Bilingualism." *Toronto Star*, 18 August.

Star Wire Services. 1971. "Fuzzy Format Gives Great Debate a Case of the Blacks." *Windsor Star*, 5 October.

Stewart, Charles J. 1975. *Central States Speech Journal* (Winter): 279–82.

Stoffman, Daniel. 1975. "Bitter Davis–Nixon Debate Crumbles into a Shouting Match." *Toronto Star*, 15 September.

Swerdlow, Joel L. 1984. *Beyond Debate*. Washington, DC: The Twentieth Century Fund.

Tarnowksi, J.-F. 1988. "Mitterrand–Barre: le duel." *La revue de cinéma* (April): 81–90.

Tiemens, R.K., et al. 1985. "An Integrative Verbal and Visual Analysis of the Carter–Reagan Debate." *Communication Quarterly* 33 (1): 34–42.

Tremblay, Bertrand, Morisset, Bois and Migneault. 1985. Subject: section 427 of the Quebec *Election Act* on debates between party leaders. Judicial Notice No. 440-200/CT, Sainte-Foy, 19 November.

Trent, J.S., and R.V. Friedenburg. 1983. *Political Campaign Communication*. New York: Praeger.

United States. *Communications Act of 1934*, June 19, 1934, ch. 652, 48 Stat. 1064 (Title 47).

———. *Federal Election Campaign Act of 1971*, Pub. L. 92-225, Feb. 7, 1972.

Van der Eijk, Cees, and Philip van Praag. 1987. *De strijd om de meerderheid: de verkiezingen van 1986*. Amsterdam: CT Press.

Warhurst, John. 1991. "Campaign Communication in Australian Elections." In *Media, Elections and Democracy*, ed. Frederick J. Fletcher. Vol. 19 of the research studies of the Royal Commission on Electoral Reform and Party Financing. Ottawa and Toronto: RCERPF/Dundurn.

White, Theodore H. 1961. *The Making of the President 1960*. New York: Atheneum.

5

IMPROVING VOTER INFORMATION ABOUT PARTIES AND CANDIDATES

~

Lyndsay Green

An informed electorate is a precondition of a healthy democracy, and effective methods of voter information are the tools for building voter knowledge. There is increasing recognition, which finds growing support in Canadian law, that having a knowledgeable electorate is not only a laudable goal but also an obligation and that voters have a "right to know" about the positions and platforms of the candidates and parties vying for their support.

Many interveners before the Royal Commission on Electoral Reform and Party Financing took the position that people have the right not only to a vote, but also to an informed vote. The arguments were made most forcefully with reference to people who have disabilities, but apply equally to all Canadians. Citing Prime Minister Brian Mulroney's commitment "to making federal elections fully accessible to all disabled Canadians by 1991," interveners emphasized that accessibility, as it is defined in the *Canada Elections Act* and interpreted by Elections Canada, ought "to include both the physical plant involved, and the relevant materials and information that are involved in the election process" (Coalition of Provincial Organizations of the Handicapped (COPOH) 1990; Canadian Association for Community Living 1990).

The Canadian Human Rights Commission (1990) submission emphasized that "accessibility" includes the right to information. "Accessibility is not limited to physical access but extends to the information that is available to assist or inform the individual in exercising his or her right to vote. It is important, therefore, that all materials, information, ballots and posters that are designed by Elections Canada and the various political parties be 'user friendly' from the perspective of disabled people."

Canadian electoral law also recognizes that the proper functioning of democracy requires fair opportunity for competitors in the electoral process. All candidates and parties do not have equal access to the electorate, and improved methods of voter information could help to improve equality of opportunity for reaching the voting public.

Improved voter information also has the potential to increase the political participation of those who are currently underrepresented in the system, such as women, native people, members of ethnocultural communities, people with disabilities and poor people, whether as voters, party members or candidates. The goal is a fairer, more representative system, and one which "more approximately mirrors the mosaic of our polity" (Lortie 1991, 8). Methods of voter information that assist candidates and parties to make their views known could lower campaign costs and reduce the need for large financial contributions from powerful sectoral interests, thereby broadening the spectrum of political representation (Paltiel 1979).

The purpose of this study is to examine methods that have been used in Canada and elsewhere to help ensure that voters have sufficient information to make an informed choice on election day. However, its concern is not with the well-established campaign communication activities of the political parties and candidates, nor with the vital information functions of the mainstream media. Rather, it attempts to identify and assess existing and projected alternatives to these channels, alternatives that might fill gaps in the information system or broaden the information flow during election campaigns. It does not, therefore, deal with the major advocacy groups that have substantial resources, but rather with service organizations and community groups. With these objectives in mind, this study examines suggestions for improving voter information and discusses factors that should be considered in assessing them. It is particularly concerned with services to information-impeded voters and examines two such groups by way of illustration.

VOTER INFORMATION METHODS

Methods Implemented by the State

In many countries, the state financially assists candidates and parties to run their campaigns, including assisting them to communicate with the electorate. The primary motive for this public financing has been to reduce campaign costs, with the goal of creating a more level playing field for contenders and reducing the dependency of political parties and candidates on powerful economic interests. However, the public funding policies are usually justified in terms of liberal democratic ideology, including the electorate's right to know and the need for equality of opportunity among parties and candidates (Paltiel 1979).

The methods of public subsidization fall into three distinct categories: direct subventions, specific grants or services and indirect subsidies. Indirect subsidies would include Canada's requirement for free-time political broadcasts. Of particular interest are indirect subsidies by which the state has improved voter information by assuming certain costs and services that were previously the obligation of the parties and candidates. Paltiel provides the following examples: "the use of public buildings for political meetings and free mailings (United Kingdom and France); the distribution of campaign pamphlets (France and Japan); free transportation for candidates in Japan and subsidized travel for delegates to nomination meetings in Norway; paper and free bill-posting in France, Finland and Japan; and the provision of ballots in France to each party" (Paltiel 1979, 12).

In 1989 the New York City (NYC) Campaign Finance Board took more direct responsibility for informing the electorate through the publication of a voter guide "to give City voters a concise, non-partisan package of information about municipal candidates, ballot proposals, and other information of relevance to voters" (NYC Campaign Finance Board 1990, 128). The guide contains two sections – one on voting, the other on the candidates. Candidate information is provided by the candidates themselves, and includes a personal profile and statements about their views and positions on issues that are important to them. Photographs are also included.

About 4.7 million copies of the voter guide were mailed to registered voters, and an additional 250 000 copies and 760 audiotapes in English and Spanish were distributed to public places. Thirty thousand advertising posters, printed in English and Spanish, were placed in subway cars for four weeks before the elections in order to make voters aware of the voter guide and understand its purpose as a nonpartisan package of candidate information.

The Board considers the project to be a success and found that response "by the public and press was extremely enthusiastic" (NYC Campaign Finance Board 1990, 128). No formal research has been done on the public's use of the guide or its effectiveness in improving voter information. However, Finance Board officials believe that, at $0.30 per copy, the publication has been a cost-effective method of assisting New York City voters to make sense of the many simultaneous voting choices they must make.[1]

Referendum or ballot pamphlets are widely used in both the United States and other jurisdictions to provide voter information.[2] The state undertakes to provide the voter with information about both sides of an issue ("Yes" and "No") by printing a booklet that contains information prepared by representatives of the opposing sides of the proposal. The booklet is mailed to every household in the jurisdiction. Although there are significant differences between ballot-issue elections or referendums and candidate elections with regard to the nature of the voter's task and information costs, it is useful to review the research on ballot pamphlets for findings that could be applied to election information.[3]

According to 1986 data, 10 states of the United States require that each registered voter be mailed a pamphlet describing referendum propositions and the arguments for and against them (Zimmerman 1986). Cronin has summarized the available research on the usefulness of the voter information pamphlets. He concludes that, where the pamphlets are available, "estimates are that between 30 and 60 percent of those who go to the polls read them and rely on them as an important source of information" (Cronin 1989, 80).

The length and complexity of the voter guides are obvious factors in their effectiveness as voter-information tools. Individual guides vary considerably, from a single 4" x 9" card used by New York State in 1979 to the two-ballot pamphlets totalling 224 pages that were distributed for the November 1990 California general election, and which included 28 propositions. The California ballot pamphlets were also available in Spanish and a cassette-recorded version was available from public libraries. Research on previous California ballot pamphlets concluded that voters rely almost entirely upon the mass media for information about propositions, and not upon the pamphlet. Analysis of the readability of the text concluded that citizens need a reading level equivalent to that of a third-year college student in order to understand the document (Magleby 1984).

As part of Britain's 1975 referendum on membership in the European Economic Community (EEC), the government printed and distributed free to every household an information pamphlet prepared by each of the two umbrella organizations, one representing those favouring membership (Britain in Europe (BIE)), and the other representing those opposed (the National Referendum Campaign (NRC)). In addition, the government information unit prepared and distributed its own separate pamphlet, setting forth the government's reasons for recommending a "Yes" vote. This meant that there were two "Yes" pamphlets and only one "No" pamphlet, and it has been argued that "the government should not have used its resources to intervene on one side, either with its own separate pamphlet or with other publicity material" (Hansard Society 1981, 187). Maintaining the neutrality of the process (or at least the image of neutrality) has been a problem in some areas.

A poll conducted on the eve of the 1975 British EEC referendum found that 75 percent of the electorate claimed to have seen the pamphlets, and 27 percent claimed to have read them from cover to cover. Nevertheless, the report of a 1979 conference on referendums, sponsored by the Hansard Society for Parliamentary Government and the American Enterprise Institute, concluded "that the money (about £4 million) would have been more effectively spent on press or television advertisements" (Hansard Society 1981, 187). The criteria for this opinion were not provided, and it may be argued that the availability of the information contributed to the credibility of the process, regardless of how widely the pamphlets were used.

A booklet was also sent to Quebec electors by the Director General of Elections of Quebec during the "sovereignty association" referendum of 20 May 1980. The text was established by the two umbrella organizations controlled by those in the legislature who aligned themselves respectively with the "Yes" and "No" sides, with equal space given to each option (Boyer 1982).[4] No research has apparently been conducted on the effectiveness of the booklet in informing voters.

Submissions to the Commission

A substantial number of submissions to the Commission raised concerns about the need for more voter education and information. Although these submissions placed greater emphasis on the need for nonpartisan information related to the electoral process, they also expressed the requirement for increased information about parties and candidates. Spokespeople for many special interest groups addressed the need for those they represented to learn more about the platforms and positions of candidates and parties. Such groups represented people with disabilities, native people, poor or illiterate people and ethnocultural communities.

Representatives of political parties who made submissions to the Commission expressed a desire for increased opportunity to communicate with the electorate. The Green Party and the Libertarian party attested to the difficulty of obtaining media coverage. Their position is supported by research findings showing that during Canadian federal elections, the media focus on the three major parties, and the minor or emerging parties receive little coverage (Fletcher 1988; Roth 1990). The Green Party further emphasized the disproportionate amount of campaign funds required to gain access to television. The Green Party spent 25 percent of its total election budget to produce the program for the two minutes of free-time broadcasting that was allocated to it.

In general, submissions about voter information emphasized the need for more information to be presented in audio and visual form, and for greater use of television and radio. This emphasis is understandable, given the high percentage of Canadians with limited or no reading skills. Interveners estimated that 24 percent of the Canadian population is illiterate, using as a standard a level of education that is less than grade nine. A recent study conducted by the National Literacy Secretariat concluded that there is another group of Canadians who can carry out simple reading tasks, but avoid situations where they have to read. As a result, it is estimated that only 62 percent of the Canadian population can meet the demands of everyday reading (Canada, Statistics Canada 1989).

Where print is used, interveners argued for the use of simpler language and larger print. As the Greater Moncton Literacy Council phrased it, "Politicians can help by printing brochures using a larger text and a common vernacular, a language of the people so to speak" (1990). The London Cross Cultural Learner Centre recommended that posters and public transit advertisements be used to reach persons such as the homeless who have limited access to other media (1990).

Voters who are literate in languages other than French and English also require increased information. The Canadian Ethnocultural Council urged parties and candidates to respect the linguistic requirements of the electorate (1990).[5] Special measures are required to communicate information about parties and candidates to Aboriginal people, some of whom may face both linguistic and geographic barriers to information (Alia 1991; Roth 1991).

Several specific proposals were submitted to the Commission for increasing information about candidates and parties. Sylvain Auclair (1990) of Montreal proposed that the government publish a newspaper with text that is submitted by parties and candidates. The Liberal Association of Saskatchewan (1990) suggested that officially registered parties be eligible to send out free election mailings. Use of the parliamentary television channel to transmit partisan information during election time was proposed by representatives of the Liberal party and the Green Party of Canada (1990). The Premier's Council on the Status of Disabled Persons of New Brunswick (1990) urged that there be a Canadian Radio-television and Telecommunications Commission (CRTC) licensing requirement to ensure that "some community-focused issues would be discussed at the national level using the national media," for example a national forum on the concerns of citizens with disabilities.

The Toronto Christian Resource Centre (1990) proposed the establishment of "an equal participation fund to allow poorer groups to participate equally in election campaigns," with a levy on political contributions proposed as one potential source of funding. The Federal Constituency Association of the Willowdale New Democratic Party (NDP) (1990) suggested that overall funding be increased for public broadcasting and alternative publications in order to increase voter information.

In summary, the submissions served to emphasize the significant number of electors who are impeded from receiving information by virtue of illiteracy, disability, culture, language or poverty. Many people are unable to receive political information in a form that they can access and special measures are advocated to ensure that these groups have an equal opportunity to be informed. In addition, inadequate media coverage is given to issues of interest and concern to many voters and there are insufficient opportunities for minor or emerging parties to communicate with the electorate.

Methods Established by Intermediaries

Nonpartisan intermediaries in both Canada and the United States have played an important role in increasing voter awareness about parties and candidates. We have examined a number of their efforts, including those by community groups and local media.

For one Ontario provincial election, the Ontario Association for Community Living prepared videotapes in which the leaders of the three major parties stated some of the issues in very simple terms. The video cassettes were made available to persons in institutions and in segregated settings. The Association (1990) found that the tapes "really provoked a lot of discussion and in fact allowed people to make some decisions about the content ... in a way that would probably otherwise not have been possible."

The Canadian Ethnocultural Council (CEC) (1990) organized an all-party debate focused on ethnocultural issues, which was broadcast by Channel 47, a multicultural television channel in Toronto, after the major networks refused to carry it. The CEC also published a special issue of its newsletter that examined the parties on a number of issues of importance to ethnocultural communities. The Saskatchewan Coalition for Social Justice (1990) currently sends questionnaires to municipal candidates, and then publicizes the results and their recommendations as to the best voter choice.

The news media inform voters about parties and candidates on a daily basis, with reports that are filtered through their own news values. However, some newspapers, especially at the community level, provide an opportunity for the candidates to express themselves without editorial intervention. Sylvain Auclair (1990) of Montreal told the Commission that he was favourably impressed by a community newspaper that provided the same amount of free space to all candidates to express their positions. Other research for the Commission has found that the provision of free space is a common practice across the country (Bell and Fletcher 1991).

The voluntary sector in the United States has traditionally played an important role in disseminating election information. Some community organizations assume this task as part of a broader mandate of public service, while others such as the League of Women Voters have a mandate of reforming the electoral process. A number of newly formed projects and organizations have as their primary objective the provision of information about candidates and issues. These projects and organizations are independent of any political party and receive their financing from nonpartisan fund-raising or fees for service. Cooper and Peters (1990) provide the following description of these projects.

The Citizens Jury is a Minnesota project for evaluating statewide elected officials, conducted by the League of Women Voters of Minnesota and the Jefferson Center. "Juries" are selected to represent the Minnesota electorate, based on a representative sample of the population. The jurors choose three key topics on which to rate the gubernatorial candidates. They hold discussions with the candidates, listen to the testimony of expert witnesses and rate each candidate in a public report. With the exception of the deliberation portion, the entire process is open to both the public and the media. A "how-to" manual is being prepared to assist others interested in introducing the concept.

The Center for National Independence in Politics (CNIP), a nonprofit, nonpartisan educational centre, prepares a series of pamphlets containing information to assist voters in examining state congressional delegates. Information includes the names of financial contributors and performance evaluations of delegates given by conservative, liberal, labour, business and other interest groups. By 1992, CNIP intends to have a 1-800 telephone number operating in all 50 states through which citizens can acquire information about candidates' backgrounds and issue-related questions. A National Political Awareness test will be made available through the media providing candidates' stands on 10 basic issues.

The Campaign Research Center (CRC) has developed a computerized database that allows interested parties to learn about campaign contributions by Political Action Committees (PACs), associations and individuals. The database also gives information about election totals, voting records and committee assignments. It is hoped that the press will make use of the database to inform the public better about the legislative process and general campaign information. The program has been operating since June 1990 and has been used by the media, advocacy groups, special interest groups, corporations, PACs, incumbents and challengers. The fees for the service are based on ability to pay (Cooper and Peters 1990).

Designing Voter Information Programs

The voter information programs discussed above vary as to who provides the information, who determines the subject matter, how accessible the information is to all voters, how accessible the system is to all candidates and parties, and the extent of interactivity and information exchange. In evaluating voter information programs, we have found the following four factors to be particularly helpful: promoting pluralistic dialogue, expanding the campaign agenda, enhancing accessibility and choosing the appropriate organization.

Plans for future voter information programs must consider not only the information methods that are currently available, but also the potential for emerging communications technologies to change the nature of the relationship between voters and candidates. New communications technologies have been used in a variety of political contexts, such as election campaigns, referendums, discussion of policy alternatives and the provision of ongoing elected-representative and citizen communication. They clearly have the potential to improve the voter's knowledge of partisan issues.

Barber has argued that, although they bring new kinds of risks, communications technologies have the potential to be an instrument for democratic discourse.[6] "The capabilities of the new technology can be used to strengthen civic education, guarantee equal access to information, and tie individuals and institutions into networks that will make real participatory discussion and debate possible across great distances" (1984, 274).

It is important, however, to approach this subject with long-range vision. Since the early 1970s it has been suggested that communications technologies could assist the democratic process. For example, papers published by the Rand Corporation during this era include the proposal for a "direct democratic legislative structure for local government" based on a system for instant referendums delivered by cable television (Zacks and Harris 1971). However, a five-year study on the impact of new media technologies on democratic politics that was published in 1988 concluded that "to date there is not all that much technology in politics" and "the impact of new media technologies on elections will not be felt fully for ten or fifteen years" (Abramson et al. 1988, 108).

How accessible the technology will be in the future and how amenable it will be to improving voter information will depend on decisions made by government, the major political parties, the media and community groups.

Promoting Pluralistic Dialogue

Abramson et al. (1988) set out the value choices that lie ahead in the application of electronics to democracy and conclude that the result could be one of two contrasting visions: "plebiscitary democracy" – the politics of polls and plebiscites, electronic voting and instant feed-back – or "the electronic commonwealth" – the televised town meetings, debates and discussions based on pluralistic dialogue. They view the congregating or conferencing capacity of the electronic commonwealth as being a democratic model that is far preferable to the isolation, priva-tization and fragmentation of plebiscitary democracy.

Voter information programs that are based on broad distribution techniques and that promote feedback and interaction are viewed as the foundation for the electronic commonwealth because they offer opportunities to learn from and be persuaded by other points of view. They provide the potential to develop a shared vision. Many of the voter information projects that were discussed earlier in this study, particularly those implemented by intermediaries, meet these objec-tives to varying degrees through their efforts to disseminate broadly multiple perspectives and to encourage discussion and dialogue.

Information programs that deal with voters in isolation and reduce the potential for dialogue would move away from the goals of the electronic commonwealth. Political parties and candidates themselves are making increased use of methods that would fall into this category, such as taped campaign messages that are delivered to voters by telephone-automated dialing equipment, computer-generated mail that targets voters according to increasingly specific criteria, and distribu-tion by mail of candidate-produced videotapes that are targeted to voter interest. The challenge is to preserve and enhance public forums.

Expanding the Campaign Agenda

Another criterion by which voter information programs should be judged is whether the information that is provided expands the campaign agenda. This criterion overlaps with the goal of pluralistic dialogue, since the latter should also result in an expanded campaign agenda. In his assessment of the media coverage of the 1984 federal election campaign, Fletcher (1988) found that two developments contributed significantly to expanding the campaign agenda and improving the quality of public debate: the National Action Committee (NAC) debate on women's issues and the series of debates on the CBC television program "The Journal." In these debates, called "The Front Benches," members of Parliament from each of the three parties were confronted by spokespeople for relevant interest groups.

The proposals made to the Commission to have "community-focused issues" included in the national agenda and the efforts to have ethnocultural issues debated nationally rather than on a local ethno-cultural channel both reflect the desire to expand the campaign agenda and reduce the marginalizing of certain issues. The proposal by the Liberal and Green parties for use of the parliamentary channel during elections would also provide a national forum for issues that may be construed as more local or regional in nature.[7]

Proposals for the provision of new information channels to parties and candidates may be of limited use to voters if political competitors are unwilling to provide substantive information. For example, one can envision the use of a series of tape-recorded messages that would be accessible by telephone, such as DIAL-A-LAW, a free program offered by the Law Society of Upper Canada. The program provides general legal information on over 100 topics through brief messages that can be accessed by telephone.[8] However, without the proper framework, the information provided by parties and candidates to such a system might be too general or vague to be of much public value.

Efforts to make such a service useful would need to be concerted, since the strategic considerations dictated by elections in a brokerage political system "mitigate against strong or specific stands by political parties" (Pammett 1988). The ambiguity of electoral appeals may, however, flow from the need to appeal in the traditional media to mass audiences. The provision of a forum that permitted fuller explanation or tailoring of messages to particular groups might provide an incentive for parties and candidates to provide more substantial materials.

Enhancing Accessibility

No single communications method will ensure access to the entire population or meet the diversity of specialized communications needs that were brought before the Commission. One reason for this is what Toffler refers to as the "de-massification of the media." Society has become multi-channelled and the mass audience has been broken "into segments and subgroups, each receiving a different configuration of programs and messages" (Toffler 1990, 334). Electoral communication will inevitably be influenced by these developments.

When Arterton (1987) examined 13 teledemocracy experiments designed to elicit citizen participation, he found that "the plethora of media is the single most difficult institutional barrier they face." Several projects "commandeered broadcast television because that medium has the most extensive reach to the citizenry. Their experience, however, documents that despite the capabilities of the medium, repetition and the use of multiple channels are necessary to involve anything approaching all of the people" (ibid., 187).

In Canada, the ability to commandeer a national audience for our television networks has been limited by the presence of the American television signals, which offer viewers a ready alternative. And audience fragmentation is increasing as specialized networks are set up to meet special purpose needs. For example, the needs of individual multicultural communities have resulted in networks such as Rim Jhim, a radio service for the Vancouver Indo-Canadian community that is broadcast on a sub-carrier frequency of an existing FM station and is received in the home through the use of a decoder.

How do specific technologies rate in terms of ensuring access to voter information programs, for voters, parties and candidates? Arterton's study found the following six categories of technology in use: mediating political discussion by means of televised call-in formats, mail-back ballots, interactive cable television, teleconferencing and video-conferencing, computer conferencing, electronic mail and videotex (interactive computer-based information systems). He concluded that "there is still a long way to go before we reach the point at which the available media will be ideal for pluralist dialogues." Audio- and video-conferencing hold prospects for the few-to-few pattern of communication. Videotex and computer conferencing offer potential benefits as well as challenges, but "access is so severely limited by cost that they cannot be considered practical, and this condition will probably last for a substantial period of time" (Arterton 1987, 189).

To combat the problem of limited access to videotex, Barber proposes a Civic Videotex Service, a nationwide, interactive and free videotex service that would provide viewers with regular news, discussions of issues, and technical, political and economic data. Barber suggests that this service "would serve the public need for equal access to civic information" (1984, 279).

The following examples of operational computer-based services that allow citizen access to elected officials provide insight into how such a system might work for informing voters during elections. The Public Electronics Network (PEN) in Santa Monica, California, allows city services to be accessed through computers that are located in public places such as the local shopping mall or through home computers. The PEN's interactive capacity allows government to respond to citizen inquiries and complaints. Citizens can direct individual comments to their representatives, and the system allows for computerized town meetings. City council members' votes are recorded to allow comparison with stated positions (Cooper and Peters 1990).

Superkiosk, a Canadian telematic project, is scheduled for completion of a service prototype in spring 1991.[9] Superkiosk is a private-public sector project designed to provide a variety of customer services through a national and/or local network of public kiosks. Among Superkiosk's proposed services is a "direct democracy" project that will allow users to respond to questions on matters of topical concern and then view the aggregate survey results. At their request, users' survey responses will be transmitted to their provincial or federal representatives. More detailed messages can be transmitted to the representative via computer keyboard or audio-recording. Each transmission will be assigned a confidential code, allowing users to access their representatives' responses at a later date.[10]

Although current access to such a system is extremely limited, the Department of Communications along with the information technology industries are forecasting a project they call "Vision 2000," a network of advanced technologies and services to be available to all Canadians by the year 2000. A spokesperson for the department says that "the objective of Vision 2000 is to develop advanced communications technologies, networks and services to allow Canadians to communicate with anyone, anywhere and at any time" (Frangini 1990).[11]

Certain activities are forerunners of this development, such as Vidéotron's interactive cable project in Quebec,[12] some of the activities of the provincial educational broadcasters,[13] the use of video-conferencing for town-hall meetings,[14] and the on-line information retrieval services being commercially offered.[15] It is not known, however, how quickly the technologies will be developed, how accessible they will be, or how much they will cost.

It is also clear that there will not be a provision for public-sector use unless there is a deliberate and concerted campaign to that end. In his study of telematics, Edwards finds that, in Canada, the business market has emerged as a priority for telematics application, and obstacles are making the services less accessible and affordable for ordinary citizens. He concludes that "if we want telematics to serve people and communities in this country, we must create effective public sector development models" (1988, 261). Abramson et al. came to the same conclusion that the market-place would not support electronic information services devoted to exchanges of civic information and recommended that "intervention in the selections of the market in favor of subsidized civic uses of computers, data bases, videotex, and two-way television must become a political priority" (1988, 279).

In any assessment of access, it is critical to recognize that more than mere physical access to a communications medium is required. Access is mediated by the financial and social cost of use, comprehension of the language used, the skill required to use the medium, awareness of the medium, confidence in the right to use the medium and perceived sociocultural distance from the medium (Hudson 1974). As an example, the computer and videotex systems discussed above are very appealing because of their assumed mass accessibility; however, they are text-based communications services, and given what we know about the reading skills of the Canadian population, universal accessibility would be more apparent than real.

The gulf would appear to be widening between the increasing points of access for the information-rich and the impoverishment of the information-poor. Publicly funded programs for voter information should give priority to reaching those people who do not already have access to a myriad of information channels, that is, those with restricted access to available communication channels because of disabilities or sociocultural, linguistic, geographic or other factors.

Choosing the Appropriate Organization

When considering which is the appropriate organization to provide information regarding voting rights and procedures, it is necessary to distinguish between *nonpartisan* voter information and the *partisan* information that voters need to make an informed choice. Both forms of information are important but the appropriate provider is likely to be different.

With regard to *partisan* information, should the state be charged with responsibility for establishing mechanisms to increase its availability? Should a new entity be created to assume this function, or should the responsibility be carried out by existing organizations? Certainly it is valid to argue that Elections Canada itself would not be the appropriate vehicle for partisan information, given its mandate as the nonpartisan agency of Parliament responsible for running federal elections. Elections Canada is attempting to increase voter awareness of the fact that it is an agency of Parliament, free of political interference, that by law it ensures fair elections and can, if necessary, take politicians to court. Elections Canada has an educational challenge before it, however. Survey results show that awareness of its status increases with the educational level of the public and is significantly higher among professional people (Canadian Gallup Poll 1984). Anything that obscures its neutrality in the public view would not be in the public interest.

Barber proposes that in the United States such a responsibility be given to a Civic Communications Cooperative whose mandate would be "to promote and guarantee civic and democratic uses of telecommunications, which remain a vital public resource." Its aims would include "pioneering and experimenting with innovative forms of civic broadcasting" and "setting guidelines for and where feasible originating videotex and other computer information services as a free public utility" (Barber 1984, 277). Intermediaries discussed above, such as the Citizens Jury, the Center for National Independence in Politics (CNIP) and Gary Schmitz's Campaign Research Center (CRC), suggest additional possibilities.

One of the most cost-effective ways to meet the needs of the "information-impeded," that is, those with restricted access to available communication channels because of disabilities or sociocultural, linguistic, geographic or other factors, would be the provision of financial assistance to the nonpartisan interest groups or media that already exist to serve them. Designated funding to nonprofit, nonpartisan organizations, such as the Ontario Association for Community Living, the Canadian Ethnocultural Council and the Saskatchewan Coalition for Social Justice, would permit them to continue to expand their efforts to communicate with their constituencies about partisan issues. The special interest media for groups such as native people, women and multicultural organizations could also provide increased nonpartisan coverage of partisan issues through public financial assistance.

To illustrate the general argument, the expressed concerns and needs of two groups, the deaf and hard-of-hearing, and the blind and visually impaired, are examined. In both cases technology exists to improve their access to voter information. The challenge is to ensure that these channels carry the necessary information to these groups in ways that are accessible to them.

DEAF AND HARD-OF-HEARING CANADIANS

Approximately 2.5 million Canadians (one-tenth of the population) are hard of hearing, of whom 270 000 are profoundly deaf. The Canadian Association of the Deaf (CAD) found in its 1989 research project into deaf literacy skills that as many as 65 percent of deaf Canadians may be classified as functionally illiterate.[16] Hearing impairment increases with age and the proportion of Canadians with hearing disabilities will increase as the population ages.[17] Interveners before the Royal Commission made the following proposals as to how parties and candidates could improve communications with the deaf and hard-of-hearing. Sign-language interpreters and assistive listening systems should be provided at nomination meetings, all-candidates meetings and public meetings. Candidates should hire a qualified sign-language interpreter for their campaigns. Campaign material published by the candidates should be interpreted in written format by a sign-language interpreter (see submissions by the CAD 1990; Ontario Advisory Council for Disabled Persons 1990; Saint John Hearing Society 1990).

Televised political advertisements should be captioned,[18] and televised debates of the party leaders should be made accessible in as many forms as possible, including both visible sign-language interpreters and captions. The CAD (1990) told the Commission that "Deaf people generally prefer to see an interpreter; hard of hearing people, senior citizens, people learning literacy skills, and immigrants learning English and French as a new language prefer captions. Both methods should be offered." It was also argued that captions should be "open" in order not to restrict their reception to people who have a closed-caption decoding machine. If captions are open, the text is visible to all viewers at the bottom of the screen. If the captions are "closed," they are only made visible through the use of a teletext decoder (submissions of the CAD 1990; Saint John Hearing Society 1990).

Captioning

Captioning is a process whereby the dialogue or narrative on audio-visual productions is displayed in printed format on the screen.[19] "Open captions" are placed directly on the video master and are visible to all viewers. "Closed captions" are transmitted in a line on the vertical blanking interval (VBI) and only appear on the screen when the viewer uses a decoding device attached to the television set.

The technology for closed-captioned television was developed by the National Captioning Institute in the United States to facilitate television viewing by the hearing-impaired without alienating other audiences, and it was introduced in Canada in 1981.[20]

The CAD has found that captions are used not only by the deaf and hard-of-hearing, but also by immigrants, senior citizens, people learning literacy skills, and by those who speak English or French but wish to improve their skills in the other language. The CAD estimates that, when all these groups are totalled, over one-third of Canadians can benefit from captions.[21]

The captioning of television broadcasts is not a licence requirement, although the Canadian Radio-television and Telecommunications Commission (CRTC) encourages broadcasters to provide programming in captioned form.[22] The Department of Communications (1989) estimated in 1989 that 10 percent of television programming is closed-captioned.[23] A 1988 figure estimated that approximately 150 hours of closed-captioned programs are available in Toronto each week (Mehler 1988).

Individual Canadian broadcasters vary as to both the amount of captioned programming they transmit and the source of the program captions. The type of captioning depends on whether the captions can be encoded into prerecorded television programs or whether they must be created simultaneously with the transmission of a program, that is, real-time or verbatim captioning.[24] Programming purchased from the United States often has captions available for purchase at approximately 10 percent of the real costs.[25]

Some broadcasters, such as CBC and CTV, create closed captions for some of their programs through in-house captioning facilities. Many broadcasters require that co-productions or programming acquired from Canadian producers be provided with captions encoded on the master tape and, since 1984, Telefilm Canada has offered assistance to closed-caption projects that receive Telefilm production financing (Canada, Telefilm Canada 1990). Some public broadcasters have received special government grants or appropriations to cover the costs of closed-captioning equipment or services. Some cable operators are captioning their community channel and offering open-captioned programming on a designated channel.

There are at least six commercial captioning companies in Canada, of which three companies in Montreal, Toronto and Vancouver are licensed by the Canadian Captioning Development Association (CCDA). The CCDA licence attests that the captioning company abides by a certain set of captioning standards and/or uses a patented captioning process.[26] Captioning charges currently run about $2 000 per program hour for post-production captioning, with the rate varying according to such factors as turnaround time required, volume discounts and the time of year (off-season is cheaper).

The federal government has demonstrated its commitment to closed captioning. As of 3 May 1985, all commercials produced by the federal government for television, including public service announcements, are required to be closed-captioned for the benefit of the hearing-impaired (Canada, Treasury Board 1985). As of 1 April 1990, the National Film Board committed itself to closed-caption all of its productions in both English and French in video format before their release for distribution.

According to the Canadian Advertising Foundation, 225 advertisers are closed-captioning their advertisements. The Foundation finds that advertisers are committed to closed-captioning because "they dare not miss any potential consumer or buyer of a product or service, especially when the additional cost is marginal." Both the cost and time requirements of closed-captioning are built into the specifications of their product (Interview, 8 March 1991).

Decoder Availability

Representatives of the deaf and hard-of-hearing expressed concern to the Commission that closed captions restrict access because a limited number of decoders are in use, a result of their high cost ($180–$200).[27] Since decoders are commercial products that are bought from a variety of sources with no requirement for registration, there is no way of knowing the precise number of caption decoders that are in use in Canada. The Ministry of Transportation and Communications estimated in 1985 that 10 000 decoders were in use in Ontario (Mehler 1988). The CRTC estimates that the total figure for all of Canada could be as high as 25 000–30 000 but is more likely closer to 16 000–17 000 (Interview, 20 February 1991).

Maclean Hunter, which serves approximately 640 000 cable subscribers in Ontario, has undertaken a $2.25 million program to provide approximately 10 000 decoders to hearing-impaired subscribers.[28] Rogers Communications Inc. made a similar proposal in its August 1990 application to assume control of Skyline Cablevision.

The Rogers proposal will make 10 000 decoders available to hearing-impaired subscribers in its cable systems who, with the addition of Skyline customers, represent 25 percent of the Canadian cable market (approximately 1.7 million subscribers in Ontario, Alberta and British Columbia).

The *Television Decoder Circuitry Act* represents one development that should eventually eliminate the need for decoders. Passed into law on 16 October 1990, this law requires that television sets sold in the United States after 1993 have built-in captioning decoder circuitry to decode closed captions. As a result, a separate decoder will no longer be required for the caption to become visible on a person's home television set.[29] Whether or not similar Canadian laws are enacted, Canadian consumers will benefit from the manufacturers' modification of their products to comply with the American law.[30]

The 1988 Federal Election

During the 1988 election campaign, Progressive Conservatives captioned their three French-language advertisements, but none of the seven

English-language spots. The NDP captioned six of nine television advertisements. The Liberal party produced seven English-language spots, none of which was closed-captioned. Its 16 French-language television advertisements were all closed-captioned. Spokespeople for the three parties all said that tight deadlines prevented the closed-captioning of all the advertisements. One spokesperson said that the additional time required for captioning was 24 to 48 hours and "would prevent the party from getting ads linked to current issues to air" (*Globe and Mail* 1988). Are time and cost significant barriers to the closed captioning of party campaign advertising?

Whether or not this situation existed in 1988, it is no longer the case. The National Captioning Centre (NCC) captions 2 500–3 000 commercials per year, and states that 12 hours is their standard turnaround time. The charge for this regular service is $375 for a 30-second commercial. For an additional $150, the NCC will provide the same length captioned commercial in four to six hours turnaround time. The NCC operates evenings and weekends (Interview, 6 March 1991).

Signing

It is estimated that 5 percent of deaf people sign (Interview, CRTC, 20 February 1991). In Canada most deaf people communicate in either American Sign Language (ASL) or Langue du signe québécois (LSQ) (Saint John Hearing Society 1990), but there are regional variations or dialects.[31] As stated earlier, deaf people generally prefer to see an interpreter, and may not be able to read captions. However, most broadcasters have opted for captions rather than signing, because of the greater number of people they have the potential to reach. One exception is the parliamentary channel, which has a visible signer on both its English- and French-language channels.[32]

Ensuring Access

The Canadian Association of the Deaf (1990) told the Commission that when it complained to the three parties about the lack of closed-captioning of television advertisements during the 1988 federal election, "one party stated they did not have the funds to consistently caption all of their ads. The other parties stated that they did not have time to caption the ads." As noted above, time and cost no longer appear to be significant obstacles.

The 1991 *Broadcasting Act* declares as broadcasting policy that "programming accessible by disabled persons should be provided within the Canadian broadcasting system as resources become available for the purpose" (s. 3(1)(*p*)), but falls short of making such accessibility mandatory.

The issue of captioning or providing visible signers for leaders debates was not specifically addressed in the submission by the Canadian Association of Broadcasters (CAB) (1990) to the Commission. However, the CAB stated its belief that "it is the broadcasters' duty to ensure that the public has adequate knowledge of the issues surrounding an election and the position of the parties and candidates. The CAB considers that broadcast licensees, in the exercise of their responsibilities, must be allowed to judge how they should respond to the needs of the public in the communities they have been licensed to serve." A coalition of four groups representing persons with disabilities appeared before the House of Commons Standing Committee on the Status of Disabled Persons to propose omnibus legislation to revise all laws and regulations to ensure compliance with the *Canadian Charter of Rights and Freedoms* and the *Canadian Human Rights Act*. The *Broadcasting Act* was specifically mentioned as needing amendment to require closed captioning of all programming (Interview, Standing Committee, 20 March 1991). The Canadian Disability Rights Council (CDRC) is taking a motion to the Federal Court of Appeal to argue that closed captioning ought to be a condition of CRTC licence, with specific reference to the licence renewals of five British Columbia broadcasters. The CDRC argues that both the CRTC and the broadcasters are bound by the Charter and the *Canadian Human Rights Act* and are accordingly forbidden to act in a discriminatory manner (Interview, CDRC, 20 March 1991).

Given that the right to accessibility of the deaf and hard-of-hearing communities is being understood as including the right to information about parties and candidates, and given the increasing availability of the technology and the numbers of people who can potentially benefit, it must be concluded that parties should caption political advertisements, and broadcasters should caption and provide visible signers for leaders debates. In considering how best to ensure the accessibility of political broadcasts, the CAD (1990) stressed that "the costs of captioning election advertisements should be treated as a normal part of election expenses – not a frill to be added on later if there are a few cents left in the budget."

According to a representative of the Department of Communications, it is essential, when drafting legislation regarding technologies to serve the disabled, to ensure that the wording is general and not technology-specific, since new and better technologies are always being developed. Measures to serve the deaf and hard-of-hearing communities that were drafted 10 years ago would have specified signing, since captioning was then still in its infancy (Interview, 28 February 1991).

BLIND AND VISUALLY IMPAIRED CANADIANS

There are over half a million blind and visually impaired people in Canada, with the largest single group being over 65. (Statistics Canada (1990) states the number as 552 580 in its Health Activity Limitation Survey conducted in 1986 and 1987.) This figure does not take into account people who are print-handicapped. The Ontario Advisory Council for Disabled Persons (1990) said that information for public distribution should be available in formats such as Braille and audio-cassette to serve the visually disabled. Information on audiocassette can be used both by people with limited literacy difficulties and those who have visual impairments. Although it is estimated that only 7 to 10 percent of the visually disabled actually use Braille, the Status of Disabled Persons Secretariat of the Department of the Secretary of State recommends the availability of Braille versions of printed material to meet their needs. Once information is in data form, the computer software is available commercially to generate a Braille version without great difficulty or expense (Interview, 8 March 1991).

A number of technological developments hold great promise for improving access to information for the visually disabled. The National Broadcast Reading Service (called "Voiceprint") and its French-language equivalent, La Magnétothèque, provide cable-delivered audio services to people who are blind, visually impaired and print-handicapped due to physical reasons (licensed 16 October 1990, launched 1 December 1990). Materials from Canadian newspapers and magazines are read 24 hours per day to provide the audience with what is effectively an "audio news-stand." The services are based in Toronto and Montreal respectively. Regional programming studios are being set up in Vancouver and in the National Capital Region, with plans for at least one regional studio operating in every province within five years.

The future also holds promise for the accessibility of campaign literature through the use of voice synthesizers. The technology, not yet in widespread use, allows people to access print by telephone from a computer-operated database that is hooked up to a voice synthesizer.

Descriptive Video Service (DVS) is another new technological development that will provide new ways for the visually handicapped to receive information. DVS allows for the production of television programs with a voice describing the action between lines of dialogue in order to give visually impaired people information about the scene. The extra audiochannel is sent by broadcast in stereo to be picked up by a third channel built into newer stereo televisions, called the separate audio program or SAP channel. If consumers do not have a stereo television they may purchase a stereo audiotelevision receiver (decoder).

Thirty-four PBS stations in the United States provide DVS on four programs, and another 14 were to begin such broadcasts by April 1991. The comments of a blind consumer about the benefits of DVS for advertisers could apply equally to political ads: "A lot of commercials have no dialogue at all. I have no idea what is being sold, so I'm not going to buy it" (*Globe and Mail* 1991).

Research on alternate distribution methods for DVS is being conducted by the Department of Communications, because of the lack of broadcast operations with the capability to broadcast in stereo and the low market penetration of stereo television. The possibility of using the vertical blanking interval, as is done for closed captioning, is being explored.

CONCLUSION

We have examined some promising efforts to increase voter information about candidates and parties. Most of these efforts have been carried out by intermediaries rather than by the state. Because neither the economic nor the political market-place will serve the needs of information-impeded groups, community action is needed.

Public funding provides one option for improving voter information, and any publicly funded programs should give priority to meeting the information needs of the "information-impeded," that is, those whose access to available communication channels is restricted because of disabilities or because of sociocultural, linguistic, geographic or other factors. In many cases, the most cost-effective way to meet these needs would be the provision of financial assistance to the nonpartisan interest groups or media that already exist to meet their needs. In the specific cases of the deaf and hard-of-hearing and the blind and visually disabled, the technological means are at hand to improve access to information, and it is incumbent upon all parties to the political process to see that these means are used.

Any proposals to allocate public funding to voter information programs should be assessed by the four criteria developed in this study, that is, according to their capacity to promote pluralistic dialogue, to expand the campaign agenda, to increase accessibility and to provide appropriate organizational control.

In conclusion, it will be critical for Elections Canada and the CRTC to monitor the possible impact of new technologies on campaign information, particularly to the information-poor. Public access to communications technologies for purposes of political and public dialogue will be critical in ensuring that all Canadians are full participants in the democratic process.

ABBREVIATIONS

c.	chapter
Pub. L.	Public Law (U.S.)
R.S.C.	Revised Statutes of Canada
S.C.	Statutes of Canada
S.Q.	Statutes of Quebec
s(s).	section(s)

NOTES

This study was completed in August 1991.

1. Information provided by the New York City Campaign Finance Board, 6 May 1991.

2. "Referendum" is used here to refer to both initiatives and referendums, but there is a difference in some jurisdictions. Under United States law "the initiative allows voters to propose a legislative measure (statutory initiative) or a constitutional amendment (constitutional initiative) by filing a petition bearing a required number of valid citizen signatures. The referendum refers a proposed or existing law or statute to voters for their approval or rejection" (Cronin 1989, 2).

3. Cronin notes that in ballot issue elections the " 'information costs' (the costs of learning about the various aspects of the issue) are generally even higher than in candidate elections. Legal and technical language on ballot issues sometimes causes confusion, and the absence of party labels usually attached to candidates denies a majority of these voters a familiar cue" (Cronin 1989, 67). Seymour-Ure, writing about the British Referendum of 1975, concluded that there was an "absence of constituency candidates, contests and campaign rituals." General elections in parliamentary democracies "are concerned with non media institutions (parties, legislature, cabinet) which interact with media in the election campaign." In the referendum, by contrast, "the media institutions were central and such non media institutions as came into existence devoted much money and energy (press conferences, advertisements) to securing media coverage" (Seymour-Ure 1978, 615).

4. Section 26 of the Quebec *Referendum Act* of 1978 requires the Director General of Elections to send to electors, no later than 10 days before the holding of a poll, a single booklet explaining each of the options submitted to the referendum. The text of the booklet is to be established by each national committee, respectively. Equal space, as fixed by the director general, must be given in this booklet to each option.

5. The Elections Canada brochure "Voting in Canada," which contains basic information on the right to vote, was published in 15 languages other than English and French.

6. Although there are obvious benefits to be gained from the use of new technologies in political discourse, it would be remiss for a study such as this not to mention the potential dangers that could result from consequences that were unintended. The opportunities for invasion of privacy have been well documented. Less emphasis has been given to the potential for communications to restrict, as well as to expand, voter rights. For example, a proposal has been made to use computers "to promote well-informed democratic legislation" by, among other things, testing citizens on their knowledge of a legislative proposal to see whether they "have sufficient understanding to warrant having their votes counted" (Bahm 1986, 55).

7. In 1988, Elections Canada used the parliamentary television channel for the first time during a federal election campaign to provide election information to the public, election administrators and media. The information program was available 24 hours per day in English and French, and presented nonpartisan information in written form by means of a revolving scroll, and through videos depicting the various stages of the electoral process.

8. Touch-tone telephone users have access through an automated answering system 24 hours a day, seven days a week. Rotary-dial users can access DIAL-A-LAW Monday to Friday during regular business hours and are connected to the tape of their choice with the help of an operator. In 1990 the service received 325 996 calls in a 10-month period (January through October), for an average of 1 100 calls daily. Research has not been conducted on the effectiveness of the program from the users' perspective.

9. "Telematics" is one of many terms used for the merging of computer and communications technologies.

10. Superkiosk participants include the federal Department of Communications, Communications Québec, Tourisme Québec, the City of Montreal, Sears, Air Canada, General Motors, Provigo and Industrielle-Alliance/General Trust. Information provided by the Canadian Workplace Automation Research Centre (CWARC), December 1990.

11. Currently 97 percent of Canadians have telephones and television sets, 70 percent have cable television and 20 percent have microcomputers in their homes (Frangini 1990).

12. Through a converter hooked up to a television set and the use of a remote control, the Videoway project allows viewers to choose from among some 120 electronic services – stock prices, the latest prices at the supermarket, movies and a dating service. An interactive function allows viewers to interact with the program visuals by changing viewing angles or adjusting the program format. The goal of Le Groupe Vidéotron Ltée is to have 1.5 million units in place in Quebec, one in every home of a Vidéotron cable subscriber (*Globe and Mail* 1990).

13. As but one example, the Open Learning Agency of British Columbia is operating the Discovery Training Network, an on-line computer database of educational and training courses and programs.

14. The Citizens' Forum on Canada's Future (Spicer Commission) used inter-active television to hold electronic town-hall meetings as a means of linking Canadians in different communities to dialogue on the future of the country. This technique has also been used by groups such as the International Joint Commission and the Canadian Association for Adult Education.

15. In Canada, customers can obtain on-line information retrieval services from at least three providers: Alex (offered by Bell Canada), GEnie (General Electric Information Services Canada) and Susy, provided by Stratford Software Corp. The customer uses a computer connected to a telephone in order to access the system services which may include electronic informa-tion, shopping, banking and communicating with other subscribers (Frangini 1990).

16. Statistical source, Canadian Association of the Deaf. Deaf people identify themselves as "culturally" deaf. "These are not people who are just hard of hearing and function as hearing people, basically, but profoundly deaf people whose preference for communication is sign language" (Canadian Association of the Deaf 1990).

17. By the year 2000, Statistics Canada forecasts the population over age 65 will reach 3.9 million, representing 13 percent of the total population.

18. Under the *Canada Elections Act*, licensed networks are required to make available to the political parties during a federal general election an aggre-gate amount of fixed time that is to be provided in the form of "free" or unpaid commercial time for the presentation of partisan political "programs." There are also provisions that oblige all broadcasters to make available to the parties a total of six and one-half hours of paid commercial time during the designated campaign period of an election.

19. Captions can be a verbatim transcription of the audio script, a condensed version, a simplified version, or can be supplementary to the audio script. Programs can be captioned in more than one language, with viewers selecting the language by tuning into the appropriate channel of their decoders.

20. A background document prepared by the NFB to launch their plan for closed captioning NFB productions states that prior to the development of closed-caption technology, major networks in the United States telecast some prime-time programming with open captions. "The ratings for those programmes dropped and it became evident that the distraction caused by 'Open Captions' for hearing audiences would put an end to 'Open Captions' on television" (Smith 1991). In 1985 TVOntario reviewed the "sparse research" done on open captioning (or subtitling) and concluded that "there appears to be a lack of consensus on whether or not this method of captioning

would be accepted by a majority of the hearing audience" (Anderson and Duggan 1985, 2).

21. Submission by the Canadian Association of the Deaf (1990). A TVOntario study (Mehler 1988) found that, for the most part, Canadian audiences for closed-captioned television are currently limited to the hearing-impaired, mainly because other applications have not yet been developed or popularized. In the United States, however, closed-captioned television has been used to teach English as a second language (ESL) and literacy to both deaf and hearing children and adults. Research conducted by the National Captioning Institute (NCI) in the United States found a large increase in the numbers of Asian immigrants using closed-captioned television to learn English at home, and sales of NCI's decoder have increased dramatically to Chinese and Korean cultural groups (ibid.). A 1990 study done by the Canadian Captioning Development Agency in conjunction with the Montreal Catholic School Board "showed that a class of functionally illiterate students responded positively to captioned videos designed to accelerate literacy learning" (submission of the Ontario Closed Caption Consumers to the CRTC Re Skyline Application, 7 November 1990).

22. CRTC Guidelines regarding the provision of VBI/SCMO Services state that "captions for the hearing-impaired should be given a high priority; line 21 of the VBI should be reserved for this purpose" (CRTC 1989).

23. The CRTC estimates the figure conservatively at 10 to 15 percent, with prime time being closer to 25 percent. The equally important question is not just how much, but what is being captioned. For example, while prime-time American programming is captioned, this may not be true of local news broadcasts (Interview, CRTC spokesperson, 20 February 1991).

24. Real-time captioning employs a technology similar to that used for court reporting: the operator is connected to the television studio by means of a computer modem, and the captions are encoded instantaneously into the television signal. Real-time broadcasting is used for many evening news broadcasts and sports events.

25. For approximately U.S.$250–$300 (1988 figures) the Canadian broadcaster is provided with the floppy disc containing the captions and the broadcast rights to the captioned version, which are purchased separately from the program itself (Mehler 1988, 4).

26. According to the National Captioning Centre (one of the licensed companies), the nonlicensed companies use American software (Interview, 6 March 1991).

27. Skyline Cablevision states that the decoders they will offer to customers as part of the proposals contained in the application to transfer control to Rogers will cost $180 each, as purchased from the National Captioning Institute in Virginia (Skyline Response to Intervention of Ontario Closed Caption Consumers, 19 November 1990). The lower volume cost is closer to $200 (U.S.).

28. No more than a couple of hundred are currently in use. Information provided by Maclean Hunter, 9 April 1991.

29. After July 1993, all television sets sold in the United States with a screen size of 13" or larger will be required to have built-in captioning decoder circuitry as a result of the *Television Decoder Circuitry Act*. The Act specifies that the apparatus be able to receive and display closed captions which have been transmitted by way of line 21 of the vertical blanking interval (VBI).

30. Skyline estimates that it will take 10 years before the entire universe of television sets will be replaced by sets with built-in decoders, since historically the trend has been that less than 10 percent of the population replaces its television set in any given year (Skyline Response to Intervention of Ontario Closed Caption Consumers, 19 November 1990).

31. "The interpreter for Question Period uses parliamentary sign, Quebec has its own sign language. The Maritimes have their own sign language that is a little bit different from the kind of English sign language that we use in English Canada based on the older British model. In the west they use a lot of finger spelling rather than signing ... accents [vary] across the country, through the generations – some older people cannot understand the signs of some [other] people and vice versa" (Canadian Association of the Deaf 1990).

32. This decision was taken because it was desirable to provide the same type of service on both language channels and the software to generate real-time or verbatim captioning in French is not yet available (Interview, House of Commons Broadcasting Service, 26 February 1991). The future was uncertain at the time of writing because the CBC had announced that it no longer intended to operate the parliamentary channel as of 31 March 1991, and a number of options were being considered by the House of Commons in order to continue this service. One option was to provide only one channel service, with a visible signer providing French-language interpretation, and captions providing the proceedings in English (Interview, House of Commons Office of Public Information, 20 March 1991). The Ontario legislature provides verbatim captions and is considering providing a French-language version on the separate audio program (SAP) channel (Interview, Ontario Legislature, 26 February 1991).

INTERVIEWS

Broadcast and Recording Service, Legislative Assembly of Ontario, Toronto, 26 February 1991, by telephone.

Canada, Department of Communications, Ottawa, 28 February 1991, by telephone.

Canada, Department of the Secretary of State, Status of Disabled Persons Secretariat, Ottawa, 8 March 1991, by telephone.

Canadian Advertising Foundation, Toronto, 8 March 1991, by telephone.

Canadian Disability Rights Council (CDRC), Winnipeg, 20 March 1991, by telephone.

Canadian Radio-television and Telecommunications Commission (CRTC), Ottawa, 20 February 1991, by telephone.

House of Commons, Broadcasting Service, Ottawa, 26 February 1991, by telephone.

House of Commons, Office of Public Information, Ottawa, 20 March 1991, by telephone.

House of Commons, Standing Committee on the Status of Disabled Persons, Ottawa, 20 March 1991, by telephone.

Maclean Hunter, Ottawa, 9 April 1991, by telephone.

National Captioning Centre (NCC), Toronto, 6 March 1991, in person.

REFERENCES

Abramson, Jeffrey B., F. Christopher Arterton and Gary R. Orren. 1988. *The Electronic Commonwealth: The Impact of New Media Technologies on Democratic Politics.* New York: Basic Books.

Alexander, Herbert E. 1989. "Money and Politics: A Conceptual Framework." In *Comparative Political Finance in the 1980s,* ed. Herbert E. Alexander. Cambridge: Cambridge University Press.

Alia, Valerie. 1991. "Aboriginal Peoples and Campaign Coverage in the North." In *Aboriginal Peoples and Electoral Reform in Canada,* ed. Robert A. Milen. Vol. 9 of the research studies of the Royal Commission on Electoral Reform and Party Financing. Ottawa and Toronto: RCERPF/Dundurn.

Anderson, Jane, and Kay Duggan. 1985. *Open Captioning Trial Project Literature Review.* Report No. 13. Toronto: TVOntario, Office of Project Research.

Arterton, F. Christopher. 1987. *Teledemocracy: Can Technology Protect Democracy?* Newbury Park: Sage Publications.

Auclair, Sylvain. 1990. Brief presented to the Royal Commission on Electoral Reform and Party Financing. Ottawa.

Bahm, A.J. 1986. *Computocracy: Our New Political Philosophy – Its Time Has Come.* Albuquerque: University of New Mexico.

Barber, Benjamin R. 1984. *Strong Democracy: Participatory Politics for a New Age.* Berkeley: University of California Press.

Barber, Benjamin, and Patrick Watson. 1988. *The Struggle for Democracy.* Boston: Little, Brown.

Bell, David V.J., and Frederick J. Fletcher, eds. 1991. *Reaching the Voter: Constituency Campaigning in Canada.* Vol. 20 of the research studies of the Royal Commission on Electoral Reform and Party Financing. Ottawa and Toronto: RCERPF/Dundurn.

Boyer, Patrick J. 1982. *Lawmaking by the People: Referendums and Plebiscites in Canada.* Toronto: Butterworths.

Canada. *Broadcasting Act,* S.C. 1991, c. 11, s. 3.

———. *Canada Elections Act,* R.S.C. 1985, c. E-2.

———. *Canadian Charter of Rights and Freedoms,* Part I of the *Constitution Act, 1982,* being Schedule B of the *Canada Act 1982* (U.K.), 1982, c. 11.

———. *Canadian Human Rights Act,* R.S.C. 1985, c. H-6.

Canada. Department of Communications. 1989. "Broadcasting for the Visually and Hearing Impaired." Press release. Ottawa: DOC.

Canada. Elections Canada. 1989. *Report of the Chief Electoral Officer of Canada.* Ottawa: Minister of Supply and Services Canada.

Canada. House of Commons. Standing Committee on the Status of Disabled Persons. 1988. *No News Is Bad News.* Ottawa: Queen's Printer.

Canada. Statistics Canada. 1989. *Survey of Literacy Skills Used in Daily Activities.* Survey conducted on behalf of the National Literacy Secretariat of the Department of the Secretary of State. Ottawa: Statistics Canada.

———. 1990. *Highlights: Disabled Persons in Canada.* Health and Activity Limitation Survey. Ottawa: Canadian Government Publishing Centre.

Canada. Telefilm Canada. 1990. Closed Captioning for the Hearing Impaired – Policies 1990–1991. Ottawa.

Canada. Treasury Board. 1985. "Management of Government Advertising." TB Circular 1985–30. Ottawa: TB.

Canadian Association for Community Living. 1990. Brief presented to the Royal Commission on Electoral Reform and Party Financing. Ottawa.

Canadian Association of Broadcasters. 1990. Brief presented to the Royal Commission on Electoral Reform and Party Financing. Ottawa.

Canadian Association of the Deaf. 1990. Brief presented to the Royal Commission on Electoral Reform and Party Financing. Ottawa.

Canadian Ethnocultural Council. 1990. Brief presented to the Royal Commission on Electoral Reform and Party Financing. Ottawa.

Canadian Gallup Poll Ltd. 1984. "Gallup National Omnibus Conducted for Elections Canada: Summary of Results." Toronto.

Canadian Human Rights Commission. 1990. Brief presented to the Royal Commission on Electoral Reform and Party Financing. Ottawa.

Canadian National Institute for the Blind. 1988. *The Right To Know.* Toronto: CNIB.

Canadian Radio-television and Telecommunications Commission. 1989. "Services Using the Vertical Blanking Interval (Television) or Subsidiary Communications Multiplex Operation (FM)." Public Notice CRTC 1989-23. Ottawa: CRTC.

Clarke, Harold, J. Jenson, L. LeDuc and J. Pammett. 1984. *Absent Mandate: The Politics of Discontent in Canada.* Toronto: Gage.

Coalition of Provincial Organizations of the Handicapped. 1990. Brief presented to the Royal Commission on Electoral Reform and Party Financing. Ottawa.

Cooper, Jamie, and Farley Peters. 1990. "Policy Alternatives on Voter Participation: A State Report." *Center For Policy Alternatives* 2(2) (December).

Cronin, Thomas E. 1989. *Direct Democracy: The Politics of Initiative, Referendum, and Recall.* Cambridge: Harvard University Press.

Edwards, Laurie. 1988. "Telematics in Canada: The Vanishing Opportunity." In *Communication Canada: Issues in Broadcasting and New Technologies,* ed. Rowland Lorimer and Donald Wilson. Toronto: Kagan and Woo.

Fletcher, Frederick J. 1988. "The Media and the 1984 Landslide." In *Canada at the Polls, 1984: A Study of the Federal General Elections,* ed. Howard Penniman. Durham: Duke University Press.

Frangini, Monica. 1990. "Videotex not a Mass Service Yet, Gov't Says." *Computing Canada* (21 June): 1, 6.

Garramone, Gina M., Allen C. Harris and Ronald Anderson. 1986. "Uses of Political Computer Bulletin Boards." *Journal of Broadcasting and Electronic Media* 30 (Summer): 325–39.

Globe and Mail. 1988. "Lobby for Deaf Is Angry over Lack of Captions in TV Ads." 17 November.

———. 1990. "Two-Way TV Turns on Videotron Boss." 10 December.

———. 1991. "Hearing Is Seeing with New Technology." 5 January.

Greater Moncton Literacy Council. 1990. Brief presented to the Royal Commission on Electoral Reform and Party Financing. Ottawa.

Green Party of Canada. 1990. Brief presented to the Royal Commission on Electoral Reform and Party Financing. Ottawa.

Hansard Society for Parliamentary Government. 1981. "Appendix." In *The Referendum Device,* ed. Austin Ranney. Washington, DC: American Enterprise Institute for Public Policy Research.

Hudson, Heather. 1974. *The Northern Pilot Project: An Evaluation.* Ottawa: Department of Communications.

Liberal Association of Saskatchewan. 1990. Testimony before the Royal Commission on Electoral Reform and Party Financing, Saskatoon, 17 April.

London Cross Cultural Learner Centre. 1990. Brief presented to the Royal Commission on Electoral Reform and Party Financing. Ottawa.

Lortie, Pierre. 1991. "The Five Main Objectives of Electoral Reform." Notes for a speech to the Symposium on Media and Elections, Royal Commission on Electoral Reform and Party Financing, Toronto, 21 February.

Magleby, David B. 1984. *Direct Legislation Voting on Ballot Propositions in the United States*. Baltimore: Johns Hopkins University Press.

Magleby, David B., and Candice J. Nelson. 1990. *The Money Chase: Congressional Campaign Finance Reform*. Washington, DC: Brookings Institution.

Meadow, Robert G. 1989. "Political Campaigns." In *Public Communication Campaigns*. 2d ed., ed. Ronald E. Rice and Charles K. Atkin. Newbury Park: Sage Publications.

Mehler, Audrey. 1988. *The Potential of Captioned Television for Adult Learners*. Working Paper No. 88-3. Toronto: TVOntario, Planning and Development Research.

New York City Campaign Finance Board. 1990. *Dollars and Disclosure: Campaign Finance Reform in New York City*. New York: The Board.

Ontario Advisory Council for Disabled Persons. 1990. Brief presented to the Royal Commission on Electoral Reform and Party Financing. Ottawa.

Ontario Association for Community Living. 1990. Brief presented to the Royal Commission on Electoral Reform and Party Financing. Ottawa.

Ontario Closed Caption Consumers. 1990. Submission to CRTC re Skyline Application, 7 November. Skyline Response, 19 November. (In the Matter of Public Hearing for Skyline Application 900563800 and 901890400.)

Organisation for Economic Co-operation and Development. 1988. *New Telecommunications Services Videotex Development Strategies*. Paris: OECD.

Paltiel, Khayyam Zev. 1979. "Public Financing Abroad: Contrasts and Effects." Paper presented to the Conference on Parties, PACs and the Campaign Finance Laws, American Enterprise Institute for Public Policy Research, Washington, DC.

————. 1989. "Canadian Election Expense Legislation, 1963–85." In *Comparative Political Finance in the 1980s*, ed. Herbert E. Alexander. Cambridge: Cambridge University Press.

Pammett, Jon H. 1988. "Political Education and Democratic Participation." In *Political Education in Canada*, ed. J.H. Pammett and Jean-Luc Pepin. Halifax: Institute for Research on Public Policy.

Premier's Council on the Status of Disabled Persons of New Brunswick. 1990. Brief presented to the Royal Commission on Electoral Reform and Party Financing. Ottawa.

Quebec. *Referendum Act*, S.Q. 1978. c. 6, s. 26.

Roth, Bob. 1990. "Muffled Voices." *Content for Canadian Journalists* (July/August): 21–22.

Roth, Lorna. 1991. "CBC Northern Service and the Federal Electoral Process: Problems and Strategies for Improvement." In *Election Broadcasting in Canada*, ed. Frederick J. Fletcher. Vol. 21 of the research studies of the Royal Commission on Electoral Reform and Party Financing. Ottawa and Toronto: RCERPF/Dundurn.

Roth, Lorna, and Gail Gutherie Valaskakis. 1989. "Aboriginal Broadcasting in Canada: A Case Study in Democratization." In *Communication For and Against Democracy*, ed. Marc Raboy and Peter A. Bruck. Montreal: Black Rose Books.

Saint John Hearing Society. 1990. Brief presented to the Royal Commission on Electoral Reform and Party Financing. Ottawa.

Saskatchewan Coalition for Social Justice. 1990. Brief presented to the Royal Commission on Electoral Reform and Party Financing. Ottawa.

Schiller, Herbert I. 1986. *Information and the Crisis Economy*. New York: Oxford University Press.

Seymour-Ure, Colin. 1978. "Press and Referenda: The Case of the British Referendum of 1975." *Canadian Journal of Political Science* 12:601–15.

Smith, Richard. 1991. "NFB Provides Service for Deaf and Hearing Impaired." Ottawa: National Film Board.

Toffler, Alvin. 1990. *Powershift: Knowledge, Wealth and Violence at the Edge of the 21st Century*. New York: Bantam Books.

Toronto Christian Resource Centre. 1990. Brief presented to the Royal Commission on Electoral Reform and Party Financing. Ottawa. (This brief is part of the brief submitted by the Metro Tenants Legal Services.)

United States. *Television Decoder Circuitry Act of 1990*, Pub. L. 101-431, Oct. 15, 1990.

Willowdale New Democratic Party. Federal Constituency Association. 1990. Brief presented to the Royal Commission on Electoral Reform and Party Financing. Ottawa.

Zacks, Leonard, and Craig Harris. 1971. *The Instant Referendum – A CATV Based Direct Democratic Legislative Structure for Local Government.* Santa Monica: Rand Corporation.

Zimmerman, Joseph F. 1986. *Participatory Democracy: Populism Revived.* New York: Praeger.

CONTRIBUTORS TO VOLUME 18

Cathy Widdis Barr	Wilfrid Laurier University
Robert Bernier	École nationale d'administration publique
Jean Crête	Université Laval
Lyndsay Green	Lyndsay Green and Associates
R.H. MacDermid	York University
Denis Monière	Université de Montréal

ACKNOWLEDGEMENTS

The Royal Commission on Electoral Reform and Party Financing and the publishers wish to acknowledge with gratitude the permission of the following to reprint and translate material:

Canadian Political Science Association.

Care has been taken to trace the ownership of copyright material used in the text, including the tables and figures. The authors and publishers welcome any information enabling them to rectify any reference or credit in subsequent editions.

~

Consistent with the Commission's objective of promoting full participation in the electoral system by all segments of Canadian society, gender neutrality has been used wherever possible in the editing of the research studies.

THE COLLECTED RESEARCH STUDIES*

---

* The titles of studies may not be final in all cases.

Commission Organization

EDITORIAL, DESIGN AND PRODUCTION SERVICES

ROYAL COMMISSION ON ELECTORAL REFORM AND PARTY FINANCING

Editors   Denis Bastien, Susan Becker Davidson, Ginette Bertrand, Louis Bilodeau, Claude Brabant, Louis Chabot, Danielle Chaput, Norman Dahl, Carlos del Burgo, Julie Desgagners, Chantal Granger, Volker Junginger, Denis Landry, André LaRose, Paul Morisset, Christine O'Meara, Mario Pelletier, Marie-Noël Pichelin, Kathryn Randle, Georges Royer, Eve Valiquette, Dominique Vincent.

LE CENTRE DE DOCUMENTATION JURIDIQUE DU QUÉBEC INC.

Hubert Reid, *President*

Claire Grégoire, *Comptroller*

Lucie Poirier, *Production Manager*
Gisèle Gingras, *Special Project Assistant*

Translators   Pierre-Yves de la Garde, Richard Lapointe, Marie-Josée Turcotte.

Technical Editors   Stéphane Côté Coulombe, *Coordinator*; Josée Chabot, Danielle Morin.

Copy Editors   Martine Germain, Lise Larochelle, Élizabeth Reid, Carole St-Louis, Isabelle Tousignant, Charles Tremblay, Sébastien Viau.

Word Processing   André Vallée.

Formatting   Typoform, Claude Audet; Linda Goudreau, *Formatting Coordinator*.

WILSON & LAFLEUR LTÉE

Claude Wilson, *President*